Non-Volatile Memory
Database Management Systems

Synthesis Lectures on Data Management

Editor
H.V. Jagadish, *University of Michigan*

Founding Editor
M. Tamer Özsu, *University of Waterloo*

Synthesis Lectures on Data Management is edited by H.V. Jagadish of the University of Michigan. The series publishes 80–150 page publications on topics pertaining to data management. Topics include query languages, database system architectures, transaction management, data warehousing, XML and databases, data stream systems, wide scale data distribution, multimedia data management, data mining, and related subjects.

Non-Volatile Memory Database Management Systems

Joy Arulraj and Andrew Pavlo

ISBN: 978-3-031-00740-8   paperback
ISBN: 978-3-031-01868-8   ebook
ISBN: 978-3-031-00095-9   hardcover

DOI 10.1007/978-3-031-01868-8

A Publication in the Springer series
SYNTHESIS LECTURES ON DATA MANAGEMENT

Lecture #55
Series Editor: H.V. Jagadish, *University of Michigan*
Founding Editor: M. Tamer Özsu, *University of Waterloo*
Series ISSN
Print 2153-5418   Electronic 2153-5426

Non-Volatile Memory Database Management Systems

Joy Arulraj
Georgia Institute of Technology

Andrew Pavlo
Carnegie Mellon University

SYNTHESIS LECTURES ON DATA MANAGEMENT #55

ABSTRACT

This book explores the implications of non-volatile memory (NVM) for database management systems (DBMSs). The advent of NVM will fundamentally change the dichotomy between volatile memory and durable storage in DBMSs. These new NVM devices are almost as fast as volatile memory, but all writes to them are persistent even after power loss. Existing DBMSs are unable to take full advantage of this technology because their internal architectures are predicated on the assumption that memory is volatile. With NVM, many of the components of legacy DBMSs are unnecessary and will degrade the performance of data-intensive applications.

We present the design and implementation of DBMS architectures that are explicitly tailored for NVM. The book focuses on three aspects of a DBMS: (1) logging and recovery, (2) storage and buffer management, and (3) indexing. First, we present a logging and recovery protocol that enables the DBMS to support near-instantaneous recovery. Second, we propose a storage engine architecture and buffer management policy that leverages the durability and byte-addressability properties of NVM to reduce data duplication and data migration. Third, the book presents the design of a range index tailored for NVM that is latch-free yet simple to implement. All together, the work described in this book illustrates that rethinking the fundamental algorithms and data structures employed in a DBMS for NVM improves performance and availability, reduces operational cost, and simplifies software development.

KEYWORDS

non-volatile memory, database management system, logging and recovery, storage management, buffer management, indexing

Contents

Acknowledgments

Many people deserve special acknowledgment for making this book possible. I thank my advisor Andy Pavlo for his unceasing support and thoughtful guidance. He was always generous with his time and gave me the freedom to pursue my research agenda. I greatly benefited from his expertise in designing and building software systems. He taught me everything from advanced topics in database systems to Wu Tang Clan. I could not have asked for a better advisor.

I have been fortunate to have had the guidance of several remarkable mentors: Todd Mowry, Greg Ganger, Sam Madden, Donald Kossmann, Garth Gibson, and Michael Stonebraker. Their valuable feedback and constructive criticism helped shape this book. I would like to express my gratitude to Sam, Mike, and Todd for their advice on the academic job market.

I am indebted to Shan Lu who fostered my interest in software systems. She took the chance to work with me and introduced me to systems research.

I have been fortunate to overlap with a multitude of exemplary researchers during my time at CMU: David Andersen, Subramanya Dulloor, Christos Faloutsos, Phil Gibbons, Anuj Kalia, Michael Kaminsky, Danai Koutra, Mike Kozuch, Viktor Leis, Hyeontaek Lim, Yixin Luo, Lin Ma, Prashanth Menon, Gennady Pekhimenko, Matthew Perron, Guru Prashanth, Ram Raghunathan, Majd Sakr, Jungmin Seo, Vivek Seshadri, Neil Shah, Sahil Singla, Anthony Tomasic, Dana Van Aken, Yingjun Wu, Huanchen Zhang, and Michael Zhang. The many members of the CMU Database group and Parallel Data Lab made for wonderful company. I am grateful to Deborah Cavlovich, Karen Lindenfelser, Jessica Parker, and Marilyn Walgora for their support.

I worked on the BzTree project (Chapter 6) during my internship at Microsoft Research. I am grateful to Justin Levandoski, Umar Farooq Minhas, and Paul Larson for their mentorship.

Many others provided helpful feedback during the course of this work, including Phil Bernstein, Shel Finkelstein, David Lomet, Chandrasekaran Mohan, and Hamid Pirahesh.

I thank my friends in Pittsburgh who often gave me reasons to laugh and think: Vivek, Ranjan, SKB, Divya, Vikram, and Lavanya. I am sure I have missed many others.

Finally, I am deeply grateful for the love and support from my parents. I thank my wife Beno for being there with me every step of the way. My brother Leo and sister-in-law Vinoliya led by example and encouragement. I dedicate this book to my family.

Joy Arulraj
February 2019

CHAPTER 1

Introduction

Changes in computer trends have given rise to new application domains, such as Internet services, that support a large number of concurrent users and systems. What makes these modern applications unlike their predecessors is the scale in which they ingest information [118]. Database management systems (DBMSs) are often the critical component of these applications because they are responsible for ensuring that operations of concurrent transactions execute in the correct order and that their changes are not lost after a system crash [45, 97]. Optimizing the DBMS's performance is important because it determines how quickly an application can take in new information and use it to make new decisions [167].

The performance of a DBMS is affected by how fast it can read and write data on non-volatile storage. DBMSs have always been designed to deal with the differences in the performance characteristics of non-volatile storage and volatile memory (DRAM). The key assumption has been that non-volatile storage is much slower than DRAM and only supports block-oriented read/writes. But new non-volatile memory (NVM)[1] technologies, that are almost as fast as DRAM and that support fine-grained read/writes, invalidate these previous design choices.

Existing DBMSs can be classified into two types based on the primary storage location of the database: (1) disk-oriented and (2) memory-oriented DBMSs. Disk-oriented DBMSs are based on the same hardware assumptions that were made in the first relational DBMSs from the 1970s, such as IBM's System R [36]. The design of these systems target a two-level storage hierarchy comprising of a fast but volatile byte-addressable memory for caching (i.e., DRAM), and a slow, non-volatile block-addressable device for permanent storage (i.e., SSD). These systems take a pessimistic assumption that a transaction could access data that is not in memory, and thus will incur a long delay to retrieve the needed data from disk. They employ legacy techniques, such as heavyweight concurrency-control schemes, to overcome these limitations [161].

Recent advances in manufacturing technologies have greatly increased the capacity of DRAM available on a single computer. But disk-oriented systems were not designed for the case where most, if not all, of the data resides entirely in memory. The result is that many of their legacy components have been shown to impede their scalability for OLTP workloads [91]. In contrast, the architecture of memory-oriented DBMSs assumes that all data fits in main memory, and it therefore does away with the slower, disk-oriented components from the system. As such, these memory-oriented DBMSs have been shown to outperform disk-oriented

---

[1]NVM is also referred to as *storage-class memory* or *persistent memory*.

DBMSs [70, 107, 108, 186]. But, they still have to employ heavyweight components that can recover the database after a system crash because DRAM is volatile.

The design assumptions underlying both disk-oriented and memory-oriented DBMSs are poised to be upended by the advent of NVM technologies, such as phase-change memory [17, 23, 173] and memristors [22, 187]. NVM supports byte-addressable loads and stores with low latency. This means that it can be used for efficient architectures employed in memory-oriented DBMSs. But unlike DRAM, all writes to NVM are potentially durable, and therefore a DBMS can directly access the tuples on NVM after a system crash without needing to reload the database first. As shown in Table 1.1, NVM differs from other storage technologies in the following ways.[2]

- **Byte-Addressability:** NVM supports byte-addressable loads and stores unlike other non-volatile devices that only support slow, bulk data transfers as blocks.

- **High Write Throughput:** NVM delivers more than an order of magnitude higher write throughput compared to SSD. More importantly, the gap between sequential and random write throughput of NVM is much smaller than other durable storage technologies.

- **Read-Write Asymmetry:** In certain NVM technologies, writes take longer to complete compared to reads. Further, excessive writes to a single memory cell can destroy it.

Table 1.1: **Technology Comparison**—Comparison of emerging NVM technologies with other storage technologies [54, 73, 144, 166]: phase-change memory (PCM) [17, 23, 173], memristors (RRAM) [22, 187], and STT-MRAM (MRAM) [72].

Attribute	NVM				SSD	HDD
	DRAM	PCM	RRAM	MRAM		
Read latency	60 ns	50 ns	100 ns	20 ns	25 μs	10 ms
Write latency	60 ns	150 ns	100 ns	20 ns	300 μs	10 ms
Sequential bandwidth	60 GB/s	10 GB/s	10 GB/s	5 GB/s	1 GB/s	0.1 GB/s
\$/GB	10	1	1	1	0.25	0.02
Addressability	Byte	Byte	Byte	Byte	Block	Block
Persistent	No	Yes	Yes	Yes	Yes	Yes
Endurance	$>10^{16}$	$>10^{10}$	10^8	10^{15}	10^5	$>10^{16}$

Although the advantages of NVM are obvious, making full use of them in a DBMS is non-trivial. Our evaluation of state-of-the-art disk-oriented and memory-oriented DBMSs on NVM shows that the two architectures achieve almost the same performance when using NVM [67]. This is because current DBMSs assume that memory is volatile, and thus their

---

[2]We discuss the implications of these design assumptions in Appendix A.3.

architectures are predicated on making redundant copies of changes on durable storage. This illustrates the need for a complete rewrite of the database system to leverage the unique properties of NVM.

1.1   BOOK OVERVIEW

This book presents the design and implementation of DBMS architectures that are explicitly tailored for NVM. The resulting NVM-centric architectures have several key advantages over current systems.

1. They adopt a logging and recovery protocol that improves the availability of the DBMS by 100× compared to the write-ahead logging protocol.

2. Their storage engines leverage the durability and byte-addressability properties of NVM to avoid unnecessary data duplication. This improves the space utilization of the NVM device and extends its lifetime by reducing the number of device writes.

3. They employ a range index tailored for NVM that is latch-free yet simple to implement. This reduces the implementation and maintenance complexity of critical DBMS components.

4. Their buffer management policy leverages the direct-addressability property of NVM to reduce data migration. This improves the system's performance on a multi-tier storage hierarchy.

Our evaluation using different online transaction processing (OLTP) and analytical processing (OLAP) benchmarks show that such NVM-centric architectures improve the runtime performance, availability, operational cost, and development cost of DBMSs [32–35, 68]. These research efforts illustrate that:

Rethinking the fundamental algorithms and data structures employed in a database management system to leverage the characteristics of non-volatile memory improves availability, operational cost, development cost, and performance.

In the remainder of this chapter, we summarize the primary contributions of this work and conclude with an outline of this book.

1.2   CONTRIBUTIONS

This book answers the following research questions with the specific contributions listed.

1. How do state-of-the-art memory-oriented and disk-oriented DBMSs perform on non-volatile memory? [32, 67] (Chapter 2)

    • A study of the impact of NVM on two OLTP DBMSs.

- We explore two possible architectures using non-volatile memory (i.e., NVM-only and NVM+DRAM architectures).

2. How should the storage engine architecture evolve to leverage NVM? [33] (Chapter 3)

- We implement three storage engine architectures in a single DBMS: (1) in-place updates with logging, (2) copy-on-write updates without logging, and (3) log-structured updates.
- We then develop NVM-optimized variants for these architectures that improve the computational overhead, storage footprint, and wear-out of NVM devices.

3. What changes are required in the logging and recovery algorithms to support fast recovery from failures? [34, 35] (Chapter 4)

- We present a logging and recovery protocol that is designed for a hybrid storage hierarchy with NVM and DRAM.
- We examine the impact of this redesign on the transactional throughput, latency, availability, and storage footprint of the DBMS.

4. How should the DBMS manage data in a multi-tier storage hierarchy comprising of DRAM, NVM, and SSD? (Chapter 5)

- We construct a new class of buffer management policies that are tailored for NVM.
- We characterize the impact of NVM on the performance of the DBMS across diverse storage hierarchy designs and varied workloads.

5. How should we adapt the design of a range index for NVM? [31] (Chapter 6)

- We propose the design of such an index that supports near-instantaneous recovery without requiring special-purpose recovery code.
- An evaluation of the impact of this redesign on the software development and maintenance complexity, performance, and availability.

1.3   OUTLINE

The remainder of this book is organized as follows. Chapter 2 presents our initial foray into the use of NVM in existing DBMSs and makes the case for a new NVM-aware DBMS. Chapter 3 covers the design of NVM-aware variants of three different storage engine architectures that leverage the persistence and byte-addressability properties of NVM. Chapter 4 makes the case for a new logging and recovery protocol, called write-behind logging, that enables a DBMS to recover nearly instantaneously from system failures. Chapter 5 introduces a new class of buffer management policies that maximize the utility of NVM in a multi-tier storage hierarchy. Chapter 6 presents the design of a latch-free range index tailored for NVM that supports near-instantaneous recovery without requiring special-purpose recovery code. Chapter 7 presents a discussion of the related work. We highlight possible areas for future work in Chapter 8 and conclude in Chapter 9.

1.4   RELATED WORK

Researchers have proposed several DBMS architectures for NVM technologies. These efforts focus on different layers of the DBMS, ranging from logging and recovery protocols to indexing data structures [32, 160]. Table 1.2 summarizes the key features of these systems. We present a detailed discussion of these systems in Chapter 7.

Table 1.2: **NVM-Centric Systems**—Summary of key features of NVM-centric systems.

Research Systems	Features
1. Logging and Recovery	
MARS [58]	Write-ahead logging scheme based on a hardware primitive
Shore-MT [100, 164, 199]	Distributed transactional log; uses NVM to buffer data on SSD
FOEDUS [110]	Dual-page primitive with write-ahead logging
SOFORT [155, 156]	Recoverable data structures; no logging; DRAM-NVM system
Hyrise-NV [179]	Recoverable data structures; no logging; NVM-only system
Write-Behind Logging [§ 4]	No physical redo and logical undo; DRAM-NVM system
II. Storage and BufferManagement	
OLTP DBMS Test-bed [§ 3]	Three NVM-only storage engine architectures
FOEDUS [110]	Mutable volatile page in DRAM and immutable snapshot on NVM
SOFORT [155, 156]	Write-optimized delta on DRAM; read-optimized storage on NVM
Three-tier Buffer Manager [190]	DRAM-NVM-SSD system; eager data migration to DRAM
Adaptive Buffer Manager [§ 5]	DRAM-NVM-SSD systemr; adaptive data migration
III. Indexing	
CDDS Btree [191]	Multi-versioned tree; in-place updates without logging
wB+tree [55, 56]	Redo-only logging; indirection slot array to reduce data movement
NVTree [205]	Append-only index updates; re-constructs internal index nodes
FPTree [159]	Hybrid DRAM-NVM index; partial index rebuild during recovery
BzTree [§ 6]	Latch-free NVM-only index; no tree-level logging protocol

CHAPTER 2

The Case for a NVM-Oriented DBMS

This chapter presents our initial foray into the use of NVM in OLTP DBMSs. We test several DBMS architectures on a hardware-based NVM emulator and explore their trade-offs using two OLTP benchmarks. The read and write latencies of the emulator are configurable, and thus we can evaluate multiple potential NVM profiles that are not specific to a particular technology. To the best of our knowledge, our investigation is the first to use emulated NVM for OLTP DBMSs.

Since it is unknown what future memory hierarchies will look like with NVM, we consider two potential use cases. The first is where the DBMS only has NVM storage with no DRAM. The second case is where NVM is added as another level of the storage hierarchy between DRAM and SSD. In both these configurations, the system still uses volatile CPU caches.

NVM storage devices are currently prohibitively expensive and only support small capacities. For this reason, we use a NVM hardware emulator developed by Intel Labs in our evaluations in this book [73]. Appendix A presents the architecture of the hardware emulator and the interfaces that it exports to the DBMS. We use the emulator's NUMA interface for evaluating the NVM-only DBMS architecture. We use the persistent memory file system (PMFS) interface in the evaluation of both the NVM-only and NVM+DRAM architectures.

We now provide a brief overview of how a processor persists data on NVM. We later present the architectures in Sections 2.2 and 2.3.

2.1 PERSISTING DATA ON NVM

The data path taken by a store instruction (MOV) to NVM is illustrated in Figure 2.1 [177]. When a processor issues a store, the data typically lands in volatile store buffers or processor caches. To ensure the durability of the data, the processor first flushes the cached changes using the cache-line write back (CLWB) instruction [23]. This instruction writes back the modified data in the cache-lines to the write pending queue (WPQ) in the memory controller. Unlike the cache-line flush (CLFLUSH) instruction that is generally used for flushing operations, CLWB does not invalidate the line from the cache and instead only transitions it to a non-modified state. This reduces the possibility of a compulsory cache miss when the same data is accessed momentarily after the line has been flushed.

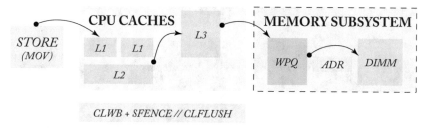

Figure 2.1: **Persisting Data on NVM**—The data path taken by a store to NVM.

After flushing the cache lines, the processor issues a SFENCE instruction to ensure that the store are ordered ahead of any subsequent store operations. At this point, the store may be buffered in the memory controller's write pending queue (WPQ). Platform-level features, such as Asynchronous DRAM Refresh (ADR), are designed to automatically flush the WPQ on power-fail or shutdown. So, the WPQ is within the power-fail safe persistence domain. Thus, a DBMS can persist data by flushing the associated cachelines using the CLWB instruction and then ordering the stores using the SFENCE instruction.

2.2   NVM-ONLY ARCHITECTURE

In the NVM-only architecture, the DBMS uses NVM exclusively for its storage. We compare a memory-oriented DBMS with a disk-oriented DBMS when both are running entirely on NVM storage using the emulator's NUMA interface. For the former, we use the H-Store DBMS [4], while for the latter we use MySQL (v5.5) with the InnoDB storage engine. We provide an overview of the H-Store DBMS in Appendix C. Both systems are tuned according to their "best practice" guidelines for OLTP workloads.

The NVM-only architecture has implications for the DBMS's recovery scheme. In all DBMSs, some form of logging is used to guarantee recoverability in the event of a failure [77]. Disk-oriented DBMSs provide durability through the use of a write-ahead log, which is a type of *physical logging* wherein updated versions of data are logged to disk with each write operation. Such an approach has a significant performance overhead for main memory-oriented DBMSs [91, 136]. Thus, others have argued for the use of *logical logging* for main memory DBMSs where the log contains a record of the high-level operations that each transaction executed.

The overhead of writing out logical log records and the size of the log itself is much smaller for logical logging. The downside, however, is that the recovery process takes longer because the DBMS must re-execute each transaction to restore the database state. In contrast, during recovery in a physical logging system, the log is replayed forward to redo the effects of committed transactions and then replayed backward to undo the effects of uncommitted transactions [77, 142]. But since all writes to memory are persistent under the NVM-only configuration, heavyweight logging protocols such as these are excessive and inefficient.

We now discuss the runtime operations of the memory-oriented and disk-oriented DBMSs that we evaluated on the NVM-only configuration in more detail (see Figure 2.2). For each architecture, we analyze the potential complications and performance pitfalls from using NVM in the storage hierarchy.

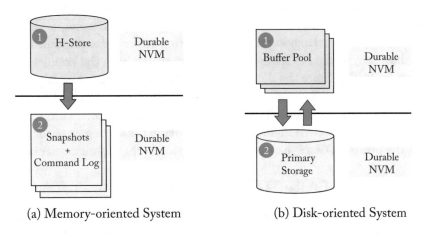

(a) Memory-oriented System   (b) Disk-oriented System

Figure 2.2: **NVM-Only Architecture**—System configurations that use NVM exclusively for storage.

2.2.1   MEMORY-ORIENTED SYSTEM

We use the emulator's NUMA interface to ensure that all of H-Store's in-memory data is stored on NVM. This data includes all tuples, indexes, and other database elements. We did not change any part of H-Store's storage manager or execution engine to use the byte-addressable NVM storage. But this means that the DBMS is not aware that writes to the memory are potentially durable.

Since H-Store was designed for DRAM, it employs a disk-oriented logical logging scheme [136] (Appendix C). To reduce recovery time, the DBMS also periodically takes a non-blocking checkpoint of all the partitions and writes them out to a disk-resident checkpoint. For our experiments in Section 2.4, we configured H-Store to write its checkpoints and log files to PMFS.

2.2.2   DISK-ORIENTED SYSTEM

In a disk-oriented DBMS, the system's internal data is divided into in-memory and disk-resident components. The DBMS maintains a buffer pool in memory to store copies of pages retrieved from the database's primary storage location on disk. We use the emulator's NUMA interface to store the DBMS's buffer pool in the byte-addressable NVM storage, while its data files and logs are stored in NVM through the PMFS interface.

Like with H-Store, MySQL is not aware that modifications to the buffer pool are persistent when using the NUMA interface. MySQL uses a *doublewrite* mechanism for flushing data to persistent storage. This involves first writing out the pages to a contiguous buffer on disk before writing them out to the data file. The doublewrite mechanism serves two purposes. First, it protects against torn writes that can occur when the DBMS has to atomically commit data that is larger the page size of the underlying storage device. Second, it also improves the performance of (synchronous) logging as writes to the log buffer are sequential. This mechanism is not useful, however, in the NVM-only architecture where both the doublewrite buffer and the data file are on NVM. Since the doublewrite mechanism maintains multiple copies of each tuple, the DBMS unnecessarily wastes storage space in the NVM. The performance difference between random and sequential I/O on NVM is also much smaller than disk, thus batching the writes together in the doublewrite buffer does not provide the same gains as it does on a disk. Furthermore, the overhead of `fsync` in PMFS is also lower than in disk-oriented file systems.

2.3 NVM+DRAM ARCHITECTURE

In this configuration, the DBMS relies on both DRAM and NVM for satisfying its storage requirements. If we assume that the entire dataset cannot fit in DRAM, the question arises of how to split data between the two storage layers. Because of the relative latency advantage of DRAM over NVM, one strategy is to attempt to keep the hot data in DRAM and the cold data in NVM. One way is to use a buffer pool to cache hot data, as in traditional disk-oriented DBMSs. With this architecture, there are two copies of cached data: one persistent copy on disk and another copy cached in the DRAM-based buffer pool. The DBMS copies pages into the buffer pool as they are needed, and then writes out dirty pages to the NVM for durability.

Another approach is to use the *anti-caching* system design proposed in [68] where all data initial resides in memory and then cold data is evicted out to disk over time. One fundamental difference in this design is that exactly one copy of the data exists at any point in time. Thus, a tuple is either in memory or the anti-cache. An overview of these two architectures is shown in Figure 2.3.

2.3.1 ANTI-CACHING SYSTEM

Anti-caching is a memory-oriented DBMS design that allows the system to manage databases that are larger than the amount of memory available without incurring the performance penalty of a disk-oriented system [68]. When the amount of in-memory data exceeds a user-defined threshold, the DBMS moves data to disk to free up space for new data. To do this, the system dynamically constructs blocks of the coldest tuples and writes them asynchronously to the anti-cache on disk. The DBMS maintains in-memory "tombstones" for each evicted tuple. When a running transaction attempts to access an evicted tuple through its tombstone, the DBMS

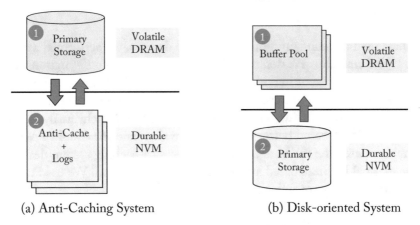

(a) Anti-Caching System   (b) Disk-oriented System

Figure 2.3: **NVM+DRAM Architecture**—System configurations that use both DRAM and NVM for storage.

aborts that transaction and fetches that it needs from the anti-cache without blocking other transactions. Once the data that the transaction needs is moved back into memory, it is restarted.

For this study, we propose an extension of anti-caching where the cold data is stored in an NVM-optimized hash table rather than disk. We modify the cold data storage manager to adapt the anti-caching system to NVM. In the original implementation, we use the BerkeleyDB [151] key-value store to manage anti-caching blocks. For NVM-backed data files, BerkeleyDB proved to be too heavyweight as we need finer-grained control over writes to NVM. To this end, we implemented a lightweight array-based block store using the emulator's PMFS interface. Elements of the array are anti-cache blocks and array indexes correspond to the anti-cache block id. If a block is transferred from the anti-cache to DRAM, the array index where the block was stored is added to a free list. When a new anti-cache block needs to be written, a vacant block is acquired from the free list. We use a slab-based allocation method, where each time the anti-cache is full, a new slab is allocated and added to the free list. If the anti-cache shrinks, then the DBMS compacts by deallocating sparse slabs.

2.3.2 DISK-ORIENTED SYSTEM

We configure a disk-oriented DBMS to run on the NVM+DRAM architecture. We allow the buffer pool to remain in DRAM and store the data and log files using the PMFS interface. The main difference between this configuration and the NVM-only MySQL configuration presented in Section 2.2.2 is that all main memory accesses in this configuration go to DRAM instead of NVM.

2.4   EXPERIMENTAL EVALUATION

To evaluate these memory configurations and DBMS designs, we performed a series of experiments on the NVM emulator. We deployed four different system configurations: two executing entirely on NVM and two executing on a hybrid NVM+DRAM hierarchy. For the NVM-only analysis, we configured MySQL to execute entirely out of NVM and compared it with H-Store configured to run entirely in NVM. For the NVM+DRAM hierarchy analysis, we configured MySQL to use a DRAM-based buffer pool and store all persistent data in PMFS. As a comparison, we implemented the NVM adaptations to the anti-caching system described above by modifying the original H-Store based anti-caching implementation. We used two benchmarks in our evaluation and a range of different configuration parameters.

2.4.1   SYSTEM CONFIGURATION

All experiments were conducted on the NVM emulator described in Appendix A.1. For each system, we evaluate the benchmarks on two different NVM latencies: 2× DRAM and 8× DRAM, where the base DRAM latency is approximately 160 ns. We consider these latencies to represent the best-case and worst-case NVM latencies, respectively. We chose this range of latencies to make our results as independent from the underlying NVM technology as possible. The sustained bandwidth of NVM is likely to be lower than that of DRAM. We leverage the bandwidth throttling mechanism in the emulator to throttle the NVM bandwidth to 9.5 GB/s, which is 8× lower than the available DRAM bandwidth on the platform [73].

2.4.2   BENCHMARKS

We use the YCSB and TPC-C benchmarks in our evaluation. A detailed description of these benchmarks is provided in Appendix B. We use H-Store's internal benchmarking framework for both the H-Store on NVM and the anti-caching analysis. For the MySQL benchmarking, we use the OLTP-Bench [71] framework.

For the TPC-C benchmark, we use 100 warehouses and 100,000 items, resulting in a total data size of 10 GB. For the anti-cache trials, we evict data from the HISTORY, ORDERS, and ORDER_LINE tables, as these are the only tables where transactions insert new data. We will now discuss the results of executing the benchmarks on each of the NVM-only and NVM-DRAM architectures described in Sections 2.2 and 2.3.

2.4.3   NVM-ONLY ARCHITECTURE

YCSB: We evaluate YCSB on each system across the range of skew parameters and workload mixtures described above. We first consider the impact of NVM latency on the throughput of memory-oriented and disk-oriented systems. The results for the read-heavy workload shown in Figure 2.4b indicate that increasing NVM latency decreases the throughput of H-Store and MySQL by 12.3% and 14.8%, respectively. There is no significant impact on H-Store's performance in the read-only workload shown in Figure 2.4a, which indicates that latency mainly impacts the performance of logging.

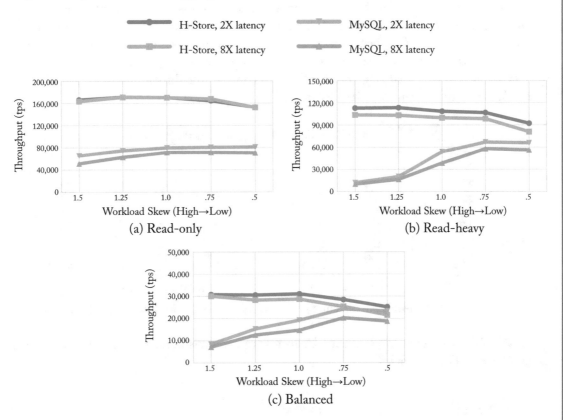

Figure 2.4: **YCSB Performance on NVM-only Architecture**—Performance comparison for the YCSB benchmark across different workload mixtures.

The throughput varies with the amount of skew in the workload. The impact of skew on H-Store's performance is more pronounced in the read-heavy workload shown in Figure 2.4b. Throughput drops by 18.2% in the read-heavy workload as the skew level is reduced. The drop in throughput is due to the application's larger working set size, which increases the number of cache misses and subsequent accesses to NVM. In contrast, MySQL performs poorly on high-skew workloads but its throughput improves by 5× as skew decreases. This is because a disk-oriented system uses locks to allow transactions to execute concurrently. Thus, if a significant portion of the transactions access the same tuples, then lock contention becomes a bottleneck.

We can summarize the above observations as follows: (1) increasing NVM latency impacts the performance of the logging mechanism; and (2) the throughput of memory-oriented and disk-oriented systems varies differently as skew decreases. We contend that the ideal system for a NVM-only architecture will possess features of both memory-oriented and disk-oriented systems.

TPC-C: For the TPC-C benchmark, most transactions insert or access new records (i.e., NewOrder), and older records are almost never accessed. As such, there is strong temporal skew built into the semantics of the benchmark. Only a subset of the tables are increasing in size, and the rest are static. In Figure 2.5a, we see that throughput of both systems only varies slightly with an increase in NVM latency, and that for both latencies the throughput of H-Store is 10× higher than that of the disk-oriented system.

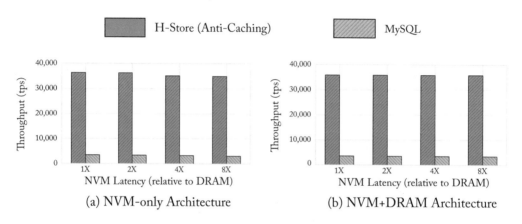

Figure 2.5: **NVM Latency Evaluation**—Performance comparison for the TPC-C benchmark using different NVM latencies.

2.4.4 NVM+DRAM ARCHITECTURE

YCSB: We use the same YCSB skew and workload mixes, but configure the amount of DRAM available to the DBMSs to be $\frac{1}{8}$ of the total database size. There are several conclusions to draw from the results shown in Figure 2.6. The first is that the throughput of the two systems trend differently as skew changes. For the read-heavy workload in Figure 2.6b, anti-caching achieves 13× higher throughput over MySQL when skew is high, but only a 1.3× improvement when skew is low. Other workload mixes have similar trends. This is because the anti-caching system performs best when there is a high skew since it needs to fetch fewer blocks and restart fewer transactions. In contrast, the disk-oriented system performs worse on the high skew workloads due to high lock contention. We note that at the lowest skew level, MySQL's throughput decreases due to lower hit rates for data in the CPU's caches.

Another notable finding is that both systems do not exhibit a major change in performance with longer NVM latencies. This is significant, as it implies that neither architecture is bottlenecked by the I/O on the NVM. Instead, the decrease in performance is due to the overhead of fetching and evicting data from NVM. For the disk-oriented system, this overhead

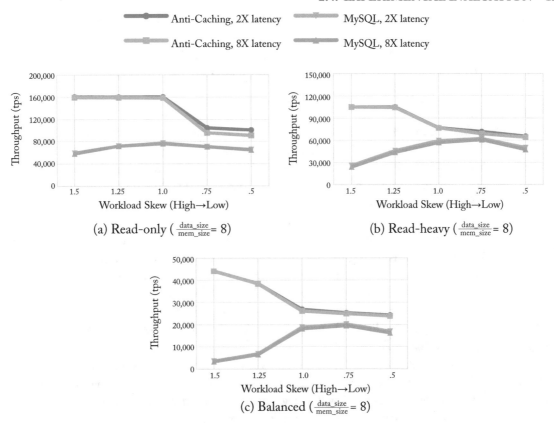

Figure 2.6: **YCSB Performance on NVM+DRAM Architecture**— Performance comparison for the YCSB benchmark across different workload mixtures.

comes from managing the buffer pool, while in the anti-caching system it is from restarting transactions and asynchronously fetching previously evicted data.

We can summarize the above observations as follows: (1) the throughput of the anti-caching system decreases as skew decreases; (2) the throughput of the disk-oriented system increases as skew decreases; and (3) neither architecture is bottlenecked by I/O when the latency of NVM is between 2–8× the latency of DRAM. Given these results, we believe that the ideal system architecture for a NVM+DRAM memory hierarchy would need to possess features of both anti-caching and disk-oriented systems to enable it to achieve high throughput regardless of skew.

TPC-C: We next ran the TPC-C benchmark on the anti-caching and disk-oriented DBMSs using different NVM latencies. The results in Figure 2.5b show that the throughput of both DBMSs do not change significantly as NVM latency increases. This is expected, since all of the transactions' write operations are initially stored on DRAM. These results corroborate previous studies that have shown the 10× performance advantage of an anti-caching system over the disk-oriented DBMS [68]. For the anti-caching system, this workload essentially measures how efficiently it can evict data to PMFS (since no transaction reads old data).

2.4.5   RECOVERY

Lastly, we evaluate recovery schemes in H-Store using the emulator's NUMA interface. We implemented logical logging (i.e., command logging) and physical logging (i.e., ARIES) recovery schemes within H-Store. For each scheme, we first measure the DBMS's runtime performance when executing a fixed number of TPC-C transactions (50,000). We then simulate a system failure and then measure how long it takes the DBMS to recover the database state from each scheme's corresponding log stored on PMFS.

For the runtime measurements, the results in Figure 2.7a show that H-Store achieves 2× higher throughput when using logical logging compared to physical logging. This is because logical logging only records the executed commands and thus is more lightweight. The amount of logging data for the workload using scheme is only 5 MB. In contrast, physical logging keeps track of all modifications made at tuple-level granularity and its corresponding log 220 MB. This reduced footprint makes logical logging more attractive for the first NVM devices that are expected to have limited capacities.

Next, in the results for the recovery times, Figure 2.7b shows that logical logging 3× is slower than physical logging. One could reduce this time in logical logging by having the DBMS checkpoint more frequently, but this will impact steady-state performance [136].

We note that both schemes are essentially doing unnecessary work, since all writes to memory when using the NUMA interface are potentially durable. A better approach is to use

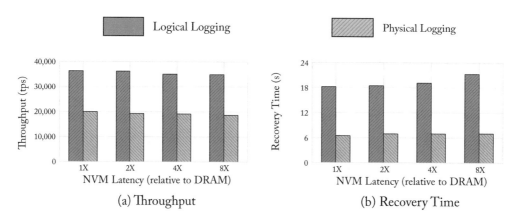

(a) Throughput   (b) Recovery Time

Figure 2.7: **Recovery Evaluation**—Comparison of recovery schemes in H-Store using the TPC-C benchmark.

a recovery scheme that is designed for NVM. This would allow a DBMS to combine the faster runtime performance of logical logging with the faster recovery of physical logging.

2.5   GOAL OF THIS DISSERTATION

In this chapter, we presented the results of our investigation on the impact of NVM on existing DBMSs. We explored two possible architectures using non-volatile memory (i.e., NVM-only and NVM+DRAM architectures). For each architecture, we evaluated memory-oriented and disk-oriented OLTP DBMSs. Our analysis shows that memory-oriented systems are better-suited to take advantage of NVM and outperform their disk-oriented counterparts. However, both memory-oriented and disk-oriented systems are doing unnecessary work in their storage and recovery methods, since all writes to NVM when using the NUMA interface are potentially durable. Because of this, we conclude that neither system is ideally suited for NVM. Instead, a new system is needed with principles of both disk-oriented and memory-oriented systems and a lightweight recovery scheme designed to utilize the non-volatile property of NVM.

In the remainder of this book, we will present the design and implementation of DBMS architectures that leverage the properties of NVM in their storage and recovery methods.

CHAPTER 3

Storage Management

In this chapter, we explore the fundamentals of storage and recovery methods in OLTP DBMSs running on a NVM-only storage hierarchy. This allows us to examine how the DBMS can leverage NVM while avoiding the overhead of dealing with the volatility of DRAM. We later extend these methods to a three-tier storage system that also includes DRAM and SSD in Chapters 4 and 5.

We implemented three storage engine architectures in a single DBMS: (1) in-place updates with logging, (2) copy-on-write updates without logging, and (3) log-structured updates. We then developed optimized variants for these approaches that reduce the computational overhead, storage footprint, and wear-out of NVM devices. For our evaluation, we configure the systems to only use NVM and volatile CPU-level caches on the hardware emulator (i.e., no DRAM).[1] Our analysis shows that the NVM-optimized storage engines improve the DBMS's throughput by a factor of 5.5× while reducing the number of writes to NVM in half.

The remainder of this chapter is organized as follows. In Section 3.1, we describe our DBMS testbed and its storage engines that we developed for this study. We then present in Section 3.2 our optimizations for these engines that leverage NVM's unique properties. We then present our experimental evaluation in Section 3.3.

3.1   DBMS TESTBED

We developed a lightweight DBMS, called N-Store, to evaluate different storage architecture designs for OLTP workloads. We did not use an existing DBMS as that would require significant changes to incorporate the storage engines into a single system. Although some DBMSs support a pluggable storage engine back-end (e.g., MySQL, MongoDB), modifying them to support NVM would still require significant changes. We also did not want to taint our measurements with features that are not relevant to our evaluation.

The DBMS's internal coordinator receives incoming transaction requests from the application and then invokes the target stored procedure. As a transaction executes in the system, it invokes queries to read and write tuples from the database. These requests are passed through a query executor that invokes the necessary operations on the DBMS's active storage engine.

The DBMS uses *pthreads* to allow multiple transactions to run concurrently in separate worker threads. It executes as a single process with the number of worker threads equal to the number of cores, where each thread is mapped to a different core. Since we do not want the

---

[1]A detailed description of the NVM hardware emulator is presented in Appendix A.

DBMS's concurrency control scheme to interfere with our evaluation, we partition the database and use a lightweight locking scheme where transactions are executed serially at each partition based on timestamp ordering [186].

Using a DBMS that supports a pluggable back-end allows us to compare the performance characteristics of different storage and recovery methods on a single platform. We implemented three storage engines that use different approaches for supporting durable updates to a database: (1) *in-place* updates engine, (2) *copy-on-write* updates engine, and (3) *log-structured* updates engine. Each engine also supports both primary and secondary indexes.

We now describe these engines in detail. For each engine, we first discuss how they apply changes made by transactions to the database and then how they ensure durability after a crash. All of these engines are based on the architectures found in state-of-the-art DBMSs. That is, they use memory obtained using the hardware emulator's allocator interface as volatile memory and do not exploit NVM's persistence. Later in Section 3.2, we present our improved variants of these engines that are optimized for NVM.

3.1.1   IN-PLACE UPDATES ENGINE (InP)

The first engine uses the most common storage engine strategy in DBMSs. With *in-place* updates, there is only a single version of each tuple at all times. When a transaction updates a field for an existing tuple, the system writes the new value directly on top of the original one. This is the most efficient method of applying changes since the engine does not make a copy of the tuple first before updating it and only the updated fields are modified. The design of this engine is based on VoltDB [15], which is a memory-oriented DBMS that does not contain legacy disk-oriented DBMS components like a buffer pool. The **InP** engine uses the STX B+tree library for all of its indexes [48].

Storage: Figure 3.1a illustrates the architecture of the **InP** engine. The storage area for tables is split into separate pools for fixed-sized *blocks* and variable-length *blocks*. Each block consists of a set of *slots*. The **InP** engine stores the table's tuples in fixed-size slots. This ensures that the tuples are byte-aligned and the engine can easily compute their offsets. Any field in a table that is larger than 8 bytes is stored separately in a variable-length slot. The 8-byte location of that slot is stored in that field's location in the tuple.

The tables' tuples are unsorted within these blocks. For each table, the DBMS maintains a list of unoccupied tuple slots. When a transaction deletes a tuple, the deleted tuple's slot is added to this pool. When a transaction inserts a tuple into a table, the engine first checks the table's pool for an available slot. If the pool is empty, then the engine allocates a new fixed-size block using the allocator interface. The engine also uses the allocator interface to maintain the indexes and stores them in memory.

Recovery: Since the changes made by transactions committed after the last checkpoint are not written to "durable" storage, the **InP** engine maintains a durable *write-ahead log* (WAL)

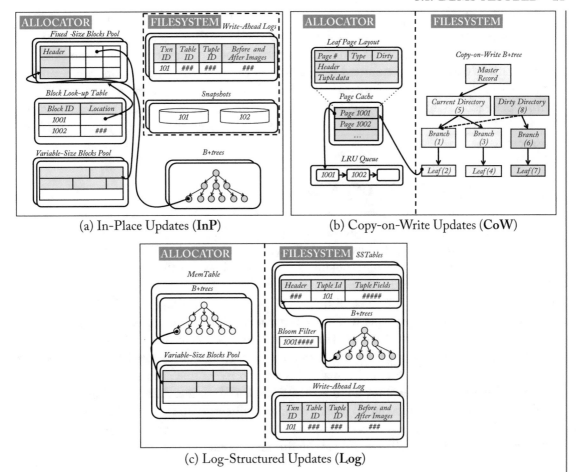

(a) In-Place Updates (**InP**)   (b) Copy-on-Write Updates (**CoW**)

(c) Log-Structured Updates (**Log**)

Figure 3.1: **Storage Engine Architectures**—Architectural layout of the three traditional storage engines supported in the DBMS testbed. The engine components accessed using the allocator interface and those accessed using the filesystem interface are bifurcated by the dashed line.

in the filesystem to assist in recovery from crashes and power failures. WAL records the transactions' changes before they are applied to DBMS [77]. As transactions execute queries that modify the database, the engine appends a new entry to the WAL for those changes. Each entry contains the transaction identifier, the table modified, the tuple identifier, and the before/after tuple images depending on the operation.

The most well-known recovery protocol for in-place updates is ARIES [142]. With ARIES, the engine periodically takes checkpoints that are stored on the filesystem to bound recovery latency and reduce the storage space consumed by the log. In our implementation, we compress (*gzip*) the checkpoints on the filesystem to reduce their storage footprint on NVM. During recovery, the engine first loads the last checkpoint. It then replays the log to ensure that the changes made by transactions committed since the checkpoint are present in the database. Modifications made by uncommitted transactions at the time of failure are not propagated to the database. The **InP** engine uses a variant of ARIES that is adapted for main memory DBMSs with a byte-addressable storage engine [136]. As we do not store physical changes to indexes in this log, all of the tables' indexes are rebuilt during recovery because they may have been corrupted.

3.1.2   COPY-ON-WRITE UPDATES ENGINE (CoW)

The second storage engine performs *copy-on-write* updates where instead of modifying the original tuple, it creates a copy of the tuple and then modifies that copy. As the **CoW** engine never overwrites committed data, it does not need to record changes in a WAL for recovery. The **CoW** engine instead uses different lookup *directories* for accessing the versions of tuples in the database. With this approach, known as *shadow paging* in IBM's System R [87], the DBMS maintains two lookup directories at all times: (1) the *current* directory and (2) the *dirty* directory. The current directory points to the most recent versions of the tuples and only contains the effects of committed transactions. The dirty directory points to the versions of tuples being modified by active transactions. To ensure that the transactions are isolated from the effects of uncommitted transactions, the engine maintains a *master record* that always points to the current directory. Figure 3.1b presents the architecture of the **CoW** engine. After applying the changes to the copy of the tuple, the engine updates the dirty directory to point to the new version of the tuple. When the transaction commits, the engine updates the master record atomically to point to the dirty directory. The engine maintains an internal page cache to keep the hot pages in memory.

System R implements shadow paging by copying the current directory to create the new dirty directory after every commit operation. But, creating the dirty directory in this manner incurs high I/O overhead. The **CoW** engine uses LMDB's CoW B+trees [57, 96, 175] to implement shadow paging efficiently. Figure 3.1b illustrates an update operation on a CoW B+tree. When the engine modifies the leaf node 4 in the current directory, it only needs to make a copy of the internal nodes lying along the path from that leaf node up to the root of the current version. The current and dirty directories of the CoW B+tree share the rest of the tree. This significantly reduces the I/O overhead of creating the dirty directory as only a fraction of the B+tree is copied. To further reduce the overhead of shadow paging, the **CoW** engine uses a group commit mechanism that batches the changes made by a group of transactions before committing the dirty directory.

Storage: The **CoW** engine stores the directories on the filesystem. The tuples in each table are stored in a HDD/SSD-optimized format where all the tuple's fields are inlined. This avoids expensive random accesses that are required when some fields are not inlined. Each database is stored in a separate file, and the master record for the database is located at a fixed offset within the file. It supports secondary indexes as a mapping of secondary keys to primary keys.

The downside of the **CoW** engine is that it creates a new copy of tuple even if a transaction only modifies a subset of the tuple's fields. The engine also needs to keep track of references to tuples from different versions of the CoW B+tree so that it can reclaim the storage space consumed by old unreferenced tuple versions [45]. As we show in Section 3.3.3, this engine has high write amplification (i.e., the amount of data written to storage is much higher compared to the amount of data written by the application). This increases wear on the NVM device thereby reducing its lifetime.

Recovery: If the DBMS crashes before the master record is updated, then the changes present in the dirty directory are not visible after restart. Hence, there is no recovery process for the **CoW** engine. When the DBMS comes back on-line, the master record points to the current directory that is guaranteed to be consistent. The dirty directory is garbage collected asynchronously since it only contains the changes of uncommitted transactions.

3.1.3 LOG-STRUCTURED UPDATES ENGINE (Log)

Lastly, the third storage engine uses a *log-structured* update policy. This approach originated from log-structured filesystems [176], and then it was adapted to DBMSs as *log-structured merge* (LSM) trees [153] for write-intensive workloads. The LSM tree consists of a collection of *runs* of data. Each run contains an ordered set of entries that record the changes performed on tuples. Runs reside either in volatile memory (i.e., *MemTable*) or on durable storage (i.e., *SSTables*) with their storage layout optimized for the underlying storage device. The LSM tree reduces write amplification by batching the updates in MemTable and periodically cascading the changes to durable storage [153]. The design for our **Log** engine is based on Google's LevelDB [66], which implements the log-structured update policy using LSM trees.

Storage: Figure 3.1c depicts the architecture of the **Log** engine. The **Log** engine uses a *leveled* LSM tree [115], where each level in the tree contains the changes for a single run. The data starts from the MemTable stored in the topmost level and propagates down to SSTables stored in lower parts of the tree over time. The size of the run stored in a given level is k times larger than that of the run stored in its parent, where k is the growth factor of the tree. The **Log** engine allows us to control the size of the MemTable and the growth factor of the tree. It first stores the tuple modifications in a memory-optimized format using the allocator interface in the MemTable. The MemTable contains indexes to handle point and range queries efficiently. When the size of the MemTable exceeds a threshold, the engine flushes it to the filesystem as an immutable SSTable stored in a separate file. The **Log** engine also constructs a Bloom filter [50] for each SSTable to quickly determine at runtime whether it contains entries associated with a tuple to avoid unnecessary index lookups.

The contents of the MemTable are lost after system restart. Hence, to ensure durability, the **Log** engine maintains a WAL in the filesystem. The engine first records the changes in the log and then applies the changes to the MemTable. The log entry contains the transaction identifier, the table modified, the tuple identifier, and the before/after images of the tuple depending on the type of operation. To reduce the I/O overhead, the engine batches log entries for a group of transactions and flushes them together.

The log-structured update approach performs well for write-intensive workloads as it reduces random writes to durable storage. The downside of the **Log** engine is that it incurs high read amplification (i.e., the number of reads required to fetch the data is much higher than that actually needed by the application). To retrieve a tuple, the **Log** engine first needs to lookup the indexes of all the runs of the LSM tree that contain entries associated with the desired tuple [1]. To reduce this read amplification, the **Log** engine performs a periodic *compaction* process that merges a subset of SSTables. First, the entries associated with a tuple in different SSTables are merged into one entry in a new SSTable. Tombstone entries are used to identify purged tuples. Then, the engine builds indexes for the new SSTable.

Recovery: During recovery, the **Log** engine rebuilds the MemTable using the WAL, as the changes contained in it were not written onto durable storage. It first replays the log to ensure that the changes made by committed transactions are present. It then removes any changes performed by uncommitted transactions, thereby bringing the MemTable to a consistent state.

3.2   NVM-AWARE ENGINES

All of the engines described above are derived from existing DBMS architectures that are predicated on a two-tier storage hierarchy comprised of volatile DRAM and a non-volatile SSD/HDD. These devices have distinct hardware constraints and performance properties. The traditional engines were designed to account for and reduce the impact of these differences. For example, they maintain two layouts of tuples depending on the storage device. Tuples stored in memory can contain non-inlined fields because DRAM is byte-addressable and handles random accesses efficiently. In contrast, fields in tuples stored on durable storage are inlined to avoid random accesses because they are more expensive. To amortize the overhead for accessing durable storage, these engines batch writes and flush them in a deferred manner.

Many of these techniques, however, are unnecessary in a system with a NVM-only storage hierarchy [67, 73, 144]. We adapt the storage and recovery mechanisms of these traditional engines to exploit NVM's characteristics. We refer to these optimized storage engines as the *NVM-aware* engines. As we show in our evaluation in Section 3.3, these engines deliver higher throughput than their traditional counterparts while still ensuring durability. They reduce write amplification using NVM's persistence thereby expanding the lifetime of the NVM device. These engines only use the emulator's allocator interface with NVM-optimized data structures [144, 191].

Table 3.1 presents an overview of the steps performed by the NVM-aware storage engines, while executing the primitive database operations. We note that the engine performs these operations within the context of a transaction. For instance, if the transaction aborts while executing an operation, it must undo the effects of earlier operations performed by the transaction.

3.2.1   IN-PLACE UPDATES ENGINE (NVM-InP)

One of the main problems with the **InP** engine described in Section 3.1.1 is that it has high rate of data duplication. When a transaction inserts a tuple, the engine records the tuple's contents in the WAL and then again in the table storage area. The **InP** engine's logging infrastructure also assumes that the system's durable storage device has orders of magnitude higher write latency compared to DRAM. It batches multiple log records and flushes them periodically to the WAL using sequential writes. This approach, however, increases the mean response latency as transactions need to wait for the group commit operation.

Given this, we designed the **NVM-InP** engine to avoid these issues. Now when a transaction inserts a tuple, rather than copying the tuple to the WAL, the **NVM-InP** engine only records a non-volatile pointer to the tuple in the WAL. This is sufficient because both the pointer and the tuple referred to by the pointer are stored on NVM. Thus, the engine can use the pointer to access the tuple after the system restarts without needing to re-apply changes in the WAL. It also stores indexes as non-volatile B+trees that can be accessed immediately when the system restarts without rebuilding.

Storage: The architecture of the **NVM-InP** engine is shown in Figure 3.2a and Table 3.1 presents an overview of the steps to perform different operations. The engine stores tuples and non-inlined fields using fixed-size and variable-length slots, respectively. To reclaim the storage space of tuples and non-inlined fields inserted by uncommitted transactions after the system restarts, the **NVM-InP** engine maintains *durability state* in each slot's header. A slot can be in one of three states—unallocated, allocated but not persisted, or persisted. After the system restarts, slots that are allocated but not persisted transition back to the unallocated state.

The **NVM-InP** engine stores the WAL as a non-volatile linked list. It appends new entries to the list using an atomic write. Each entry contains the transaction identifier, the table modified, the tuple identifier, and pointers to the operation's changes. The changes include tuple pointers for insert operation and field pointers for update operations on non-inlined fields. The engine persists this entry before updating the slot's state as persisted. If it does not ensure this ordering, then the engine cannot reclaim the storage space consumed by uncommitted transactions after the system restarts, thereby causing non-volatile memory leaks. After all of the transaction's changes are safely persisted, the engine truncates the log.

Table 3.1: **Operations Performed by NVM-Aware Engines**—An overview of the steps performed by the NVM-aware storage engines, while executing primitive database operations. The syncing mechanism is implemented using CLFLUSH and SFENCE instructions on the hardware emulator.

	NVM-InP Engine	NVM-CoW Engine	NVM-Log Engine
INSERT	• Sync tuple with NVM • Record tuple pointer in WAL • Sync log entry with NVM • Mark tuple state as persisted • Add tuple entry in indexes	• Sync tuple with NVM • Store tuple pointer in dirty dir. • Update tuple state as persisted • Add tuple entry in secondary indexes	• Sync tuple with NVM • Record tuple pointer in WAL • Sync log entry with NVM • Mark tuple state as persisted • Add tuple entry in MemTable
UPDATE	• Record tuple changes in WAL • Sync log entry with NVM • Perform modifications on the tuple • Sync tuple changes with NVM	• Make a copy of the tuple • Apply changes on the copy • Sync tuple with NVM • Store tuple pointer in dirty dir. • Update tuple state as persisted • Add tuple entry in secondary indexes	• Record tuple changes in WAL • Sync log entry with NVM • Perform modifications on the tuple • Sync tuple changes with NVM
DELETE	• Record tuple pointer in WAL • Sync log entry with NVM • Discard entry from table and indexes • Reclaim space at the end of transaction	• Remove tuple pointer from dirty dir. • Discard entry from secondary indexes • Recover tuple space immediately	• Record tuple pointer in WAL • Sync log entry with NVM • Mark tuple tombstone in MemTable • Reclaim space during compaction
SELECT	• Find tuple pointer using index/table • Retrieve tuple contents	• Locate tuple pointer in appropriate dir. • Fetch tuple contents from dir.	• Find tuple entries in relevant LSM runs • Rebuild tuple by coalescing entries

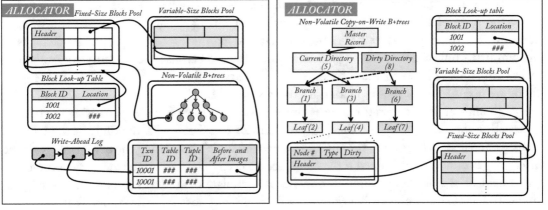

(a) In-Place Updates (NVM-**InP**)   (b) Copy-on-Write Updates (NVM-**CoW**)

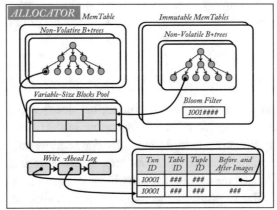

(c) Log-Structured Updates NVM-(**Log**)

Figure 3.2: **NVM-Aware Engines**—Architectural layout of the NVM-optimized storage engines.

The engine supports primary and secondary indexes using non-volatile B+trees that it maintains using the allocator interface. We modified the STX B+tree library so that all operations that alter the index's internal structure are atomic [144, 191]. For instance, when adding an entry to a B+tree node, instead of inserting the key in a sorted order, it appends the entry to a list of entries in the node. This modification is necessary because if the entry crosses cache line boundaries, the cache line write-backs required to persist the entry need not happen atomically. Our changes to the library ensure that the engine can safely access the index immediately after the system restarts as it is guaranteed to be in a consistent state.

Recovery: The effects of committed transactions are durable after the system restarts because the **NVM-InP** engine immediately persists the changes made by a transaction when it commits. So, the engine does not need to replay the log during recovery. But the changes of uncommitted transactions may be present in the database because the memory controller can evict cache lines containing those changes to NVM at any time [143]. The **NVM-InP** engine therefore needs to undo those transactions using the WAL.

To undo an insert operation, the engine releases the tuple's storage space using the pointer recorded in the WAL entry and then removes entries associated with the tuple in the indexes. In case of an update operation, the engine restores the tuple's state using the before image. If the after image contains non-inlined tuple fields, then the engine frees up the memory occupied by those fields. For a delete operation, it only needs to update the indexes to point to the original tuple. To handle transaction rollbacks and DBMS recovery correctly, the **NVM-InP** engine releases storage space occupied by tuples or non-inlined fields only after it is certain that they are no longer required. As this recovery protocol does not include a redo process, the **NVM-InP** engine has a short recovery latency that only depends on the number of uncommitted transactions.

3.2.2   COPY-ON-WRITE UPDATES ENGINE (NVM-CoW)

The original **CoW** engine stores tuples in self-containing blocks without pointers in the CoW B+tree on the filesystem. The problem with this engine is that the overhead of propagating modifications to the dirty directory is high; even if a transaction only modifies one tuple, the engine needs to copy the entire block to the filesystem. When a transaction commits, the **CoW** engine uses the filesystem interface to flush the dirty blocks and updates the master record (stored at a fixed location in the file) to point to the root of the dirty directory [57]. These writes are expensive as they need to switch the privilege level and go through the kernel's VFS path.

The **NVM-CoW** engine employs three optimizations to reduce these overheads. First, it uses a non-volatile copy-on-write B+tree that it maintains using the allocator interface. Second, the **NVM-CoW** engine directly persists the tuple copies and only records non-volatile tuple pointers in the dirty directory. Lastly, it uses the lightweight durability mechanism of the allocator interface to persist changes in the CoW B+tree.

Storage: Figure 3.2b depicts the architecture of the **NVM-CoW** engine. The storage area for tuples is spread across separate pools for fixed-sized and variable-length data. The engine maintains the durability state of each slot in both pools similar to the **NVM-InP** engine. The **NVM-CoW** engine stores the current and dirty directory of the non-volatile copy-on-write B+tree using the allocator interface. We modified the B+tree from LMDB [57] to handle modifications at finer granularity to exploit NVM's byte addressability. The engine maintains the master record using the allocator interface to support efficient updates. When the system restarts, the engine can safely access the current directory using the master record because that directory is guaranteed to be in a consistent state. This is because the data structure is append-only and the data stored in the current directory is never overwritten.

The execution steps for this engine are shown in Table 3.1. The salient feature of this engine's design is that it avoids the transformation and copying costs incurred by the **CoW** engine. When a transaction updates a tuple, the engine first makes a copy and then applies the changes to that copy. It then records only the non-volatile tuple pointer in the dirty directory. The engine also batches transactions to amortize the cost of persisting the current directory. To commit a batch of transactions, it first persists the changes performed by uncommitted transactions. It then persists the contents of the dirty directory. Finally, it updates the master record using an atomic durable write to point to that directory. The engine orders all of these writes using memory barriers to ensure that only committed transactions are visible after the system restarts.

Recovery: As the **NVM-CoW** engine never overwrites committed data, it does not have a recovery process. When the system restarts, it first accesses the master record to locate the current directory. After that, it can start handling transactions. The storage space consumed by the dirty directory at the time of failure is asynchronously reclaimed by the NVM-aware allocator.

3.2.3   LOG-STRUCTURED UPDATES ENGINE (NVM-Log)

The **Log** engine batches all writes in the MemTable to reduce random accesses to durable storage [129, 153]. The benefits of this approach, however, are not as evident for a NVM-only storage hierarchy because the performance gap between sequential and random accesses is smaller. The original log-structured engine that we described in Section 3.1.3 incurs significant overhead from periodically flushing MemTable to the filesystem and compacting SSTables to bound read amplification. Similar to the **NVM-InP** engine, the **NVM-Log** engine records all the changes performed by transactions on a WAL stored on NVM.

Our **NVM-Log** engine avoids data duplication in the MemTable and the WAL as it only records non-volatile pointers to tuple modifications in the WAL. Instead of flushing MemTable out to the filesystem as a SSTable, it only marks the MemTable as immutable and starts a new MemTable. This immutable MemTable is physically stored in the same way on NVM as the mutable MemTable. The only difference is that the engine does not propagate writes to the immutable MemTables. We also modified the compaction process to merge a set of these MemTables to generate a new larger MemTable. The **NVM-Log** engine uses a NVM-aware recovery protocol that has lower recovery latency than its traditional counterpart.

Storage: As shown in Figure 3.2c, the **NVM-Log** engine uses an LSM tree to store the database. Each level of the tree contains a sorted run of data. Similar to the **Log** engine, this engine first stores all the changes performed by transactions in the MemTable which is the topmost level of the LSM tree. The changes include tuple contents for insert operation, updated fields for update operation and tombstone markers for delete operation. When the size of the MemTable exceeds a threshold, the **NVM-Log** engine marks it as immutable and starts a new MemTable. We modify the periodic compaction process the engine performs for bounding read amplification to merge a set of immutable MemTables and create a new MemTable. The engine constructs a Bloom filter [50] for each immutable MemTable to minimize unnecessary index lookups.

Similar to the **Log** engine, the **NVM-Log** engine maintains a WAL. The purpose of the WAL is not to rebuild the MemTable, but rather to undo the effects of uncommitted transactions from the MemTable. An overview of the operations performed by the **NVM-Log** engine is shown in Table 3.1. Like the **NVM-InP** engine, this new engine also stores the WAL as a non-volatile linked list of entries. When a transaction inserts a tuple, the engine first flushes the tuple to NVM and records the non-volatile tuple pointer in a WAL entry. It then persists the log entry and marks the tuple as persisted. Finally, it adds an entry in the MemTable indexes. After the transaction commits, the engine truncates the relevant log entry because the changes recorded in MemTable are durable. Its logging overhead is lower than the **Log** engine as it records less data and maintains the WAL using the allocator interface. The engine uses non-volatile B+trees [144, 191], described in Section 3.2.1, as MemTable indexes. Hence, it does not need to rebuild its indexes upon restarting.

Recovery: When the transaction commits, all the changes performed by the transaction are persisted in the in-memory component. During recovery, the **NVM-Log** engine only needs to undo the effects of uncommitted transactions on the MemTable. Its recovery latency is therefore lower than the **Log** engine as it no longer needs to rebuild the MemTable.

3.3   EXPERIMENTAL EVALUATION

In this section, we present our analysis of the six different storage engine implementations. Our DBMS testbed allows us to evaluate the throughput, the number of reads/writes to the NVM device, the storage footprint, and the time that it takes to recover the database after restarting. We also use the *perf* toolkit to measure additional, lower-level hardware metrics of the system for each experiment [6].

The experiments were all performed on the NVM hardware emulator described in Appendix A. The engines access NVM using the allocator and filesystem interfaces of the emulator. We use the Intel memory latency checker [195] to validate the emulator's latency and bandwidth settings. We set up the DBMS to use eight partitions in all of the experiments. We configure the node size of the STX B+tree and the CoW B+tree implementations to be 512 B and 4 KB, respectively. All transactions execute with the same serializable isolation level and durability guarantees.

3.3.1   BENCHMARKS

We use the YCSB and TPC-C benchmarks for our evaluation. A detailed description of these benchmarks is provided in Appendix B. The tables in each database are partitioned in such way that there are only single-partition transactions [162]. The database for the YCSB benchmark contains 2 million tuples (~2 GB). For each workload mixture and skew setting pair, we pre-generate a fixed workload of 8 million transactions that is divided evenly among the DBMS's partitions. Using a fixed workload that is the same across all the engines allows us to compare their storage footprints and read/write amplification. We configure the TPC-C workload to contain eight warehouses and 100,000 items. We map each warehouse to a single partition. The initial storage footprint of the database is approximately 1 GB.

3.3.2   RUNTIME PERFORMANCE

We begin with an analysis of the impact of NVM's latency on the performance of the storage engines. To obtain insights that are applicable for various NVM technologies, we run the benchmarks under three latency configurations on the emulator: (1) default DRAM latency configuration (160 ns); (2) a *low* NVM latency configuration that is 2× higher than DRAM latency (320 ns); and (3) a *high* NVM latency configuration that is 8× higher than DRAM latency (1280 ns). We execute all workloads three times on each engine and report the average throughput.

YCSB: Figures 3.3 to 3.5 present the throughput observed with the YCSB benchmark while varying the workload mixture and skew settings under different latency configurations. We first consider the read-only workload results shown in Figures 3.3a, 3.4a, and 3.5a. These results provide an upper bound on performance since transactions do not modify the database and the engines therefore do not need to flush changes from CPU caches to NVM during execution.

The most notable observation is that the **NVM-InP** engine is not faster than the **InP** engine for both skew settings. This is because both engines perform reads using the allocator interface. The **CoW** engine's throughput is lower than the in-place updates engine because for every transaction, it fetches the master record and then looks-up the tuple in the current directory. As the **NVM-CoW** engine accesses the master record and the non-volatile copy-on-write B+tree efficiently using the allocator interface, it is 1.9–2.1× faster than the **CoW** engine. The **Log** engine is the slowest among all the engines because it coalesces entries spread across different LSM tree components to reconstruct tuples. The **NVM-Log** engine accesses the immutable MemTables using the allocator interface and delivers 2.8× higher throughput compared to its traditional counterpart. We see that increasing the workload skew improves the performance of all the engines due to caching benefits. The benefits are most evident for the **InP** and **NVM-InP** engines; they achieve 1.3× higher throughput compared to the low skew setting. The perfor-

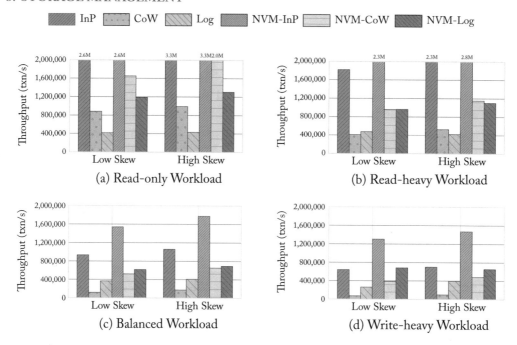

Figure 3.3: **YCSB Performance (DRAM Latency)**—The throughput of the engines for the YCSB benchmark without any latency slowdown.

mance gains due to skew are minimal in case of the **Log** and **NVM-Log** engines due to tuple coalescing costs.

We also observe that the performance gap between the two types of engines decreases in the read-only workload when we increase the NVM latency. In the high latency configuration, the **NVM-CoW** and the **NVM-Log** engines are 1.4× and 2.5× faster than their traditional counterparts. This is because the benefits of accessing data structures using the allocator interface are masked by slower NVM loads. The engines' throughput decreases sub-linearly with respect to the increased NVM latency. For example, with 8× higher latency, the throughput of the engines only drop by 2–3.4×. The NVM-aware engines are more sensitive to the increase in latency as they do not incur tuple transformation and copying costs that dampen the effect of slower NVM accesses in the traditional engines.

For the read-heavy workload, the results shown in Figures 3.3b, 3.4b, and 3.5b indicate that the throughput decreases for all the engines compared to the read-only workload because they must flush transactions' changes to NVM. Unlike before where the two engines had the same performance, in this workload, we observe that the **NVM-InP** engine is 1.3× faster than the **InP** engine due to lower logging overhead. The performance of the **CoW** engine drops compared to its performance on the read-only workload because of the overhead of persisting

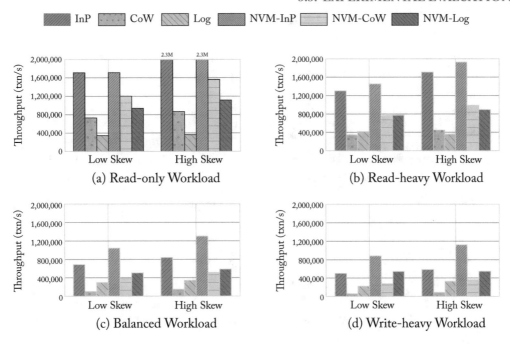

Figure 3.4: **YCSB Performance (Low Latency)**—The throughput of the engines for the YCSB benchmark under the low NVM latency configuration (2×).

the current directory. The drop is less prominent in the high skew workload because the updates are now concentrated over a few hot tuples and therefore the number of CoW B+tree nodes that are copied when creating the dirty directory is smaller.

The benefits of our optimizations are more prominent for the balanced and write-heavy workloads. For the **NVM-InP** and the **NVM-Log** engines, we attribute this to lower logging overhead. In case of the **NVM-CoW** engine, this is because it does not have to copy and transform tuples from the filesystem whenever it modifies them. This allows this engine to achieve 4.3–5.5× higher throughput than the **CoW** engine. The performance gap between the **Log** and the **CoW** engines decreases because the former incurs lower tuple coalescing costs in these workloads. The **Log** engine is therefore 1.6–4.1× faster than the **CoW** engine. It still lags behind the **InP** engine, however, because batching updates in the MemTable are not as beneficial in the NVM-only storage hierarchy. With increased latency, the throughput of all the engines decreases less on these write-intensive workloads compared to the workloads that contain more reads. The throughput does not drop linearly with increasing NVM latency. With an 8× increase in latency, the throughput of the engines only drops by 1.8–2.9×. We attribute this to the effects of caching and memory-level parallelism in the emulator.

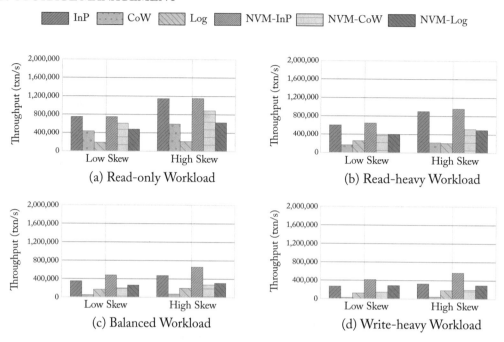

Figure 3.5: **YCSB Performance (High Latency)**—The throughput of the engines for the YCSB benchmark under the high NVM latency configuration (8×).

TPC-C: Figure 3.6 shows the engines' throughput while executing TPC-C under different latency configurations. Among all the engines, the **NVM-InP** engine performs the best. The NVM-aware engines are 1.8–2.1× faster than the traditional engines. The **NVM-CoW** engine exhibits the highest speedup of 2.3× over the **CoW** engine. We attribute this to the write-intensive nature of the TPC-C benchmark. Under the high NVM latency configuration, the NVM-aware engines deliver 1.7–1.9× higher throughput than their traditional counterparts. These trends closely follow the results for the write-intensive workload mixture in the YCSB benchmark. The benefits of our optimizations, however, are not as significant as previously observed with the YCSB benchmark. This is because the TPC-C transactions' contain more complex program logic and execute more queries per transaction.

3.3.3   READS AND WRITES

We next measure the number of times that the storage engines access the NVM device while executing the benchmarks. This is important because the number of write cycles per bit is limited in different NVM technologies, as shown in Table 1.1. We compute these results using hardware performance counters on the emulator with the *perf* framework [6]. These counters track the number of loads (i.e., reads) from and stores (i.e., writes) to the NVM device during

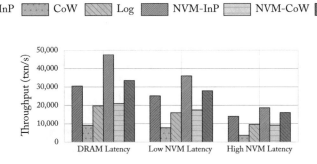

Figure 3.6: **TPC-C Throughput**—The performance of the engines for TPC-C benchmark for all three NVM latency settings.

execution. In each trial, the engines' access measurements are collected after loading the initial database.

YCSB: The results for NVM reads and writes while executing the YCSB benchmark are shown in Figures 3.7 and 3.8, respectively. In the read-only workload, we observe that the **Log** engine performs the most load operations due to tuple coalescing. The NVM-aware engines perform up to 53% fewer loads due to better cache locality as they do not perform any tuple deserialization operations. When we increase the workload skew, there is a significant drop in the NVM loads performed by all the engines. We attribute this to caching of hot tuples in the CPU caches.

In the write-intensive workloads, we observe that the **CoW** engine now performs the most NVM stores. This is because it needs to copy several pages while creating the dirty directory. This engine also performs the largest number of load operations. The copying mechanism itself requires reading data off NVM. Further, the I/O overhead of maintaining this directory reduces the number of hot tuples that can reside in the CPU caches.

On the write-heavy workload, the NVM-aware engines perform 17–48% fewer stores compared to their traditional counterparts. We attribute this to their lightweight durability mechanisms and smaller storage footprints that enable them to make better use of hardware caches. Even with increased workload skew, the NVM-aware engines perform 9–41% fewer NVM writes. We note that the NVM accesses performed by the storage engines correlate inversely with the throughput delivered by these engines, as shown in Section 3.3.2.

TPC-C: Figure 3.9 presents the NVM accesses performed while executing the TPC-C benchmark. NVM-aware engines perform 31–42% fewer writes compared to the traditional engines. We see that the access patterns are similar to that observed with the write-intensive workload mixture in the YCSB benchmark. The **Log** engine performs more writes in this benchmark compared to the YCSB benchmark because it has more indexes. This means that

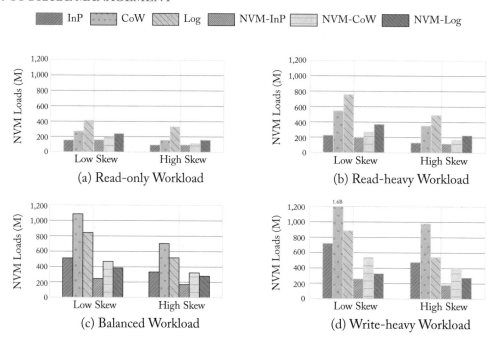

Figure 3.7: **YCSB Reads**—The number of load operations executed by the engines while running the YCSB workload.

updating a tuple requires updating several indexes as well.

3.3.4   RECOVERY

In this experiment, we evaluate the recovery latency of the storage engines. For each benchmark, we first execute a fixed number of transactions and then force a hard shutdown of the DBMS (SIGKILL). We then measure the amount of time for the system to restore the database to a consistent state. That is, a state where the effects of all committed transactions are durable, and the effects of uncommitted transactions are removed. The number of transactions that need to be recovered by the DBMS depends on the frequency of checkpointing for the **InP** engine and on the frequency of flushing the MemTable for the **Log** engine. The **CoW** and **NVM-CoW** engines do not perform any recovery mechanism after the OS or DBMS restarts because they never overwrite committed data. They have to perform garbage collection to clean up the previous dirty directory. This is done asynchronously and does not have a significant impact on the throughput of the DBMS.

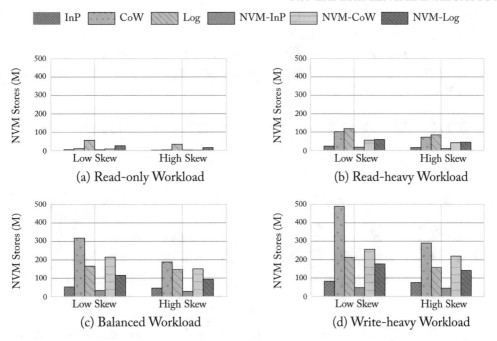

Figure 3.8: **YCSB Writes**—The number of store operations executed by the engines while running the YCSB workload.

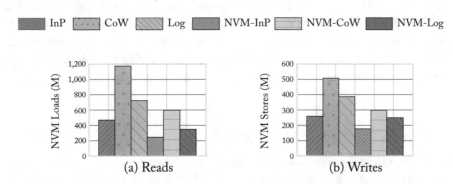

Figure 3.9: **TPC-C Reads & Writes**—The number of load and store operations executed by the engines while running the TPC-C benchmark.

YCSB: The results in Figure 3.10a show the recovery measurements for the YCSB benchmark. We do not show the **CoW** and **NVM-CoW** engines as they never need to recover. We observe that the latency of the **InP** and **Log** engines grows linearly with the number of transactions that need to be recovered. This is because these engines first redo the effects of committed transactions before undoing the effects of uncommitted transactions. In contrast, the **NVM-InP** and **NVM-Log** engines' recovery time is independent of the number of transactions executed. These engines only need to undo the effects of transactions that are active at the time of failure and not the ones since the last checkpoint or flush. So the NVM-aware engines have a short recovery that is always less than a second.

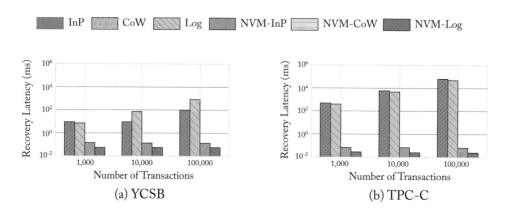

Figure 3.10: **Recovery Latency**—The amount of time that the engines take to restore the database to a consistent state after a restart.

TPC-C: The results for the TPC-C benchmark are shown in Figure 3.10b. The recovery latency of the **NVM-InP** and **NVM-Log** engines is slightly higher than that in the YCSB benchmark because the TPC-C transactions perform more operations. However, the latency is still independent of the number of transactions executed unlike the traditional engines because the NVM-aware engines ensure that the effects of committed transactions are persisted immediately.

3.3.5   EXECUTION TIME BREAKDOWN

We next analyze the time that the engines spend in their internal components during execution. We only examine YCSB with low skew and low NVM latency configuration, which allows us to better understand the benefits and limitations of our implementations. We use event-based sampling with the *perf* framework [6] to track the cycles executed within the engine's components. We start this profiling after loading the initial database.

The engine's cycles are classified into four categories: (1) *storage* management operations with the allocator and filesystem interfaces; (2) *recovery* mechanisms like logging; (3) *index* accesses and maintenance; and (4) *other* miscellaneous components. This last category is different for each engine; it includes the time spent in synchronizing the engine's components and performing engine-specific tasks, such as compaction in case of the **Log** and **NVM-Log** engines.

As our testbed uses a lightweight concurrency control mechanism, these results do not contain any overhead from locking or latching [186].

The most notable result for this experiment, as shown in Figure 3.11, is that on the write-heavy workload, the NVM-aware engines only spend 13–18% of their time on recovery-related tasks compared to the traditional engines that spend as much as 33% of their time on them. We attribute this to the lower logging overhead in the case of the **NVM-InP** and **NVM-Log** engines, and the reduced cost of committing the dirty directory in the **NVM-CoW** engine. We observe that the proportion of the time that the engines spend on recovery mechanisms increases as the workload becomes write-intensive. This explains why the benefits of our optimizations are more prominent for the balanced and write-heavy workloads.

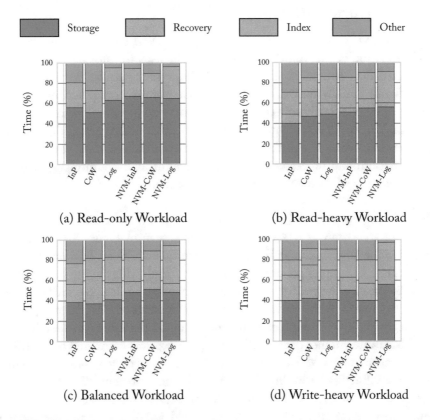

Figure 3.11: **Execution Time Breakdown**—The time that the engines spend in their internal components when running the YCSB benchmark.

These results highlight the benefits of optimizing the memory allocator to leverage NVM's characteristics. This is because the NVM-aware engines spend most of their time performing storage management operations since their recovery mechanisms are so efficient. Interestingly, the engines performing CoW updates spend a higher proportion of time on recovery-related tasks compared to other engines, particularly on the read-heavy workload. This highlights the cost of creating and maintaining the dirty directory for large databases, even using an efficient CoW B+tree. Another observation from Figure 3.11 is that the **Log** and **NVM-Log** engines spend a higher fraction of their time accessing and maintaining indexes. This is because they perform multiple index lookups on the LSM tree to reconstruct tuples. We observe that the **NVM-Log** engine spends less time performing the compaction process compared to the **Log** engine. This is due to the reduced overhead of maintaining the MemTables using the allocator interface.

3.3.6 STORAGE FOOTPRINT

In this experiment, we compare the engines' usage of NVM storage at runtime. The storage footprint of an engine is the amount of space that it uses for storing tables, logs, indexes, and other internal data structures. This metric is important because we expect that the first NVM products will initially have a higher cost than current storage technologies [109]. For this experiment, we periodically collect statistics maintained by our allocator and the filesystem meta-data during the workload execution. This is done after loading the initial database for each benchmark. We then report the peak storage footprint of each engine. For all of the engines, we allow their background processes (e.g., group commit, checkpointing, garbage collection, compaction) to execute while we collect these measurements.

YCSB: We use the balanced workload mixture and low skew setting for this experiment. The initial size of the database is 2 GB. The results shown in Figure 3.12a indicate that the **CoW** engine has the largest storage footprint. Since this workload contains transactions that modify the database and tuples are accessed more uniformly, this engine incurs high overhead from continually creating new dirty directories and copying tuples. The **InP** and **Log** engines rely on logging to improve their recovery latency at the expense of a larger storage footprint. The **InP** engine checkpoints have a high compression ratio and therefore consume less space.

The NVM-aware engines have smaller storage footprints compared to the traditional engines. This is because the **NVM-InP** and **NVM-Log** engines only record non-volatile pointers to tuples and non-inlined fields in the WAL. As such, they consume 17–21% less storage space than their traditional counterparts. For the **CoW** engine, its large storage footprint is due to duplicated data in its internal cache. In contrast, the **NVM-CoW** engine accesses the non-volatile CoW B+tree directly using the allocator interface, and only records non-volatile tuple pointers in this tree and not entire tuples. This allows it to use 25% less storage space.

TPC-C: The graph in Figure 3.12b shows the storage footprint of the engines while executing TPC-C. For this benchmark, the initial size of the database is 1 GB, and it grows to 2.4 GB. Transactions inserting new tuples increase the size of the internal data structures in the **CoW** and **Log** engines (i.e., the CoW B+trees and the SSTables stored in the filesystem).

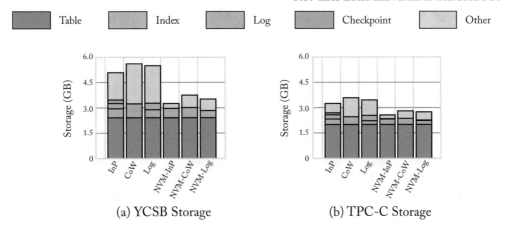

Figure 3.12: **Storage Footprint**—The amount of storage occupied in NVM by the internal components of the engines.

By avoiding unnecessary data duplication using NVM's persistence property, the NVM-aware engines have 31–38% smaller storage footprints. The space savings are more significant in this benchmark because the workload is write-intensive with longer running transactions. Thus, the logs in the **InP** and the **Log** engines grow more quickly compared to the small undo logs in their NVM-aware counterparts.

3.3.7 ANALYTICAL COST MODEL

We next present a cost model to estimate the amount of data written to NVM per operation, by the traditional and NVM-optimized storage engines. This model highlights the strengths and weaknesses of these engines.

We begin the analysis by stating the assumptions we use to simplify the model. First, the database operations are presumed to be always successful. The amount of data written to NVM while performing an aborted operation will depend on the stage at which the operation fails. We therefore restrict our analysis to only successful operations. Second, the engines handle fixed-length and variable-length tuple fields differently. The fixed-length fields are stored in-line, while the variable-length fields are stored separately. To illustrate this difference, we assume that the update operation alters one fixed-length field and one variable-length field. Note that the tuple itself can contain any number of fixed-length and variable-length fields depending on the database schema.

Let us now describe some notation. We denote the size of the tuple by T. This depends on the specific table on which the engine performs the database operation. Let the size of the fixed-length field and the variable-length field altered by the update operation be F and V, respectively. These parameters depend on the table columns that are modified by the engine. The size of a pointer is represented by p. The NVM-optimized engines use non-volatile pointers to tuples and variable-length tuple fields to reduce data duplication. We use θ to denote the write-amplification factor of the engines performing log-structured updates. θ could be attributed to the periodic compaction mechanism that these engines perform to bound read-amplification and depends on the type of LSM tree. Let B represent the size of a node in the CoW B+tree used by the **CoW** and **NVM-CoW** engines. We indicate small fixed-length writes to NVM, such as those used to maintain the status of tuple slots, by ϵ.

Given this notation, we present the cost model in Table 3.2. The data written to NVM is classified into three categories: (1) memory, (2) log, and (3) table storage. We now describe some notable entries in the table. While performing an insert operation, the **InP** engine writes three physical copies of a tuple. In contrast, the **NVM-InP** engine only records the tuple pointer in the log and table data structures on NVM. In the case of the **CoW** and **NVM-CoW** engines, there are two possibilities depending on whether a copy of the relevant B+tree node is absent or present in the dirty directory. For the latter, the engines do not need to make a copy of the node before applying the desired transformation. We distinguish these two cases in the relevant table entries using vertical bars. Note that these engines have no logging overhead. The performance gap between the traditional and the NVM-optimized engines, particularly for write-intensive workloads, directly follows from the cost model presented in the table.

3.3.8   IMPACT OF B+TREE NODE SIZE

We examine the sensitivity of our experimental results to size of the B+tree nodes in this section. The engines performing in-place and log-structured updates use the STX B+tree [48] for maintaining indexes, while the engines performing CoW updates use the append-only B+tree [57, 96, 175] for storing the directories. In all our experiments, we use the default node size for both the STX B+tree (512 B) and CoW B+tree (4 KB) implementations. For this analysis, we vary the B+tree node size and examine the impact on the engine's throughput, while executing different YCSB workloads under low NVM latency (2×) and low workload skew settings. We restrict our analysis to the NVM-aware engines as they are representative of other engines.

The graphs, shown in Figure 3.13, indicate that the impact of B+tree node size is more significant for the CoW B+tree than the STX B+tree. In case of the CoW B+tree, we observe that increasing the node size improves the engine's performance on read-heavy workloads. This can be attributed to smaller tree depth, which in turn reduces the amount of indirection in the data structure. It also reduces the amount of metadata that needs to be flushed to NVM to ensure recoverability. However, the engine's performance on write-heavy workloads drops as the B+tree nodes get larger. This is because of the copying overhead when performing updates in the dirty directory of the CoW B+tree. We found that the engines performing copy-on-write updates perform well on both types of workloads when the node size is 4 KB. With the STX B+tree, our experiments suggest that the optimal node size is 512 B. This setting provides a nice balance

Table 3.2: **Analytical Cost Model**—Cost model for estimating the amount of data written to NVM, while performing insert, update, and delete operations, by each engine.

		Insert		Update		Delete
InP	Memory	$: T$	Memory	$: F + V$	Memory	$: \epsilon$
	Log	$: T$	Log	$: 2 \times (F + V)$	Log	$: T$
	Table	$: T$	Table	$: F + V$	Table	$: \epsilon$
CoW	Memory	$: B + T \parallel T$	Memory	$: B + F + V \parallel F + V$	Memory	$: B + \epsilon \parallel \epsilon$
	Log	$: 0$	Log	$: 0$	Log	$: 0$
	Table	$: B \parallel T$	Table	$: B \parallel F + V$	Table	$: B \parallel \epsilon$
Log	Memory	$: T$	Memory	$: F + V$	Memory	$: \epsilon$
	Log	$: T$	Log	$: 2 * (F + V)$	Log	$: T$
	Table	$: \theta \times T$	Table	$: \theta \times (F + V)$	Table	$: \epsilon$
NVM-InP	Memory	$: T$	Memory	$: F + V + p$	Memory	$: \epsilon$
	Log	$: p$	Log	$: F + p$	Log	$: p$
	Table	$: p$	Table	$: 0$	Table	$: \epsilon$
NVM-CoW	Memory	$: T$	Memory	$: T + F + V$	Memory	$: \epsilon$
	Log	$: 0$	Log	$: 0$	Log	$: 0$
	Table	$: B + p \parallel p$	Table	$: B + p \parallel p$	Table	$: B + \epsilon \parallel \epsilon$
NVM-Log	Memory	$: T$	Memory	$: F + V + p$	Memory	$: \epsilon$
	Log	$: p$	Log	$: F + p$	Log	$: p$
	Table	$: \theta \times T$	Table	$: \theta \times (F + p)$	Table	$: \epsilon$

between cache misses, instructions executed, TLB misses, and space utilization [89]. Hence, in all of our experiments in Section 3.3, we configured the B+trees used by all the engines to their optimal performance settings.

3.3.9   NVM INSTRUCTION SET EXTENSIONS

In this experiment, we analyze the impact of newly proposed NVM-related instruction set extensions [23] on the performance of the engines. As we describe in Appendix A.2, we implement the *sync* primitive using the CLWB and SFENCE instructions.

The CLWB instruction writes back a target cache line to NVM similar to the CLFLUSH instruction. It is, however, different in two ways: (1) it is a weakly ordered instruction and can thus perform better than the strongly ordered CLFLUSH instruction; and (2) it can retain a copy of the line in the cache hierarchy in exclusive state, thereby reducing the possibility of cache

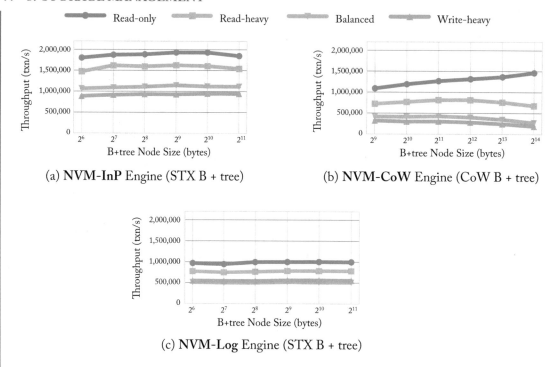

Figure 3.13: **B+tree Node Size**—The impact of B+tree node size on the performance of the NVM-aware engines. The engines run the YCSB workloads under low NVM latency (2×) and low workload skew settings.

misses during subsequent accesses. In contrast, the CLFLUSH instruction always invalidates the cache line, which means that data has to be retrieved again from NVM.

To understand the performance impact of the sync primitive comprising of CLWB and SFENCE instructions, we emulate its latency using RDTSC and PAUSE instructions. We note that our software-based latency emulation does not capture all the complex interactions in real processors. However, it still allows us to perform a useful *what-if* analysis before these instruction set extensions are available. We vary the latency of the sync primitive from 10–10,000 ns and compare it with the currently used sync primitive. Since the traditional engines use PMFS [73], which is loaded in as a kernel module, they require more changes for this experiment. We therefore restrict our analysis to the NVM-aware engines. We execute different YCSB workloads under low NVM latency (2×) and low workload skew settings.

The results in Figure 3.14 show that the engines are sensitive to the performance of the sync primitive. Performance measurements of the engines while using the current sync primitive are shown on the left side of each graph to serve as a baseline. We observe that the throughput of all the engines drops significantly with the increasing sync primitive latency. This is expected as these engines make extensive use of this primitive in their non-volatile data structures. The impact is therefore more pronounced on write-intensive workloads.

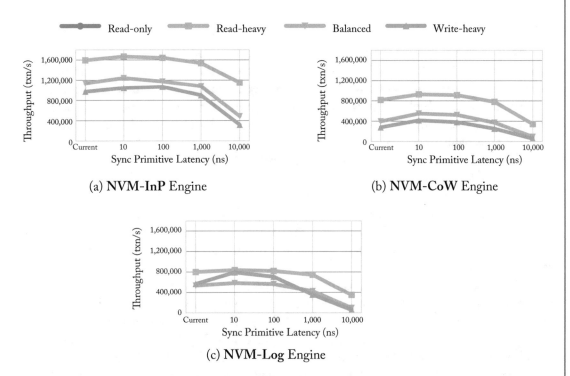

Figure 3.14: **NVM Instruction Set Extensions**—The impact of *sync* primitive latency on the performance of the NVM-aware engines. The engines run the YCSB workloads under low NVM latency (2×) and low skew settings. Performance obtained using the prior primitive, built using the SFENCE and CLFLUSH instructions, is shown on the left side of each graph to serve as a baseline.

We note that the **NVM-CoW** engine is slightly less sensitive to latency of the sync primitive than the **NVM-InP** and **NVM-Log** engines. We attribute this to the fact that this engine primarily uses data duplication to ensure recoverability and only uses the sync primitive to ensure the consistency of the CoW B+tree. In case of the **NVM-Log** engine, its performance while executing the write-heavy workload is interesting. Its throughput becomes less than the throughput on the balanced workload only when the latency of the sync primitive is above 1000 ns. This is because the engine needs to reconstruct tuples from entries spread across different LSM tree components.

We conclude that the trade-offs that we identified in these NVM-aware engines in the main body of the chapter still hold at higher sync primitive latencies. Overall, we believe that these new instructions will be required to ensure recoverability and improve the performance of future NVM-aware DBMSs.

3.3.10 DISCUSSION

Our analysis shows that the NVM access latency has the most impact on the runtime performance of the engines, more so than the amount of skew or the number of modifications to the database in the workload. This difference due to latency is more pronounced with the NVM-aware variants; their absolute throughput is better than the traditional engines, but longer latencies cause their performance to drop more significantly. This behavior is because heavyweight durability mechanisms no longer bottleneck them.

The NVM-aware engines also perform fewer store operations, which will help extend NVM device lifetimes. We attribute this to the reduction in redundant data that the engines store when a transaction modifies the database. Using the allocator interface with non-volatile pointers for internal data structures also allows them to have a smaller storage footprint. This in turn avoids polluting the CPU's caches with unnecessary copying and transformation operations. It also improves the recovery times of the engines that use a WAL since they no longer record redo information.

Overall, we find that the **NVM-InP** engine performs the best across a broad set of workload mixtures and skew settings for all NVM latency configurations. The **NVM-CoW** engine did not perform as well for write-intensive workloads, but may be a better fit for DBMSs that support non-blocking read-only transactions. For the **NVM-Log** engine, many of its design assumptions are not copacetic for a single-tier storage hierarchy. The engine is essentially performing in-place updates like the **NVM-InP** engine but with the additional overhead of maintaining its legacy components.

3.4   SUMMARY

This chapter presented the fundamentals of storage and recovery methods in OLTP DBMSs running on a NVM-only storage hierarchy. We implemented three storage engines in a modular DBMS testbed with different architectures: (1) in-place updates, (2) copy-on-write updates, and (3) log-structured updates. We then developed optimized variants of each of these engines that better make use of NVM's characteristics.

Our experimental analysis with two different OLTP workloads showed that our NVM-aware engines outperform the traditional engines by up to 5.5× while reducing the number of writes to the storage device by more than half on write-intensive workloads. We found that the NVM access latency has the most impact on the runtime performance of the engines, more so than the workload skew or the number of modifications to the database in the workload. Our evaluation showed that the NVM-aware in-place updates engine achieved the best throughput among all the engines with the least amount of wear on the NVM device.

In this chapter, we focused on a NVM-only storage hierarchy. It is possible today to replace DRAM with NV-DIMM [25], and run an NVM-only DBMS unmodified on this storage system. Further, some NVM technologies, such as STT-RAM [72], are expected to deliver lower read and write latencies than DRAM. NVM-only DBMSs would be a good fit for these technologies.

However, for slower NVM technologies, such as PCM [17, 23, 173] and RRAM [22, 187], a two-tier storage system with DRAM and NVM is another viable alternative. We will present a logging and recovery protocol designed for such a system in the next chapter.

CHAPTER 4

Logging and Recovery

A DBMS must guarantee the integrity of a database against application, operating system, and device failures [77]. It ensures the durability of updates made by a transaction by writing them out to durable storage, such as SSD, before returning an acknowledgment to the application. Such storage devices, however, are much slower than DRAM, especially for random writes, and only support bulk data transfers as blocks.

During transaction processing, if the DBMS were to overwrite the contents of the database before committing the transaction, then it must perform random writes to the database at multiple locations on disk. DBMSs try to minimize random writes to disk by flushing the transaction's changes to a separate log on disk with only sequential writes on the critical path of the transaction. This method is referred to as *write-ahead logging* (WAL).

NVM upends the design assumptions underlying the WAL protocol. Although the performance advantages of NVM are obvious, it is still not clear how to make full use of it in a DBMS running on a hybrid storage hierarchy with both DRAM and NVM. In Chapter 3, we show that optimizing the storage methods for NVM improves both the DBMS performance and the lifetime of the storage device. These techniques, however, cannot be employed in a hybrid storage hierarchy, as they target a NVM-only system.

Another line of research focuses on using NVM only for storing the log and managing the database still on disk [100]. This is a more cost-effective solution, as the cost of NVM devices are expected to be higher than that of disk. But this approach only leverages the low-latency sequential writes of NVM, and does not exploit its ability to efficiently support random writes and fine-grained data access. Given this, we contend that it is better to employ logging and recovery algorithms that are designed for NVM.

We designed such a protocol that we call *write-behind logging* (WBL). WBL not only improves the runtime performance of the DBMS, but it also enables it to recovery nearly instantaneously from failures. The way that WBL achieves this is by tracking *what* parts of the database have changed rather than *how* it was changed. Using this logging method, the DBMS can directly flush the changes made by transactions to the database instead of recording them in the log. By ordering writes to NVM correctly, the DBMS can guarantee that all transactions are durable and atomic. This allows the DBMS to write fewer data per transaction, thereby improving a NVM device's lifetime.

To evaluate our approach, we implemented it in the Peloton [9] in-memory DBMS and compared it against WAL using three storage technologies: NVM, SSD, and HDD. These experiments show that WBL with NVM improves the DBMS's throughput by 1.3× while also reducing the database recovery time and the overall system's storage footprint. Our results also show that WBL only achieves this when the DBMS uses NVM; the DBMS actually performs worse than WAL when WBL is deployed on the slower, block-oriented storage devices (i.e., SSD, HDD). This is expected since our protocol is explicitly designed for fast, byte-addressable NVM.

The remainder of this chapter is organized as follows. We begin in Section 4.1 with an overview of the recovery principles of a DBMS. We then discuss logging and recovery implementations in modern DBMSs. We start with the ubiquitous WAL protocol in Section 4.2, followed by our new WBL method in Section 4.3. In Section 4.4, we discuss how this logging protocol can be used in replicated environments. We present our experimental evaluation in Section 4.5.

4.1   RECOVERY PRINCIPLES

A DBMS guarantees the integrity of a database by ensuring (1) that all of the changes made by committed transactions are durable and (2) that none of the changes made by aborted transactions or transactions that were running at the point of a failure are visible after recovering from the failure. These are referred to as *durability* and *atomicity* constraints, respectively [26, 77].

There are three types of failures that a DBMS must protect against: (1) transaction failure, (2) system failure, and (3) media failure. The first happens when a transaction is aborted either by the DBMS due to a conflict with another transaction or because the application chose to do so. System failures occur due to bugs in the DBMS/OS or hardware failures. Finally, in the case of a data loss or corruption on durable storage, the DBMS must recover the database from an archival version.

Almost every DBMS adopts the *steal* and *no-force* policies for managing the data stored in the volatile buffer pool and the database on durable storage [77]. The former policy allows a DBMS to flush the changes of uncommitted transactions at any time. With the latter, the DBMS is not required to ensure that the changes made by a transaction are propagated to the database when it commits. Instead, the DBMS records a transaction's changes to a *log* on durable storage before sending an acknowledgment to the application. Further, it flushes the modifications made by uncommitted transactions to the log before propagating them to the database.

During recovery, the DBMS uses the log to ensure the atomicity and durability properties. The recovery algorithm reverses the updates made by failed transactions using their *undo* information recorded in the log. In case of a system failure, the DBMS first ensures the durability of updates made by committed transactions by reapplying their *redo* information in the log on the database. Afterward, the DBMS uses the log's undo information to remove the effects of transactions that were aborted or active at the time of the failure. DBMSs can handle media failures by storing the database, the log, and the archival versions of the database (i.e., checkpoints) on multiple durable storage devices.

To appreciate why WBL is better than WAL when using NVM, we now discuss how WAL is implemented in both disk-oriented and in-memory DBMSs.

4.2   WRITE-AHEAD LOGGING

The most well-known recovery method based on WAL is the ARIES protocol developed by IBM in the 1990s [142]. ARIES is a *physiological logging* protocol where the DBMS combines a physical redo process with a logical undo process [77]. During normal operations, the DBMS records transactions' modifications in a durable log that it uses to restore the database after a crash.

In this section, we provide an overview of ARIES-style WAL. We begin with discussing the original protocol for a disk-oriented DBMS and then describe optimizations for in-memory DBMSs. Our discussion is focused on DBMSs that use the multi-version concurrency control (MVCC) protocol for scheduling transactions [34, 148]. MVCC is the most widely used concurrency control scheme in DBMSs developed in the last decade, including Hekaton [70], Mem-SQL, and HyPer. The DBMS records the *versioning* meta-data alongside the tuple data, and uses it determine whether a tuple version is visible to a transaction. When a transaction starts, the DBMS assigns it a unique *transaction identifier* from a monotonically increasing global counter. When a transaction commits, the DBMS assigns it a unique *commit timestamp* by incrementing the timestamp of the last committed transaction. Each tuple contains the following meta-data.

- **TxnId:** A placeholder for the identifier of the transaction that currently holds a latch on the tuple.
- **BeginCTS & EndCTS:** The commit timestamps from which the tuple becomes visible and after which the tuple ceases to be visible, respectively.
- **PreV:** Reference to the previous version (if any) of the tuple.

Figure 4.1 shows an example of this versioning meta-data. A tuple is visible to a transaction if and only if its last visible commit timestamp falls within the `BeginCTS` and `EndCTS` fields of the tuple. The DBMS uses the previous version field to traverse the version chain and access the earlier versions, if any, of that tuple. In Figure 4.1, the first two tuples are inserted by the transaction with commit timestamp 1001. The transaction with commit timestamp 1002 updates the tuple with ID 101 and marks it as deleted. The newer version is stored with ID 103. Note that the `PreV` field of the third tuple refers to the older version of tuple. At this point in time, the transaction with identifier 305 holds a latch on the tuple with ID 103. See [34, 120] for a more detailed description of in-memory MVCC.

We now begin with an overview of the runtime operation of the DBMS during transaction processing and its commit protocol. Table 4.1 lists the steps in a WAL-based DBMS to execute

Tuple ID	Txn ID	Begin CTS	End CTS	Prev V	Data
101	–	1001	1002	–	X
102	–	1001	∞	–	Y
103	305	1002	∞	101	X′

Figure 4.1: **Tuple Version Meta-data**—The additional data that the DBMS stores to track tuple versions in an MVCC protocol.

database operations, process transaction commits, and take checkpoints. Later, in Section 4.3, we present our WBL protocol for NVM systems.

4.2.1   RUNTIME OPERATION

For each modification that a transaction makes to the database, the DBMS creates a log record that corresponds to that change. As shown in Figure 4.2, a log record contains a unique log sequence number (LSN), the operation associated with the log record (i.e., INSERT, UPDATE, or DELETE), the transaction identifier, and the table modified. For INSERT and UPDATE operations, the log record contains the location of the inserted tuple or the newer version. Each record also contains the *after-images* (i.e., new values) of the tuples modified, as shown in Table 4.1. In case of UPDATE and DELETE operations, it contains the location of the older version or the deleted tuple, respectively. This is known as the *before-images* (i.e., old values) of the modified tuples and is used to ensure failure atomicity.

Checksum	LSN	Log Record Type	Transaction Commit Timestamp	Table ID	Insert Location	Delete Location	After Image

Figure 4.2: **Structure of WAL Record**—Structure of the log record constructed by the DBMS while using the WAL protocol.

A disk-oriented DBMS maintains two meta-data tables at runtime that it uses for recovery. The first is the *dirty page table* (DPT) that contains the modified pages that are in DRAM but have not been propagated to durable storage. Each of these pages has an entry in the DPT that marks the log record's LSN of the oldest transaction that modified it. This allows the DBMS to identify the log records to replay during recovery to restore the page. The second table is the *active transaction table* (ATT) that tracks the status of the running transactions. This table records the LSN of the latest log record of all active transactions. The DBMS uses this information to undo their changes during recovery.

To bound the amount of work to recover a database after a restart, the DBMS periodically takes checkpoints at runtime. ARIES uses *fuzzy checkpointing* where the checkpoint can contain the effects of both committed and uncommitted transactions [142]. Consequently, the DBMS

Table 4.1: **Operations Performed by DBMS:**—An overview of the steps performed by the DBMS during its runtime operation, commit processing, and checkpointing.

	Runtime Operation	Commit Processing	Checkpointing
WAL	• Execute the operation • Write changes to table heap on DRAM • Construct a log record based on operation (contains afterimage of tuple). • Append log record to log entry buffer.	• Collect log entries from log entry buffers • Sync the collected entries on durable storage • Mark all the transactions as committed • Inform workers about group commit	• Construct checkpoint containing after-images of visible tuples • Write out transactionally consistent checkpoint to durable storage • Truncate unnecessary log records
WBL	• Execute the operation • Write changes to table heap on DRAM • Add an entry to the DTT for that modification (does not contain after-image of tuple)	• Determine dirty tuples using the DTT • Compute c_p and c_d for this group commit • Sync dirty blocks to durable storage • Sync a log entry containing c_p and c_d • Inform workers about group commit	• Construct a checkpoint containing only the active commit identifier gaps (no after-images) • Write out transactionally consistent checkpoint to durable storage • Truncate unnecessary log records

must write out the DPT and ATT as a part of the checkpoint so that it can restore committed transactions and undo uncommitted transactions during recovery. After all the log records associated with a transaction are safely persisted in a checkpoint, the DBMS can remove those records from the log.

With an in-memory DBMS, transactions access tuples through pointers without indirection through a buffer pool [34]. The ARIES protocol can, therefore, be simplified and optimized for this architecture. Foremost is that a MVCC DBMS does not need to perform fuzzy checkpointing [168]. Instead, it constructs transactionally consistent checkpoints that only contain the changes of committed transactions by skipping the modifications made by transactions that began after the checkpoint operation started. Hence, a MVCC DBMS neither stores the before-images of tuples in the log nor tracks dirty data (i.e., DPT) at runtime. Its recovery component, however, maintains an ATT that tracks the LSN of the latest log record written by each active transaction.

4.2.2 COMMIT PROTOCOL

We now describe how a WAL-based DBMS processes and commits transactions. When a transaction begins, the DBMS creates an entry in the ATT and sets it status as *active*. For each modification that the transaction makes to the database, the DBMS constructs the corresponding log record and appends it to the log buffer. It then updates the LSN associated with the transaction in the ATT.

The DBMS flushes all the log records associated with a transaction to durable storage (using the `fsync` command) before committing the transaction. This is known as *synchronous logging*. Finally, the DBMS marks the status of the transaction in the ATT as *committed*. The ordering of writes from the DBMS to durable storage while employing WAL is presented in Figure 4.3. The changes are first applied to the table heap and the indexes residing in volatile storage. At the time of commit, WAL requires that the DBMS flush all the modifications to the durable log. Then, at some later point, the DBMS writes the changes to the database in its next checkpoint.

As transactions tend to generate multiple log records that are each small in size, most DBMSs use *group commit* to minimize the I/O overhead [69]. It batches the log records for a group of transactions in a buffer and then flushes them together with a single write to durable storage. This improves the transactional throughput and amortizes the synchronization overhead across multiple transactions.

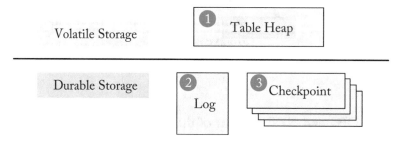

Figure 4.3: **WAL Commit Protocol**—The ordering of writes from the DBMS to durable storage while employing the WAL protocol.

4.2.3 RECOVERY PROTOCOL

The traditional WAL recovery algorithm (see Figure 4.4) comprises of three phases: (1) analysis, (2) redo, and (3) undo. In the *analysis phase*, the DBMS processes the log starting from the latest checkpoint to identify the transactions that were active at the time of failure and the modifications associated with those transactions. In the subsequent *redo phase*, the DBMS processes the log forward from the earliest log record that needs to be redone. Some of these log records could be from transactions that were active at the time of failure as identified by the analysis phase. During the final *undo phase*, the DBMS rolls back uncommitted transactions (i.e., transactions that were active at the time of failure) using the information recorded in the log. This recovery algorithm is simplified for the MVCC DBMS. During the redo phase, the DBMS skips replaying the log records associated with uncommitted transactions. This obviates the need for an undo phase.

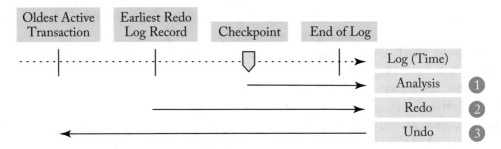

Figure 4.4: **WAL Recovery Protocol**—The phases of the recovery protocol.

Figure 4.5 shows the contents of the log after a system failure. The records contain the after-images of the tuples modified by the transactions. At the time of system failure, only transactions 80 and 81 are uncommitted. During recovery, the DBMS first loads the latest checkpoint that contains an empty ATT. It then analyzes the log to identify which transactions must be redone and which are uncommitted. During the redo phase, it reapplies the changes

LSN	WRITE AHEAD LOG
1	BEGIN CHECKPOINT
2	END CHECKPOINT (EMPTY ATT)
3	TXN 1: INSERT TUPLE 100 (NEW: X)
4	TXN 2: UPDATE TUPLE 2 (NEW: Y')
...	...
22	TXN 20: DELETE TUPLE 20
23	TXN 1, 3,..., 20: COMMIT
24	TXN 2: UPDATE TUPLE 100 (NEW: X')
25	TXN 21: UPDATE TUPLE 21 (NEW: Z')
...	...
84	TXN 80: DELETE TUPLE 80
85	TXN 2, 21,..., 79: COMMIT
86	TXN 81: UPDATE TUPLE 100 (NEW: X'')
	SYSTEM FAILURE

Figure 4.5: **WAL Example**—Contents of the WAL during recovery.

made by transactions committed since the latest checkpoint. It skips the records associated with the uncommitted transactions 80 and 81. After recovery, the DBMS can start executing new transactions.

Correctness: For active transactions, the DBMS maintains the before-images of the tuples they modified. This is sufficient to reverse the changes of any transaction that aborts. The DBMS ensures that the log records associated with a transaction are forced to durable storage before it is committed. To handle system failures during recovery, the DBMS allows for repeated undo operations. This is feasible because it maintains the undo information as before-images and not in the form of compensation log records [26, 77].

Although WAL supports efficient transaction processing when memory is volatile and durable storage cannot support fast random writes, it is inefficient for NVM storage [33]. Consider a transaction that inserts a tuple into a table. The DBMS first records the tuple's contents in the log, and it later propagates the change to the database. With NVM, the logging algorithm can avoid this unnecessary data duplication. We now describe the design of such an algorithm geared toward a DBMS running on a hybrid storage hierarchy comprising of DRAM and NVM.

4.3   WRITE-BEHIND LOGGING

WBL leverages fast, byte-addressable NVM to reduce the amount of data that the DBMS records in the log when a transaction modifies the database. The reason why NVM enables a better logging protocol than WAL is three-fold. Foremost, the write throughput of NVM is more than an order of magnitude higher than that of an SSD or HDD. Second, the gap between sequential and random write throughput of NVM is smaller than that of older storage technologies. Finally, individual bytes in NVM can be accessed by the processor, and hence there is no need to organize tuples into pages or go through the I/O subsystem.

WBL reduces data duplication by flushing changes to the database in NVM during regular transaction processing. For example, when a transaction inserts a tuple into a table, the DBMS records the tuple's contents in the database *before* it writes any associated meta-data in the log. Thus, the log is always (slightly) behind the contents of the database, but the DBMS can still restore it to the correct and consistent state after a restart.

We begin this section with an overview of the runtime operations performed by a WBL-based DBMS. We then present its commit protocol and recovery algorithm. Table 4.1 provides a summary of the steps during runtime, recovery, and checkpointing. Although our description of WBL is for MVCC DBMSs, we also discuss how to adapt the protocol for a single-version system.

4.3.1   RUNTIME OPERATION

WBL differs from WAL in many ways. Foremost is that the DBMS does not construct log records that contain tuple modifications at runtime. This is because the changes made by transactions are guaranteed to be already present on durable storage before they commit. As transactions update the database, the DBMS inserts entries into a *dirty tuple table* (DTT) to track their changes. Each entry in the DTT contains the transaction's identifier, the table modified, and additional meta-data based on the operation associated with the change. For INSERT and DELETE, the entry only contains the location of the inserted or deleted tuple, respectively. Since UPDATEs are executed as a DELETE followed by an INSERT in MVCC, the entry contains the location of the new and old version of the tuple. DTT entries never contain the after-images of tuples and are removed when their corresponding transaction commits. As in the case of WAL, the DBMS uses this information to ensure failure atomicity. But unlike in disk-oriented WAL, the DTT is never written to NVM. The DBMS only maintains the DTT in memory while using WBL.

4.3.2   COMMIT PROTOCOL

Relaxing the ordering of writes to durable storage complicates WBL's commit and recovery protocols. When the DBMS restarts after a failure, it needs to locate the modifications made by transactions that were active at the time of failure so that it can undo them. But these changes can reach durable storage even before the DBMS records the associated meta-data in the log. This is because the DBMS is unable to prevent the CPU from evicting data from its volatile caches to NVM. Consequently, the recovery algorithm must scan the entire database to identify the dirty modifications, which is prohibitively expensive and increases the recovery time.

The DBMS avoids this problem by recording meta-data about the clean and dirty modifications that have been made to the database by tracking two commit timestamps in the log. First, it records the timestamp of the latest committed transaction all of whose changes and updates of prior transactions are safely persisted on durable storage (c_p). Second, it records the commit timestamp (c_d, where $c_p < c_d$) that the DBMS *promises* to not assign to any transaction before the subsequent group commit finishes. This ensures that any dirty modifications that were flushed to durable storage will have only been made by transactions whose commit timestamp is earlier than c_d.

While recovering from a failure, the DBMS considers all the transactions with commit timestamps earlier than c_p as committed, and ignores the changes of the transactions whose commit timestamp is later than c_p and earlier than c_d. In other words, if a tuple's begin timestamp falls within the (c_p, c_d) pair, then the DBMS's transaction manager ensures that it is not visible to any transaction that is executed after recovery.

When committing a group of transactions, as shown in Table 4.1, the DBMS examines the DTT entries to determine the dirty modifications. For each change recorded in the DTT, the DBMS persists the change to the table heap using the device's sync primitive (see Appendix A.2). It then constructs a log entry containing c_p and c_d to record that any transaction with commit timestamps earlier than c_p has committed, and to indicate that it will not issue a commit timestamp later than c_d for any of the subsequent transactions before the next group commit. It appends this commit record (see Figure 4.6) to the log. The DBMS flushes the modifications of all the transactions with commit timestamps less than c_p before recording c_p in the log. Otherwise, it cannot guarantee that those transactions have been committed upon restart.

Checksum	LSN	Log Record Type	Persisted Commit Timestamp (C_p)	Dirty Commit Timestamp (C_d)

Figure 4.6: **Structure of WBL Record**—Structure of the log record constructed by the DBMS while using the WBL protocol.

For long-running transactions that span a group commit window, the DBMS also records their commit timestamps in the log. Without this information, the DBMS cannot increment c_p before the transaction commits. During recovery, it uses this information to identify the changes made by uncommitted transactions. With WBL, the DBMS writes out the changes to locations spread across the durable storage device. For example, if a transaction updates tuples stored in two tables, then the DBMS must flush the updates to two locations in the durable storage device. This design works well for NVM as it supports fast random writes. But it is not a good choice for slower devices that incur expensive seeks to handle random writes. To abort a transaction, the DBMS uses the information recorded in the DTT to determine the changes made by the transaction. It then discards those changes and reclaims their table heap storage.

The diagram in Figure 4.7 shows WBL's ordering of writes from the DBMS to durable storage. The DBMS first applies the changes on the table heap residing in volatile storage. But unlike WAL, when a transaction commits, the DBMS flushes all of its modifications to the durable table heap and indexes. Subsequently, the DBMS appends a record containing c_p and c_d to the log.

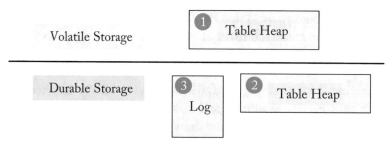

Figure 4.7: **WBL Commit Protocol**—The ordering of writes from the DBMS to durable storage while employing the WBL protocol.

4.3.3   RECOVERY PROTOCOL

Before describing WBL's recovery algorithm, we first introduce the notion of a *commit timestamp gap*. A commit timestamp gap refers to the range of timestamps defined by the pair (c_p, c_d). The

DBMS must ignore the effects of transactions that fall within such a gap while determining the tuple visibility. This is equivalent to undoing the effects of any transaction that was active at the time of failure. The set of commit timestamp gaps that the DBMS needs to track increases on every system failure. To limit the amount of work performed while determining the visibility of tuples, the DBMS's garbage collector thread periodically scans the database to undo the dirty modifications associated with the currently present gaps. Once all the modifications in a gap have been removed by the garbage collector, the DBMS stops checking for the gap in tuple visibility checks and no longer records it in the log.

The example in Figure 4.8 depicts a scenario where successive failures result in multiple commit timestamp gaps. At the end of the first group commit operation, there are no such gaps and the current commit timestamp is 101. The DBMS promises to not issue a commit timestamp higher than 199 in the time interval before the second commit. When the DBMS restarts after a system failure, it adds (101, 199) to its set of gaps. The garbage collector then starts cleaning up the effects of transactions that fall within this gap. Before it completes the scan, there is another system failure. The system then also adds (301, 399) to its gap set. Finally, when the garbage collector finishes cleaning up the effects of transactions that fall within these two gaps, it empties the set of gaps that the DBMS must check while determining the visibility of tuples.

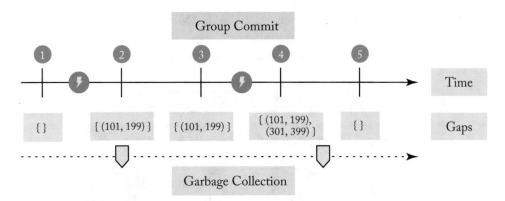

Figure 4.8: **WBL Commit Timestamp Gaps**—An illustration of successive system failures resulting in multiple commit timestamp gaps. The effects of transactions in those gaps are eventually undone by the garbage collector.

With WBL, the DBMS does not need to periodically construct WAL-style physical checkpoints to speed up recovery. This is because each WBL log record contains all the information needed for recovery: the list of commit timestamp gaps and the commit timestamps of long running transactions that span across a group commit operation. The DBMS only needs to retrieve this information during the analysis phase of the recovery process. It can safely remove all the log records located before the most recent log record. This ensures that the log's size is always bounded.

As shown in Figure 4.9, the WBL recovery protocol only contains an analysis phase. During this phase, the DBMS scans the log backward until the most recent log record to determine the currently existing commit timestamp gaps and timestamps of long-running transactions. There is no need for a redo phase because all the modifications of committed transactions are already present in the database. WBL also does not require an WAL-style undo phase. Instead, the DBMS uses the information in the log to ignore the effects of uncommitted transactions.

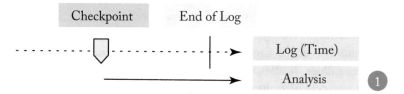

Figure 4.9: **WBL Recovery Protocol**—The phases of the recovery protocol.

Figure 4.10 shows the contents of the log after a system failure. This example is based on the same the workload used in Figure 4.5. We note that transactions 2 and 80 span across a group commit operation. At the time of system failure, only transactions 80 and 81 are uncommitted. During recovery, the DBMS loads the latest log record to determine the currently existing commit timestamp gaps and timestamps of long-running transactions. After this brief analysis phase, it can immediately start handling transactions again.

LSN	WRITE BEHIND LOG
1	BEGIN CHECKPOINT
2	END CHECKPOINT (EMPTY CTG)
3	{ (1, 100) }
4	{ 2, (21, 120) }
5	{ 80, (81, 180) }
	SYSTEM FAILURE

Figure 4.10: **WBL Example**—Contents of the WBL during recovery.

Correctness: When a transaction modifies the database, the DBMS only writes those changes to DRAM. Then when that transaction commits, the DBMS persists its changes to the table heap on durable storage. This prevents the system from losing the effects of any committed transaction, thereby ensuring the durability property. It ensures atomicity by tracking the uncommitted transactions using commit timestamp gaps. WBL allows repeated undo operations as it maintains logical undo information about uncommitted transactions.

Single-Versioned System: In a single-versioned DBMS with WBL, the system makes a copy of a tuple's before-image before updating it and propagating the new version to the database. This is necessary to support transaction rollbacks and to avoid *torn writes*. The DBMS stores the before-images in the table heap on durable storage. The DBMS's recovery process then only consists of an analysis phase; a redo phase is not needed because the modifications for all committed transactions are already present in the database. The DBMS, however, must roll back the changes made by uncommitted transactions using the before-images. As this undo process is done on demand, the DBMS starts handling transactions immediately after the analysis phase. Similar to the multi-versioned case, the DBMS uses the commit timestamps to determine the visibility of tuples and identify the effects of uncommitted transactions.

4.4   REPLICATION

With both the WAL and WBL protocols described above, the DBMS can recover from system and transaction failures. These protocols, however, are not able to handle media failures or corrupted data. This is because they rely on the integrity of durable data structures (e.g., the log) during recovery. These failures are instead overcome through replication, wherein the DBMS propagates changes made by transactions to multiple servers. When the *primary* server incurs a media failure, replication ensures that there is no data loss since the *secondary* servers can be configured to maintain a transactionally consistent copy of the database.

But replicating a database using WBL DBMS is different than in a WAL DBMS. With WAL, the DBMS sends the same log records that it stores on its durable storage device over the network. The secondary server then applies them to their local copy of the database. But since WBL's log records only contain timestamps and not the actual data (e.g., after-images), the DBMS has to perform extra steps to make WBL compatible with a replication protocol.

We now describe the different replication schemes for a primary-secondary configuration. We later present how a DBMS transforms WBL log records to work with these schemes.

4.4.1   REPLICATION SCHEMES

There are two schemes for replicating a database in a primary-secondary configuration that each provide different consistency guarantees: (1) synchronous and (2) asynchronous. Figure 4.11 presents the steps executed by the DBMS during replication. With *synchronous* replication, the primary server sends log records and waits for acknowledgments from the secondary servers that they have flushed the changes to durable storage (steps ❶,❷,❸,❹ are on the transaction's critical path). In *asynchronous* replication, the primary server does not wait for acknowledgments from any of the secondary servers (steps ❶,❷).

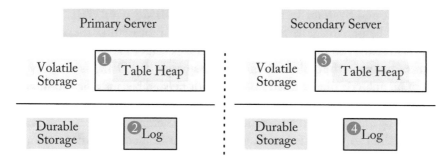

Figure 4.11: **Replication**—The steps taken by the DBMS during replication.

4.4.2   RECORD FORMAT

The primary server in a WBL-based system cannot simply send its log records to the secondary servers because they do not contain the after-images of the modified tuples. Thus, to support replication, the DBMS must construct additional WAL records that contain the physical modifications to the database and send them to the secondary servers. As we show in Section 4.5.3, this additional step adds minimal computational overhead since replication is bound by network communication costs.

We now describe the failover procedure in the secondary server when the primary server goes down. By design, the DBMS only transfers the changes associated with the committed transactions to the secondary servers. Consequently, there is no need for an undo process on the secondary servers on a failover. After a failover, the secondary server can immediately start handling transactions on a transactionally consistent database. But if the DBMS uses asynchronous replication, then the effects of recently committed transactions might not be present in the secondary server.

4.5   EXPERIMENTAL EVALUATION

We now present our analysis of the logging protocols. We implemented both WAL and WBL in Peloton, an in-memory HTAP DBMS that supports NVM [9]. We compare the DBMS's runtime performance, recovery times, and storage footprint for two OLTP workloads. We then analyze the effect of using WBL in a replicated system. Next, we compare WBL against an instant recovery protocol based on WAL [83, 90]. Finally, we examine the impact of storage latency, group commit latency, and new CPU instructions for NVM on the system's performance.

We performed these experiments on the hardware emulator described in Appendix A.1. We configured the NVM latency to be 4× that of DRAM and validated these settings using Intel's memory latency checker [33]. The emulator also includes two additional storage devices:

- **HDD:** Seagate Barracuda (3 TB, 7200 RPM, SATA 3.0)
- **SSD:** Intel DC S3700 (400 GB, SATA 2.6)

We modified Peloton to use the emulator's allocator and filesystem interfaces to store its logs, checkpoints, and table heap on NVM (see Appendix A.1). When employing WAL, the DBMS maintains the log and the checkpoints on the filesystem, and uses fsync to ensure durability. When it adopts WBL, the DBMS uses the allocator for managing the durable table heap and indexes. Internally, it stores indexes in persistent B+trees [53, 56]. It relies on the allocator's *sync* primitive to ensure database durability. All the transactions execute with the same snapshot isolation level and durability guarantees. To evaluate replication, we use a second emulator with the same hardware that is connected via 1 Gb Ethernet with 150 μs latency.

4.5.1   BENCHMARKS

We use the YCSB and TPC-C benchmarks for our evaluation. Appendix B presents a detailed description of these benchmarks. For the YCSB benchmark, we use a database with 2 million tuples (~2 GB). We configure the TPC-C workload to contain eight warehouses and 100,000 items. We map each warehouse to a single partition. The initial storage footprint of the TPC-C database is approximately 1 GB.

4.5.2   RUNTIME PERFORMANCE

We begin with an analysis of the recovery protocols' impact on the DBMS's runtime performance. To obtain insights that are applicable for different storage technologies, we run the YCSB and TPC-C benchmarks in Peloton while using either the WAL or WBL. For each configuration, we scale up the number of worker threads that the DBMS uses to process transactions. The clients issue requests in a closed loop. We execute all the workloads three times under each setting and report the average throughput and latency. To provide a fair comparison, we disable checkpointing in the WAL-based configurations, since it is up to the administrator to configure the checkpointing frequency. We note that throughput drops by 12–16% in WAL when the system takes a checkpoint.

YCSB: We first consider the read-heavy workload results shown in Figure 4.12a. These results provide an approximate upper bound on the DBMS's performance because the 90% of the transactions do not modify the database and therefore the system does not have to construct many log records. The most notable observation from this experiment is that while the DBMS's throughput with the SSD-WAL configuration is 4.5× higher than that with the SSD-WBL configuration, its performance with the NVM-WBL configuration is comparable to that obtained with the NVM-WAL configuration. This is because NVM supports fast random writes unlike HDD.

The NVM-based configurations deliver 1.8–2.3× higher throughput over the SSD-based configurations. This is because of the ability of NVM to support faster reads than SSD. The gap between the performance of the NVM-WBL and the NVM-WAL configurations is not prominent on this workload as most transactions only perform reads. The throughput of all the

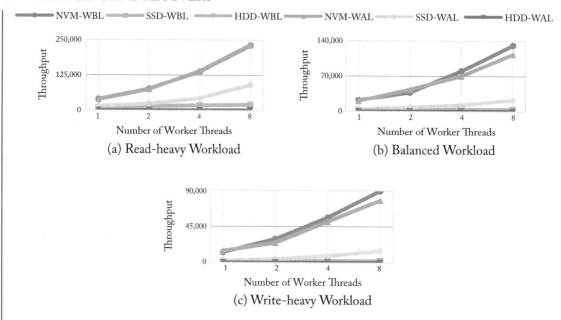

Figure 4.12: **YCSB Throughput**—The throughput of the DBMS for the YCSB benchmark with different logging protocols and durable storage devices.

configurations increases with the number of worker threads as the increased concurrency helps amortize the logging overhead. While the WAL-based DBMS runs well for all the storage devices on a read-intensive workload, the WBL-based DBMS delivers lower performance while running on the HDD and SSD due to their slower random writes.

The benefits of WBL are more prominent for the balanced and write-heavy workloads presented in Figures 4.12b and 4.12c. We observe that the NVM-WBL configuration delivers 1.2–1.3× higher throughput than the NVM-WAL configuration because of its lower logging overhead. That is, under WBL the DBMS does not construct as many log records as it does with WAL and therefore it writes less data to durable storage. The performance gap between the NVM-based and SSD-based configurations also increases on write-intensive workloads. With the read-heavy workload, the NVM-WBL configuration delivers only 4.7× higher throughput than the SSD-WBL configuration. But on the balanced and write-heavy workloads, NVM-WBL provides 10.4–12.1× higher throughput.

The transactions' average response time is presented in Figure 4.13. As expected, the HDD-based configurations incur the highest latency across all workloads, especially for WBL. For example, on the write-heavy workload, the average latency of the HDD-WBL configuration is 3.9× higher than the HDD-WAL configuration. This is because the random seek time of HDDs constrains the DBMS performance. The SSD-based configurations have up to two orders of magnitude lower transaction latency compared to HDD configurations because of their better write performance. On the write-heavy workload shown in Figure 4.12c, the transaction latency of the NVM-WBL configuration is 21% and 65% lower than that observed with NVM-WAL and SSD-WAL, respectively. We attribute this to WAL's higher overhead and higher write latency of SSD.

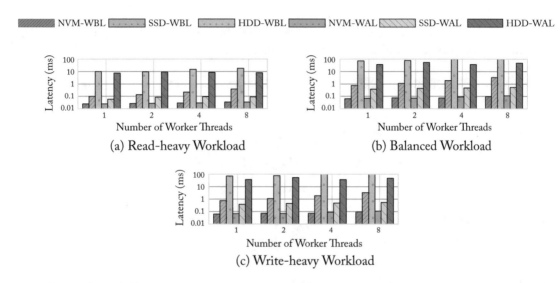

Figure 4.13: **YCSB Latency**—The latency of the DBMS for the YCSB benchmark with different logging protocols and durable storage devices.

TPC-C: Figures 4.14 and 4.15 show the throughput and latency of the DBMS while executing TPC-C with varying number of worker threads. Like with YCSB, the DBMS achieves the highest throughput and the lowest latency using the NVM-WBL configuration. The NVM-WAL and SSD-WAL configurations provide 1.3× and 1.8× lower throughput compared to NVM-WBL. We attribute this to a large number of writes performed per transaction in TPC-C. We observe that the performance obtained across all configurations on the TPC-C benchmark is lower than that on the YCSB benchmark. This is because the transactions in TPC-C contain more complex program logic and execute more queries per transaction.

4.5.3   RECOVERY TIME

We evaluate the recovery time of the DBMS using the different logging protocols and storage devices. For each benchmark, we first execute a fixed number of transactions and then force a hard shutdown of the DBMS (SIGKILL). We then measure the amount of time for the system to restore the database to a consistent state. That is, a state where the effects of all committed transactions are durable and the effects of uncommitted transactions are removed. Recall

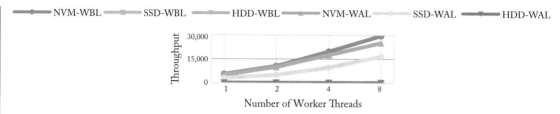

Figure 4.14: **TPC-C Throughput**—The measured throughput for the TPC-C benchmark with different logging protocols and durable storage devices.

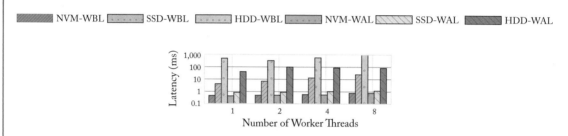

Figure 4.15: **TPC-C Latency**—The latency of the DBMS for the TPC-C benchmark with different logging protocols and durable storage devices.

from Section 4.2 that the number of transactions that the DBMS processes after restart in WAL depends on the frequency of checkpointing. With WBL, the DBMS performs garbage collection to clean up the dirty effects of uncommitted transactions at the time of failure. This garbage collection step is done asynchronously and does not have a significant impact on the throughput of the DBMS.

YCSB: The results in Figure 4.16a present the recovery measurements for the YCSB benchmark. The recovery times of the WAL-based configurations grow linearly in proportion to the number of transactions that the DBMS recovers. This is because the DBMS needs to replay the log to restore the effects of committed transactions. In contrast, with WBL, we observe that the recovery time is independent of the number of transactions executed. The system only reverses the effects of transactions that were active at the time of failure as the changes made by all the transactions committed after the last checkpoint are already persisted. The WBL-based configurations, therefore, have a short recovery.

TPC-C: The results for the TPC-C benchmark in Figure 4.16b show that the recovery time of the WAL-based configurations is higher than that in the YCSB benchmark. This is because the TPC-C transactions perform more operations, and consequently require a longer redo phase. The recovery time of the WBL-based configurations, however, is still independent

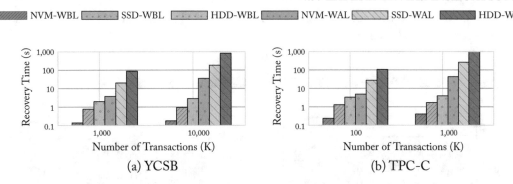

Figure 4.16: **Recovery Time**—The time taken by the DBMS to restore the database to a consistent state after a restart with different logging protocols.

of the number of transactions executed unlike their WAL counterparts because they ensure that the effects of committed transactions are persisted immediately on durable storage.

4.5.4 STORAGE FOOTPRINT

We compare the storage utilization of the DBMS using either the WAL and WBL protocols while running on NVM. This metric is important because we expect that the first NVM products will initially be more expensive than current technologies [109], thus using less storage means a lower procurement cost.

We measure Peloton's storage footprint as the amount of space that it uses in either DRAM or NVM to store tables, logs, indexes, and checkpoints. We periodically collect statistics from the DBMS's storage manager and the filesystem meta-data during the workload execution. We perform these measurements after loading the initial database and report the peak storage footprint of the DBMS for each trial. For all of the configurations, we allow the DBMS's background processes (e.g., group commit, checkpointing, garbage collection) to execute while we collect these measurements.

YCSB: We use the balanced workload mixture for this experiment with an initial database size of 2 GB. The results in Figure 4.17a show that the WAL-based configuration has a larger storage footprint than WBL. This is because WAL constructs log records that contain the physical changes associated with the modified tuples. In contrast, as described in Section 4.3.1, WBL's log records do not contain this information. Another important difference is that while the WAL-based DBMS periodically constructs transactionally consistent checkpoints of the database, WBL only requires the DBMS to write log records that contain the list of currently existing commit identifier gaps. As such, its logical checkpoints have a smaller storage footprint than WAL's physical checkpoints. Unlike WAL, WBL persists the indexes on durable storage to avoid rebuilding it during recovery. The WBL-based DBMS consume 26% less storage space on NVM than its WAL counterpart.

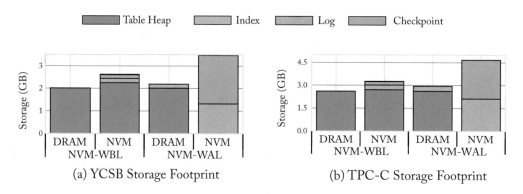

Figure 4.17: **Storage Footprint**—The storage space occupied by the internal components of the DBMS while using different recovery protocols.

TPC-C: The graph in Figure 4.17b shows the storage footprint of the engines while executing TPC-C. For this benchmark, the initial size of the database is 1 GB and it grows to 2.4 GB. Transactions inserting new orders increase the size of the table heap, log, and checkpoints in the WAL-based configuration. By reducing unnecessary data duplication using NVM's persistence property, the NVM-WBL configuration has a 31% smaller storage footprint on NVM. The space savings are more significant in this benchmark because the workload is write-intensive with longer running transactions. Thus, the log in the WAL-based configuration grows more quickly compared to the smaller undo log in WBL.

4.5.5 REPLICATION

We now examine the impact of replication on the runtime performance of the DBMS while running the YCSB benchmark and using the NVM-based configurations. The results shown in Figure 4.18 indicate that the synchronous replication scheme reduces the throughput. On the read-heavy workload, the throughput drops by 3.6× with both NVM-WAL and NVM-WBL configurations. This shows that the overhead of constructing WAL-style log records when using WBL is lower than the overhead of sending the log records over the network. Under the asynchronous replication scheme, the DBMS's throughput drops by less than 1.1× across all the workloads. The DBMS should, therefore, be configured to use this replication scheme when the user can afford to lose the effects of some recently committed transactions on a media failure.

The impact of replication is more prominent in the write-heavy workload shown in Figure 4.18c. We observe that throughput of the DBMS drops by 10.1× when it performs synchronous replication. This is because the round-trip latency between the primary and secondary

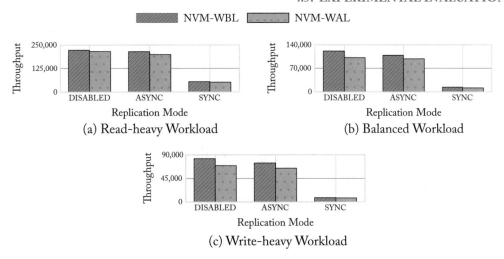

Figure 4.18: **Replication**—The throughput of the DBMS for the YCSB benchmark with different replication schemes and logging protocols.

server (150 μs) is higher than the durable write latency (0.6 μs) of NVM. The networking cost is, thus, the primary performance bottleneck in replication. We conclude that a faster replication standard, such as the NVMe over Fabrics [149], is required for efficient transaction processing in a replicated environment containing NVM [208]. With this technology, the additional latency between a local and remote NVM device is expected to be less than a few microseconds. As every write to NVM must be replicated in most datacenter usage models, we expect WBL to outperform WAL in this replicated environment because it executes fewer NVM writes. We plan to investigate this in future work.

4.5.6   IMPACT OF NVM LATENCY

In this experiment, we analyze how the latency of the NVM affects the runtime performance of the WBL and WAL protocols in the DBMS. We ran YCSB under three latency configurations for the emulator: (1) default DRAM latency (160 ns); (2) a *low* latency that is 2× slower than DRAM (320 ns); and (3) a *high* latency that is 4× slower than DRAM (640 ns). We use the emulator's throttling mechanism to reduce the NVM bandwidth to be 8× lower (9.5 GB/s) than DRAM.

The key observation from the results in Figure 4.19 is that the NVM-WAL configuration is more sensitive to NVM latency compared to NVM-WBL. On the write-heavy workload shown in Figure 4.19c, with a 4× increase in NVM latency, the throughput of NVM-WAL drops by 1.3×, whereas NVM-WBL only drops by 1.1×. This is because the DBMS performs fewer stores to NVM with WBL. We observe that NVM latency has a higher impact on the performance for write-intensive workloads. On the read-heavy workload shown in Figure 4.19a, the throughput of the DBMS only drops by 1.1–1.3× with a 4× increase in latency. We attribute this to the effects of caching and memory-level parallelism.

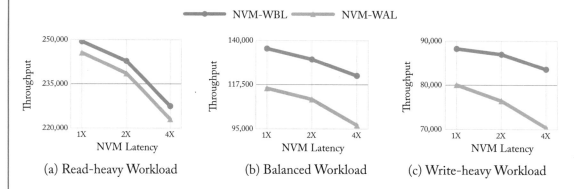

Figure 4.19: **Impact of NVM Latency**—The throughput for the YCSB benchmark with different logging protocols and NVM latency settings.

4.5.7 NVM INSTRUCTION SET EXTENSIONS

We next measure the impact of proposed NVM-related instruction set extensions on the DBMS's performance with the NVM-WBL configuration [23]. We examine the impact of using the CLWB instruction for flushing the cache-lines instead of the CLFLUSH instruction. The CLWB instruction reduces the possibility of compulsory cache misses during subsequent data accesses.

Figure 4.20 presents the throughput of the DBMS with the NVM-WBL configuration while using either the CLWB or CLFLUSH instructions in its *sync* primitive. The throughput obtained with the NVM-WAL configuration, that does not use the *sync* primitive, is provided for comparison. We observe that the throughput under the NVM-WBL configuration exceeds that obtained with NVM-WAL when the DBMS uses the CLWB instruction. We attribute this to the effects of caching. The impact of the CLWB instruction is more prominent on the write-intensive workloads, where the WBL-based DBMS delivers 1.7× higher throughput when using the CLWB instruction instead of the CLFLUSH instruction. Thus, an efficient cache flushing primitive is critical for a high-performance NVM-aware DBMS.

4.5.8 INSTANT RECOVERY PROTOCOL

We now compare WBL against an instant recovery protocol based on WAL [83, 90]. This protocol uses *on-demand* single-tuple redo and single-transaction undo mechanisms to support almost instantaneous recovery from system failures. While processing transactions, the DBMS reconstructs the desired version of the tuple on demand using the information in the write-

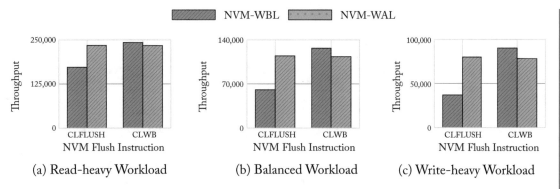

Figure 4.20: **NVM Instruction Set Extensions (CLFLUSH vs. CLWB)**—The throughput of the DBMS for the YCSB benchmark under the NVM-based configurations with different flush instructions.

ahead log. The DBMS can, therefore, start handling new transactions almost immediately after a system failure. The downside is that the DBMS performance is lower than that observed after the traditional ARIES-style recovery while the recovery is not yet complete.

Unlike the WAL-based instant recovery protocol, WBL relies on NVM's ability to support fast random writes. It does not contain a redo process. To better understand the impact of the instant-recovery protocol on the performance of the DBMS, we implemented it in our DBMS. We run the read-heavy YCSB workload on the DBMS, while varying the fraction of the tuples in the table that must be reconstructed from 0.001 to 0.1. With more frequent checkpointing, a smaller fraction of tuples would need to be reconstructed. We configure the length of a tuple's log record chain to follow a uniform distribution over the following ranges: (0, 100) and (0, 10).

The results shown in Figures 4.21a and 4.21b indicate that the performance drops with longer log record chains, especially when a larger fraction of tuples need to be reconstructed. When the maximum length of a long record chain is limited to 10 records, the throughput drops by 1.5× when the DBMS needs to reconstruct 10% of the tuples in comparison to the throughput observed after recovery. In contrast, when the length is limited to 100 records, the throughput drops by 8×. After the recovery process is complete, the performance of the DBMS converges to that observed after the traditional recovery. We conclude that the instant recovery protocol works well when the DBMS runs on a slower durable storage device. However, on a fast NVM device, WBL allows the DBMS to deliver high performance immediately after recovery. Unlike WAL, as we showed in Section 4.5.4, it improves device utilization by reducing data duplication.

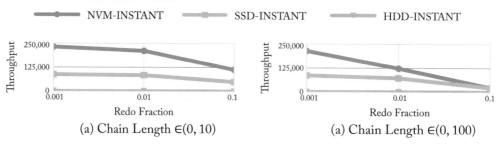

Figure 4.21: **Instant Recovery Protocol**—The throughput of the DBMS for YCSB with the instant logging protocol on different storage devices.

4.5.9   IMPACT OF GROUP COMMIT LATENCY

In this experiment, we analyze how the group commit latency affects the runtime performance of the WBL and WAL protocols in the DBMS. As the DBMS sends the results back to the client only after completing the group commit operation, this parameter affects the latency of the transaction. We run the write-heavy YCSB workload under different group commit latency settings ranging from 10–10,000 μs.

The most notable observation from the results in Figure 4.22 is that different group commit latency settings work well for different durable storage devices. Setting the group commit latency to 10, 100, and 1,000 μs works well for the NVM, SSD, and HDD, respectively. We observe that there is a two orders of magnitude gap between the optimal group commit latency settings for NVM and HDD. The impact of this parameter is more pronounced in the case of NVM compared to the slower durable storage devices. When the group commit latency of the DBMS running on NVM is increased from 10 to 1,000 μs, the throughput drops by 62×.

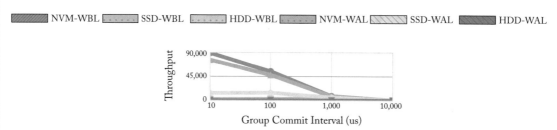

Figure 4.22: **Group Commit Latency**—Impact of the group commit latency setting on the throughput of the DBMS for the write-heavy YCSB workload with different logging protocols and durable storage devices.

4.6 SUMMARY

This chapter presented the write-behind logging protocol for emerging NVM technologies. We examined the impact of this redesign on the transactional throughput, latency, availability, and storage footprint of the DBMS. Our evaluation of recovery algorithm in Peloton showed that across different OLTP workloads it reduces the system's recovery time by $100\times$ and shrinks the storage footprint by $1.5\times$.

In this chapter, we focused on a two-tier storage system comprising of volatile DRAM and a durable storage device that is either NVM, SSD, or HDD. A DBMS operating a three-tier storage hierarchy can also employ WBL. In this case, the DBMS stores the less frequently accessed tuples in the database on SSD. It manages the log and more frequently accessed tuples on NVM. As the bulk of the data is stored on SSD, the DBMS only requires a NVM device with smaller storage capacity, thus shrinking the overall storage system cost. We explore the fundamentals of buffer management in such a three-tier storage hierarchy in the next chapter.

CHAPTER 5

Buffer Management

The design of the buffer manager in traditional DBMSs is influenced by the difference in the performance characteristics of DRAM and SSD. The canonical data migration policy employed by the buffer manager is predicated on the assumptions that the DBMS can only operate on data residing on DRAM, and that SSD is orders of magnitude slower than DRAM [45, 97]. But NVM upends these design assumptions.

This chapter explores the changes required in the buffer manager of the DBMS to leverage the unique properties of NVM in systems that still include DRAM and SSD. We describe a set of data migration optimizations enabled by NVM. The key idea is that since the DBMS can directly operate on NVM-resident data, it can adopt a *lazy data migration* policy for copying data over to DRAM. We illustrate that these optimizations have to be tailored depending on the characteristics of the storage hierarchy and the workload. We then make the case for a continuous adaptation mechanism in the buffer manager, called *adaptive data migration*, that achieves a near-optimal data migration policy for an arbitrary workload and storage hierarchy without requiring any manual tuning. We finally present a storage system recommender for identifying the optimal storage hierarchy for a workload given a cost budget.

There have been prior efforts on buffer management in a three-tier storage system including NVM [116, 190]. Renen et al. present a buffer manager that eagerly migrates data from SSD to DRAM. When a page is evicted from DRAM, the buffer manager considers admitting it into the NVM buffer. The fundamental idea is to only admit recently referenced pages. The buffer manager maintains an admission queue to keep track of pages considered for admission and only admits pages that were recently denied admission. Kwon et al. present the architecture of a three-tier file-system that transparently migrates data among different levels in the storage system [116]. This file-system is optimized for a specific NVM technology that is 2× slower than DRAM. So it does not cache NVM-resident data on DRAM. For the same reason, it bypasses DRAM while performing synchronous write operations.

In this chapter, we introduce a taxonomy of data migration policies that subsumes the specific schemes adopted by prior systems. We derive insights that are applicable for a broader range of three-tier storage systems and NVM technologies. In particular, we explore how the optimal data migration policy depends on workload and storage system characteristics.

The remainder of this chapter is organized as follows. We begin in Section 5.1 with an overview of buffer management principles. We present the NVM-related data flow optimization in Section 5.2. We then describe the adaptive data migration technique in Section 5.3.

Section 5.4 presents the design of the storage system recommender. Section 5.5 describes the trace-driven buffer manager used in our analysis. We present our experimental evaluation in Section 5.6 and conclude in Section 5.7.

5.1   BUFFER MANAGEMENT PRINCIPLES

The buffer manager in a DBMS is responsible for bringing pages from durable storage to main memory as and when they are needed [171]. The buffer manager partitions the available memory into a set of fixed-size *slots*, which is collectively termed as a *buffer pool*. The higher-level components of the DBMS, such as the query execution engine, need not concern themselves with whether a page is in the buffer pool or not. The execution engine only needs to request the buffer manager to retrieve a page using the page's logical identifier. If the page is not already present in the buffer pool, the buffer manager transparently retrieves the page from non-volatile storage. After updating a page, the execution engine must inform the buffer manager that it has modified the page so that it propagates the changes to the copy of the page on storage. When the page is no longer needed, the execution engine must request the buffer manager to release it.

The buffer manager maintains some meta-data about each page in the buffer pool. This meta-data includes the number of *active references* made to the page and whether the page has been modified since it was brought into the buffer pool from storage. When a page is requested, the buffer manager first checks if it is present in the buffer pool. If the page is already present in memory, then it increments the number of active references to the page and returns the address of the slot containing the page. If the page is not present, then the buffer manager chooses a slot for replacement based on the buffer *replacement policy* (e.g., least recently used) [152]. If the page selected for replacement contains any modifications, then the buffer pool overwrites the corresponding page on non-volatile storage. It finally reads in the requested page from storage into the replacement slot and returns the slot's address.

Prior research has shown that there is significant overhead associated with buffer management in a DBMS. When all the data fits in main memory, the cost of maintaining a buffer pool is nearly one-third of all the CPU cycles used by the DBMS [91]. This is because the buffer manager must keep track of meta-data about pages in the pool to enforce the buffer replacement policy and synchronize concurrent accesses from different threads to the pool. The overhead associated with managing disk-resident data has given rise to a class of new in-memory DBMSs that manage the entire database in main memory and do not contain a buffer pool [16, 69, 139].

In-memory DBMSs provide better throughput and lower latency than disk-based DBMSs due to this main memory orientation [107]. The fundamental limitation of in-memory DBMSs, however, is that they can deliver this improved performance only when the database is smaller than the amount of physical memory (DRAM) available in the system. If the dataset grows larger than the memory capacity, then the operating system will start to page virtual memory, and main memory accesses will cause page faults [184]. The execution of transactions is stalled until the pages are retrieved from non-volatile storage. The performance of an in-memory DBMS drops by up to 66% when the dataset exceeds the memory capacity, even if the working set fits in memory [183].

Several techniques have been proposed to improve the performance of in-memory DBMSs while operating on larger-than-memory databases [70, 75, 85, 95, 109, 123, 128, 133, 140, 172, 181, 201]. These techniques exploit the skewed access patterns observed in modern database applications. In these workloads, certain data tuples are *hot* and are accessed more frequently than other *cold* tuples. It is advantageous to cache the hot data in memory since it is likely to be modified during this period. But then once the age of particular tuple crosses some threshold, the buffer manager can migrate the cold tuple out to cheaper secondary storage. With this data migration technique, the DBMS can still deliver high performance for transactions that operate on hot in-memory tuples while still being able to access the cold data if needed at a later point in time. But *when* and *where* the buffer manager migrates data between the different tiers in a storage system is highly dependent on the properties of the underlying storage technologies.

5.2   NVM-AWARE BUFFER MANAGEMENT

In a disk-centric DBMS, the buffer manager caches data residing on SSD in the buffer pool located on DRAM, as illustrated in Figure 5.1a. Since DRAM accesses are 100× faster than SSD operations, DBMSs manage a large buffer pool on DRAM. It is, however, difficult to deploy high-capacity DRAM systems due to three factors. First, it drives up the total cost of the system since DRAM is 100× more expensive than SSDs. Second, increasing DRAM capacity raises the total system power consumption. Lefurgy et al. report that as much as 40% of the total system energy is consumed by DRAM in commercial servers [121]. Lastly, DRAM scaling faces significant challenges due to limitations in scaling techniques used in earlier generations for transistors and capacitors [137].

NVM overcomes these limitations of DRAM by providing higher memory capacity, while still being competitive with respect to performance, cost, and power. Figure 5.1b presents a candidate storage hierarchy where NVM replaces DRAM. This architecture delivers performance comparable to that of a DRAM-SSD hierarchy when NVM latency is less than 2× that of DRAM. Otherwise, the replacement of DRAM with slower NVM technologies reduces the performance of the DBMS.

Figure 5.1c presents the architecture of a hybrid storage hierarchy with both DRAM and NVM. Such a configuration can simultaneously reduce the overall cost of the system while still not sacrificing performance. The NVM buffer caches a significant fraction of the working set during system execution, thereby reducing SSD accesses. The DRAM buffer serves as a cache on top of NVM and only stores the hottest pages in the database. A DRAM buffer with only 6% the capacity of the underlying NVM device bridges most of the latency gap between DRAM and NVM.

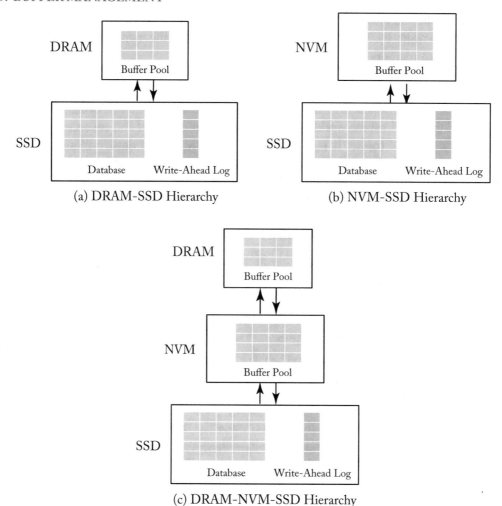

Figure 5.1: **Storage Hierarchy Architectures**—Candidate storage hierarchy organizations: (1) traditional storage hierarchy with DRAM and SSD; (2) storage hierarchy consisting of only NVM and no DRAM; and (3) storage hierarchy consisting of both NVM and DRAM.

5.2.1   NEW DATA MIGRATION PATHS

NVM introduces new data migration paths in the storage hierarchy. Consequently, the buffer manager has more options for moving data between the different tiers in the storage hierarchy. Leveraging these data migration paths to reduce data movement improves the DBMS's performance. The buffer manager also reduces the number of writes to NVM using these paths to extend the lifetime of devices with limited write-endurance [173].

Although the processor can access data stored on DRAM and NVM at cache-line granularity, we refrain from exploiting this property in our buffer manager [170, 190]. We contend that the block abstraction will continue to be employed in these tiers for two reasons. First, encryption, compression, and data validation algorithms are block-oriented. Second, maintaining the same granularity across all tiers of the hierarchy simplifies buffer management and eliminates the overhead associated with maintaining fine-grained meta-data.

Figure 5.2 presents the data flow paths in the NVM-aware multi-tier buffer manager. The default read path comprises of three steps: moving data from SSD to NVM (❶), then to DRAM (❷), and lastly to the processor cache (❸). Similarly, the default write path consists of three steps: moving data from processor cache to DRAM (❹), then to NVM (❺), and finally to SSD (❻).

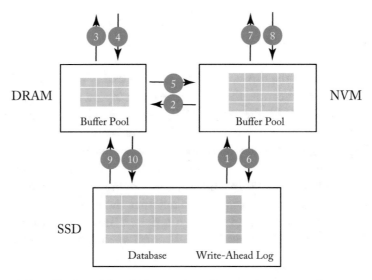

Figure 5.2: **Data Flow Paths**—The different data flow paths in a multi-tier storage hierarchy consisting of DRAM, NVM, and SSD.

In the rest of this section, we describe how the buffer manager leverages other data flow paths shown in Figure 5.2 to minimize the impact of NVM on the DBMS's performance and extend the lifetime of the NVM device by reducing write operations.

5.2.2 BYPASS DRAM DURING READS

Unlike existing storage technologies, such as SSDs, the processor can directly access data on NVM via read operations. This data flow path is labeled as ❻ in Figure 5.2. To access a block on SSD, in a disk-centric DBMS, the DBMS must copy it over to DRAM (❾), before it can operate on the copied data. With NVM, the buffer manager can leverage the new data flow path (❻) to *lazily* migrate data from NVM to DRAM while serving read operations.

Let $\mathcal{D}_r$ represent the number of references to a block on durable storage before the buffer manager copies the block over to DRAM. With existing storage technologies, $\mathcal{D}_r = 1$. We refer to this data migration policy as *eager migration*. With NVM, the buffer manager can employ a wider range of *lazy migration* policies with higher values of $\mathcal{D}_r$. Such policies reduce upward data migration between NVM and DRAM during read operations. They are beneficial when the capacity of DRAM is smaller than that of NVM. A lazy migration strategy ensures that colder data (i.e., data that has not been frequently referred) on NVM do not evict hotter data in DRAM.

The optimal value of $\mathcal{D}_r$ depends on the application's workload. If the working set fits within the DRAM buffer, then the buffer manager employs a more eager migration policy ($\mathcal{D}_r \leq 3$). A lazier policy would delay the data migration to DRAM, thereby increasing the impact of NVM latency on performance. If the working set does not fit in DRAM, but fits in the NVM buffer, then the buffer manager employs a lazy migration policy with higher $\mathcal{D}_r$. This strategy ensures that only the hot data is stored in DRAM.

In addition to considering the size of the working set, the buffer manager picks $\mathcal{D}_r$ depending on the ratio between the capacities of the DRAM and NVM buffers. In a storage hierarchy where the ratio approaches one, the buffer manager adopts a more eager policy to leverage the space available in DRAM. Higher values of $\mathcal{D}_r$ work well when the ratio approaches zero. In this case, lazy migration ensures that the DRAM buffer is used to only store the hot data.

With the eager migration policy, the buffer manager always brings the block to DRAM while serving the read operation. Consequently, if the application then updates the same block, the writes are performed on DRAM. In contrast, a lazy migration policy increases the number of writes on NVM. This is because it is more likely that the block being updated is residing on NVM when the buffer manager adopts such a policy. This is not a problem for DBMS applications with skewed access patterns [41, 182]. Such applications tend to modify hot data that is cached in DRAM even when the buffer manager employs a lazy migration policy.

5.2.3   BYPASS DRAM DURING WRITES

The buffer manager does not have complete autonomy over when to flush data to storage [26, 77]. It must coordinate with the log manager to ensure that all of the changes made by committed transactions are durable, and that none of the changes made by aborted or active transactions are visible after the DBMS recovers from the failure. These constraints are referred to as the *atomicity* and *durability* properties.

If a transaction modifies a block and commits, and the buffer manager has not written the updated block to storage, then a system crash will leave the block in its old invalid state. This violates the durability property. On the other hand, if the buffer manager decides to write a modified block belonging to an active transaction, it violates the atomicity property. To prevent such scenarios, the buffer manager must refrain from making completely autonomous replacement decisions.

Since the contents of the DRAM buffer are lost after a system failure, the log manager records information needed to recover from a failure on durable storage. Before updating a page, the DBMS writes its old contents to the log (i.e., the before image of the page). Similarly, when a page is about to be evicted from the buffer pool, its current contents are recorded in the log (i.e., the after image of the page). When recovering from a failure, the DBMS uses the information in the log to restore the database to a transactionally consistent state. To bound the amount of storage space taken up by the log records on NVM, the DBMS periodically takes checkpoints at runtime.

Ensuring the persistence of blocks containing log and checkpoint records is critical for the recoverability of the DBMS. The DBMS's performance is affected by the I/O overhead associated with existing secondary storage technologies, such as SSDs. As transactions tend to generate multiple log records that are each small in size, most DBMSs use the *group commit* optimization to reduce the I/O overhead [69]. The DBMS first batches the log records for a group of transactions in the DRAM buffer (❹) and then flushes them together with a single write to SSD (❻). This improves the operational throughput and amortizes the I/O overhead across multiple transactions.

With NVM, the buffer manager provides *synchronous persistence* with lower overhead by taking advantage of the ability to directly persist data on NVM during write operations [35, 116]. This data flow path is labeled as ❽ in Figure 5.2. The write operation bypasses DRAM since the data must be eventually persisted, and this data flow optimization shrinks the overall latency of the operation, especially on NVM devices whose write latencies are comparable to that of DRAM. In addition to reducing the synchronous persistence overhead by eliminating the redundant write to DRAM, it also avoids potential eviction of other hot data blocks from the DRAM buffer.

5.2.4   BYPASS NVM DURING READS

We next present how the buffer manager reduces the number of writes to NVM using an alternate data flow path during read operations. The default read path consists of moving the data from SSD to NVM (❶) and eventually migrating it to DRAM (❷). This optimization makes use of the direct data flow path from SSD to DRAM, which is labeled as ❾ in Figure 5.2.

When the buffer manager observes that a requested page is not present in either the DRAM or NVM buffers, it copies the data on SSD directly to DRAM, thus bypassing NVM during read operations. If the data read into the DRAM buffer is not subsequently modified, and is selected for replacement, then the buffer manager discards it. If the page is modified and later selected for eviction from DRAM, the buffer manager copies it to NVM (❺).

In case of a modified page, bypassing NVM during read operations eliminates the first write to NVM. The buffer manager installs a copy of the page on NVM only after it has been evicted from DRAM. If instead, the page were installed on NVM during the read operation, then it is written twice: once at fetch time and again when the page is evicted from DRAM.

For a page that is only read and not modified, this lazy data migration policy eliminates an unnecessary write to NVM when the page is fetched from SSD.

5.2.5   BYPASS NVM DURING WRITES

To reduce the number of writes to NVM, the buffer manager skips migrating data to NVM while serving write operations by using an alternate data flow path. The default write path consists of moving the data from DRAM to NVM (❺) and then eventually migrating it to SSD (❻). Instead of using the default path, this technique makes use of the data flow path from DRAM to SSD (❿).

Bypassing NVM during writes ensures that only pages frequently swapped out of DRAM are stored on NVM [190]. If the buffer manager employs an eager migration policy while copying data into DRAM, then this optimization prevents infrequently accessed pages residing in the DRAM buffer from polluting the NVM buffer. However, with a lazy migration policy, adopting this technique results in hot pages being loaded more slowly into the NVM buffer.

Let $\mathcal{N}_w$ represent the average number of references to a block on DRAM before the buffer manager copies the block over to NVM. With the default write path, $\mathcal{N}_w = 1$. The buffer manager can support a wider range of data migration policies with NVM while serving write operations. Higher values of $\mathcal{N}_w$ reduce data migration from DRAM to NVM during write operations. Such a policy is beneficial when the capacity of DRAM is comparable to that of NVM. In such a storage hierarchy, a lazy migration strategy ensures that colder data on DRAM does not evict warmer data in the NVM buffer. This optimization reduces the number of writes to NVM since only warmer pages identified by the buffer manager are stored in the NVM buffer.

5.3   ADAPTIVE DATA MIGRATION

The buffer manager's *data migration policy* consists of the frequencies with which it should bypass DRAM and NVM while serving read and write operations (Sections 5.2.2 to 5.2.5). All of the above data flow optimizations are moot unless the buffer manager effectively adapts the data migration policy based on the characteristics of the workload and the storage hierarchy. The crux of our approach is to track the *target metrics* on recent query workload at runtime, and then periodically adapt the policy in the background. Over time, this process automatically optimizes the policy for the application's workload and the storage hierarchy, and amortizes the adaptation cost across multiple queries. We now describe the information that the buffer manager collects to guide this process.

The buffer manager keeps track of two target metrics while executing the workload. These include the operational throughput (T) of the buffer manager and the number of write operations (W) performed on NVM. The goal is to determine the optimal configuration of the data migration policies that maximizes the throughput and minimizes writes to NVM. The *cost function* associated with a candidate data migration policy configuration consists of two weighted components associated with these target metrics:

$$Cost(T, W) = \lambda_1 * T - \lambda_2 * W.$$

To adapt the buffer manager's data migration policy, we employ an iterative search method called *simulated annealing* (SA) [111]. This technique searches for a policy configuration that maximizes the cost function presented. An attractive feature of SA is that it avoids getting caught at local optima, which are configurations that are better than any other nearby configurations, but are not the globally optimal configuration [101]. It is a probabilistic hill climbing algorithm that migrates through a set of local optima in search of the global extremum.

SA consists of two stochastic processes for generating candidate policy configurations and for accepting a new configuration. Algorithm 5.1 presents the algorithm for tuning the data migration policy using SA. At each time step, SA randomly selects a new configuration (C') close to the current one (C). It then evaluates the cost of that configuration (E'). Lastly, it decides to accept the configuration C' or stay with C based on whether the cost of C' is lower or higher than that of the current configuration. If C' is better than C, then it immediately transitions to C'. Otherwise, it randomly accepts the new configuration with higher cost (C') based on the Boltzmann acceptance probability factor.

SA is theoretically guaranteed to reach the global optima with high probability. The control parameter T determines the magnitude of the perturbations of the energy function E. SA gradually decreases T over time. During the initial steps of SA, at high temperatures, the probability of uphill moves in the energy function ($\Delta E > 0$) is large. Despite temporarily increasing the energy, such non-beneficial downhill steps ($\Delta E < 0$) allows for a more extensive search for the global optimal configuration. Over time, SA reduces the temperature. This gradual cooling mechanism corresponds to slowly decreasing the probability of accepting worse configurations as it explores the configuration state space.

5.4   STORAGE HIERARCHY SELECTION

We have so far focused on identifying an optimal data migration policy configuration for a particular workload given a storage hierarchy. The tuning algorithm presented in Section 5.3 assumes that we have already provisioned a multi-tier storage hierarchy that is a good fit for the workload. It is unclear, however, how to select such a hierarchy for a particular workload given a cost or performance constraint.

In this section, we formulate an analytical model of a hierarchical storage system to improve the intuition behind provisioning a multi-tier storage hierarchy. We then identify the limitations of the model and present a recommender system that addresses them.

5.4.1   HIERARCHICAL STORAGE SYSTEM MODEL

We can model the multi-tier storage system as a linear hierarchy with n levels, $L_1, L_2, \ldots, L_n$. The performance of a particular level L_i in the hierarchy is determined by two factors: the average

---

Algorithm 5.1 Data Migration Policy Tuning Algorithm

Require: temperature reduction parameter α,
threshold for number of accepted transitions γ,
initial data policy configuration C_0,
initial temperature T_0,
final temperature T_{min}

function UPDATE-CONFIGURATION($\alpha, \gamma, C_0, T_0, T_{min}$)

 # Initialization
 current configuration $C = C_0$
 energy $E = \text{cost}(C)$
 temperature $T = T_0$
 # Iterative Search
 while $T > T_{min}$ **do**
  while number of accepted transitions $< \gamma$ **do**
   new configuration $C' = \text{neighbor}(C)$
   energy $E' = \text{cost}(C')$
   energy delta $\Delta E = E' - E$
   Boltzmann acceptance probability $P = e^{\frac{-\Delta E}{T}}$
   if $\Delta E < 0$ or with acceptance probability P **then**
    # Accept new policy configuration
    $C = C'$
  # Reduce temperature
  $T = T * \alpha$

---

access time t_i and the device capacity C_i [103]. We assume that a copy of all blocks in level i exists in every level greater than i (i.e., in all lower levels in the hierarchy). The maximum information that can be stored in the system is equal to the capacity of the lowest level C_n, since copies of all blocks stored in the higher levels of the system must be present in L_n.

We can characterize the performance impact of the device capacity at a particular level by the probability of finding the requested data block in that level. This is termed as the *hit ratio* H. H is a monotonically increasing function with respect to device capacity C. Let the cost per storage unit (e.g., per GB) of the device technology used at a particular level be given by the *cost function* $P(t_i)$. It decreases monotonically with respect to the access time t_i of the device technology.

Since a copy of all data blocks at level i exists in every level greater than i, the probability of a hit in level L_i and misses in the higher levels, is given by:

$$h_i = H(C_i) - H(C_{i-1}).$$

Here, h_i represents the relative number of successful data accesses at level i in the storage hierarchy. The *effective average access time* per block request, is then given by:

$$T = \sum_{i=1}^{n} h_i \left(\sum_{j=1}^{i} t_j \right).$$

To maximize the operational throughput of the DBMS, we need to minimize T subject to storage system cost constraints. Given a storage system cost budget B, the goal is to select the device technology t_i and determine the device capacity C_i for each level in the storage hierarchy. We formulate this problem as follows:

Minimize:

$$T = \sum_{i=1}^{n} (1 - H(C_{i-1})) t_i.$$

Subject to the storage system cost constraint:

$$\sum_{i=1}^{n} P(t_i) C_i \leq B.$$

5.4.2 STORAGE HIERARCHY RECOMMENDER SYSTEM

H is a function of the workload locality and does not have a closed-form expression [103]. Consequently, instead of deriving an explicit solution to this optimization problem, the recommender system resorts to measuring the actual throughput on a particular workload to identify the optimal storage hierarchy. The goal of the recommender system is to identify a multi-tier storage hierarchy consisting of DRAM, NVM, and/or SSD that maximizes a user-defined objective function given a cost constraint. It searches across candidate storage hierarchies that meet the user-specified budget.

We represent the set of candidate DRAM devices by $\{D_0, D_1, D_2, \ldots, D_p\}$, the set of candidate NVM devices by $\{N_0, N_1, N_2, \ldots, N_q\}$, and the set of candidate SSD devices by $\{S_0, S_1, S_2, \ldots, S_r\}$. These devices have varying capacities and costs. We are provided with a cost function P that returns the cost of a particular device. For instance, $P(D_i)$ returns the cost of the DRAM device with capacity D_i.

We can prune the set of candidate storage hierarchies by only considering devices whose capacities are powers of two. With this restriction, the size of set of candidate storage hierarchies is relatively small (p, q, and $r < 10$). The recommender system does a *pure grid search* over the entire set [43]. During a particular trial on a grid, we only consider device triples $\{D_i, N_j, S_k\}$ that meet the user-specified budget B, as given by:

$$P(D_i) + P(N_j) + P(S_k) \leq B.$$

The system then measures the operational throughput on the storage hierarchy corresponding to the device triple $\{D_i, N_j, S_k\}$. We configure $D_0 = 0$ to model storage hierarchies containing only NVM and SSD devices (i.e., those that do not have DRAM). Similarly, we set $N_0 = 0$ and $S_0 = 0$ to model storage hierarchies without NVM and SSD, respectively. We note that the entire database must fit in the lowest level of storage hierarchy. Since the cost of NVM is more than $10\times$ lower than that of SSD, the latter device will likely continue to occupy the lowest level.

5.5   TRACE-DRIVEN BUFFER MANAGER

We developed a trace-driven buffer manager to evaluate different storage hierarchy designs and data migration policies. We gather traces from a real DBMS by running OLTP, OLAP, and HTAP workloads. The trace contains information about individual buffer pool operations.

At the beginning of the trace period, we take a snapshot of the DBMS's meta-data regarding the blocks stored in memory and on storage. This snapshot does not contain any user data. The buffer manager only simulates the movement of user data blocks and not their actual contents. This allows us to effectively run simulations of buffer management operations on large databases.

During simulation, the trace requests are handed off to the buffer manager's worker threads. The buffer manager runs on top of a multi-tier storage hierarchy consisting of DRAM, NVM, and/or SSD. For instance, in case of a three-tier DRAM-NVM-SSD storage hierarchy, it maintains two buffer pools on DRAM and NVM. While processing the trace requests, the buffer manager issues read and write operations to the appropriate devices in the storage hierarchy depending on the data migration policy.

We use the hardware emulator developed by Intel Labs to emulate NVM [73, 208]. The buffer manager uses the filesystem interface exported by the emulator. This allows the buffer manager to use the POSIX filesystem interface to read and write data to files stored on NVM. This interface is implemented by the *persistent memory filesystem*, a special filesystem optimized for NVM. Typically, in a block-oriented filesystem, file I/O requires two copies; one involving the block device and another involving the user buffer. The emulator's optimized filesystem, however, requires only one copy between the file and the user buffers.

5.6   EXPERIMENTAL EVALUATION

We now present an analysis of the proposed buffer management policies for a multi-tier storage hierarchy comprising of NVM. To perform a fair comparison, we implemented all the policies in the same trace-driven buffer manager. We illustrate the following.

- NVM improves throughput by reducing accesses to canonical storage devices due to its higher capacity-cost ratio compared to DRAM.

- The selection of a multi-tier storage hierarchy for a given workload depends on the working set size, the frequency of persistent writes, the system cost budget, and the performance and cost characteristics of NVM.

- Tuning the buffer management policy for the workload and the storage hierarchy shrinks the number of writes to NVM and improves throughput.

5.6.1   EXPERIMENTAL SETUP

We perform our experiments on the NVM hardware emulator described in Appendix A. By default, we set the capacity of the DRAM and NVM buffers to be 2 GB and 128 GB, respectively. Unless otherwise stated, we configured the NVM latency to be 2× that of DRAM and validated these settings using Intel's memory latency checker. The emulator's storage hierarchy also includes two additional devices:

- **HDD:** Seagate Barracuda (3 TB, 7200 RPM, SATA 3.0)
- **SSD:** Intel DC S3700 (400 GB, SATA 2.6)

Workloads: We use the TPC-C, Voter, CH-benCHmark, and AuctionMark workloads from the OLTP-Bench testbed in our evaluation [8, 71]. Appendix B presents a detailed description of these benchmarks. These workloads differ in their workload skews and frequencies of persistent writes.

Trace Collection: We ran the benchmarks on an instrumented Postgres DBMS (v9.4) [12]. All the transactions execute with the same serializable isolation level and durability guarantees. To collect the traces, we ran each benchmark for three hours including a 30-min warm-up period. At the end of the warm-up period, we take a snapshot of the DBMS's metadata regarding the location of blocks in volatile memory and on durable storage. We then start recording the buffer pool references in the trace. During simulation, the buffer manager first loads the snapshot before executing the operations recorded in the trace.

The amount of data referenced at least once in a trace is termed as its *footprint*. An important issue in using trace-driven simulations to study storage hierarchy design is that the traces must have a sufficiently large footprint for the storage configurations of interest [99]. Table 5.1 presents the footprints of the traces associated with different benchmarks. For all experiments, we used half of the trace to warm-up the simulator. We collect system statistics only after the buffer pools have been warmed up.

5.6.2   WORKLOAD SKEW CHARACTERIZATION

We begin with a characterization of the workload skew present in the different workloads. Figure 5.3 shows the cumulative distribution function (CDF) of the number of buffer pool accesses per block in the workload traces.

Table 5.1: **Trace Footprints**—Footprints of the traces associated with different benchmarks.

Benchmark	Footprint
TPC-C	203 GB
CH-benCHmark	154 GB
Voter	185 GB
AuctionMark	117 GB

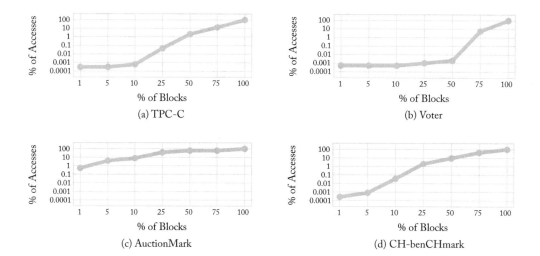

Figure 5.3: **Workload Skew Characterization**—CDF of the number of times a block is referenced in the traces associated with different workloads. Due to the inherent skew present in certain workloads, most of the buffer pool accesses are made to a small fraction of blocks.

For the TPC-C benchmark shown in Figure 5.3a, 13% of buffer pool references are made to 75% of the blocks and 25% of the blocks only account for 0.05% of the accesses. This illustrates that this workload is not highly skewed and has a large working set. Similarly, the CH-benCHmark also exhibits low skew as depicted in Figure 5.3d. 50% and 75% of the blocks account for 9% and 43% of the buffer pool references, respectively.

Figure 5.3b shows that the Voter benchmark exhibits the lowest degree of skew among all workloads since 75% of the referenced blocks account for only 6% of buffer pool references. This is because the workload mostly consists of short-lived transactions that generate many writes to the log. In contrast, AuctionMark exhibits the highest degree of skew among all workloads. 0.001% of the blocks account for 8% of the buffer pool references and 61% of the buffer pool accesses are made to 25% of the blocks. We attribute this to the temporally skewed item access patterns in AuctionMark.

5.6.3   IMPACT OF NVM ON RUNTIME PERFORMANCE

In this section, we compare the buffer manager's throughput on similarly priced NVM-SSD and DRAM-SSD storage hierarchies to examine the impact of NVM on runtime performance. We do not consider a DRAM-NVM-SSD hierarchy in this experiment to isolate the utility of NVM. We configured the cost budget to be $150. The cost of NVM is derived from the current price of Intel's 3D XPoint-based Optane SSD 905P [24]. Given this budget, the capacity of the NVM and DRAM devices are 16 GB and 128 GB, respectively. Note that the latter device's capacity is 8× higher than that of the former due to NVM's higher capacity-cost ratio. To obtain insights that are applicable for a broader range of NVM technologies, we quantify the impact of NVM on different latency configurations. We ran the experiment under three NVM latency configurations for the emulator ranging from 2–8× DRAM latency (320–1280 ns).

The results shown in Figure 5.4 illustrate that the NVM-SSD hierarchy outperforms its DRAM-based counterpart on most workloads and latency configurations. On the TPC-C benchmark, we observe that with the 2× latency configuration, the NVM-based hierarchy outperforms the DRAM-SSD hierarchy by 3.7×. This is because NVM reduces the number of SSD accesses by 19× due to its larger capacity over DRAM. The reduction in time spent on disk operations negates the performance impact of slower NVM operations. With the 4× latency configurations, the performance gap drops to 2.1×. This illustrates the impact of NVM's higher latency relative to DRAM. Both storage hierarchies deliver similar throughput on the 8× latency configuration. In this setting, slower NVM operations nullify the benefits of its higher capacity.

The impact of NVM is more pronounced on the Voter benchmark. This benchmark saturates the DBMS with many short-lived transactions that each update a small number of tuples. The buffer manager frequently flushes dirty blocks to durable storage while executing this workload. NVM improves runtime performance by efficiently absorbing these writes. As shown in Figure 5.4b, the performance gap between the two storage hierarchies varies from 10× to 2.8× on the 2× and 8× latency configurations, respectively.

On the AuctionMark workload shown in Figure 5.4c, the NVM-SSD hierarchy outperforms its DRAM-based counterpart by 2.2× with the 2× latency configuration. However, the trend reverses on the 8× latency configuration, where the latter hierarchy delivers 1.8× higher throughput than the former. We attribute this to the workload's smaller working set that fits in the DRAM buffer.

The results for the CH-benCHmark workload, shown in Figure 5.4d, illustrate that the NVM-based hierarchy delivers 5.1× higher throughput compared to its DRAM-based counterpart on the 2× latency configuration. We attribute this to the larger working set associated

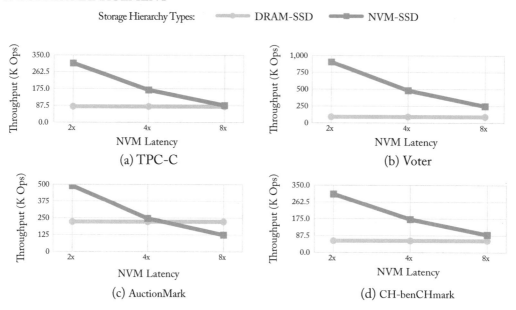

Figure 5.4: **Performance Impact of NVM**—Comparison of the buffer manager's throughput on similarly priced NVM-SSD and DRAM-SSD storage hierarchies under different NVM latency configurations.

with this workload. Even on the 8× latency configuration, the former storage hierarchy delivers 51% higher throughput than the latter. This demonstrates the performance impact of NVM on HTAP workloads.

Performance Impact of NVM with Slower Storage: We next compare the buffer manager's throughput on similarly priced NVM- and DRAM-based hierarchies that use a HDD instead of a SSD for secondary storage. The results in Figure 5.5 show that the utility of NVM is higher when operating on top of HDD relative to a SSD.

On the TPC-C benchmark, as shown in Figure 5.5a, NVM-HDD outperforms its DRAM-based counterpart by 18× on a 2× latency configuration. This is larger than the 2.8× performance gap between the NVM-SSD and DRAM-SSD hierarchies on the same configuration. This shows that the utility of the NVM buffer is higher on top of HDD due to the latter's higher latency compared to SSD. Even on the 8× latency configuration, NVM-HDD hierarchy delivers 15.3× higher throughput than DRAM-HDD. This is because the working set does not fit in the DRAM buffer. However, it fits in the NVM buffer. NVM absorbs the bulk of the buffer pool references, thereby shrinking the impact of HDD on runtime performance.

The benefits of NVM are more prominent on the Voter benchmark shown in Figure 5.5b. The NVM-based hierarchy outperforms its HDD-based counterpart by 73× on the 2× latency

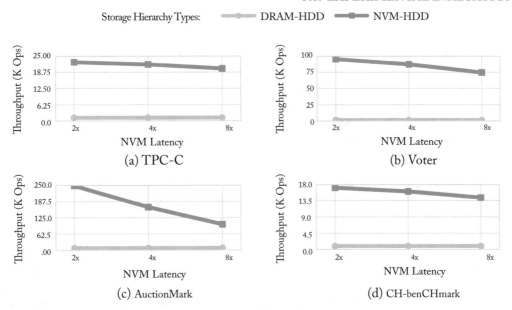

Storage Hierarchy Types: ●──● DRAM-HDD ■──■ NVM-HDD

(a) TPC-C

(b) Voter

(c) AuctionMark

(d) CH-benCHmark

Figure 5.5: **Performance Impact of NVM with Slower Storage**—Comparison of the buffer manager's throughput on similarly priced NVM-HDD and DRAM-HDD storage hierarchies under different NVM latency configurations.

configuration. On this workload, the NVM buffer reduces HDD writes by 7× in comparison to the DRAM buffer. With the 8× configuration, the performance gap marginally drops to 58×. Slower HDD operations dampen the performance impact of NVM latency on this workload.

NVM-HDD outperforms its DRAM-based counterpart across all latency configurations on the AuctionMark workload, as shown in Figure 5.5c. The performance gap between the NVM-SSD and NVM-HDD hierarchies (1.9×) is smaller than that between the DRAM-SSD and DRAM-HDD hierarchies (28×).

These results illustrate that NVM shrinks the performance impact of slower HDD operations by reducing capacity cache misses. This implies that the first place to spend money when designing a multi-tier storage hierarchy is on the cheaper tier (NVM) rather than the faster one (DRAM).

5.6.4 STORAGE HIERARCHY RECOMMENDATION

We next focus on the storage hierarchy recommendation problem presented in Section 5.4. In this experiment, we compare the *performance/price numbers* of multi-tier storage hierarchies. If the cost of a storage hierarchy is \$ C and the throughput it delivers is $\mathcal{T}$ operations per second, then the performance/price number is given by $\frac{\mathcal{T}}{C}$. This represents the number of operations executed per second per dollar. Given a system cost budget and a target workload, the recommender system identifies the storage hierarchy with the highest performance/price number.

Each storage system consists of at most three devices: DRAM, NVM, and SSD. We vary the capacity of the DRAM and NVM devices from 256 MB through 16 GB, and from 64 GB through 256 GB, respectively. We configured the capacity of the SSD device to be 1 TB. We examine the runtime performance of the buffer manager on both two- and three-tier storage hierarchies: DRAM-SSD, NVM-SSD, and DRAM-NVM-SSD. We configured the NVM latency to be 2× that of DRAM.

Storage System Cost: Figure 5.6a presents the cost of candidate storage hierarchies. The cost of the DRAM-SSD hierarchy increases from $202 to $356 when we vary the capacity of the DRAM device from 256 MB through 16 GB. The cost of the NVM-SSD hierarchy raises from $262 to $450 when we vary the capacity of the NVM device from 64 GB through 256 GB.

Storage Hierarchy Recommendation: The performance/price numbers of candidate storage hierarchies across different workloads is presented in Figure 5.6. The recommender system performs a grid search to identify the storage hierarchy with the highest performance/price number on a target workload given a cost budget.

For the TPC-C benchmark, as shown in Figure 5.6b, the storage system that delivers the highest performance/price number consists of 2 GB DRAM and 128 GB NVM on top of SSD. Expanding the capacity of the DRAM buffer to 16 GB improves performance by 12%. But, this also raises the storage system cost by 40%. Similarly, reducing the capacity of the DRAM buffer to 256 MB shrinks performance and cost by 15% and 5%, respectively. The recommended storage hierarchy outperforms its NVM-SSD counterpart by 21%. This is because the DRAM buffer reduces the time spent on NVM read operations by 63%.

The optimal storage system for the Voter workload consists of 1 GB DRAM and 128 GB NVM, as shown in Figure 5.6c. While executing this workload, the buffer manager frequently flushes dirty blocks to durable storage. In the absence of NVM, the buffer manager spends more time flushing data to SSD. So the performance/price number on a similarly priced 16 GB DRAM-SSD system is 10× lower than its NVM-based counterpart.

On the AuctionMark workload, as shown in Figure 5.6d, a NVM-SSD system consisting of 128 GB NVM delivers the highest performance/price number. It delivers 2.2× higher throughput compared to a similarly priced DRAM-SSD system with 16 GB DRAM. This illustrates the utility of NVM's higher capacity-cost ratio relative to DRAM. Adding a 2 GB DRAM buffer on top of NVM does not improve performance on this workload. Instead, it reduces throughput by 6%. The I/O overhead associated with data migration between DRAM and NVM overrides the utility of caching data on DRAM.

For the CH-benCHmark workload, the results in Figure 5.6e show that the maximal performance/price number is delivered by a DRAM-NVM-SSD system with 1 GB DRAM

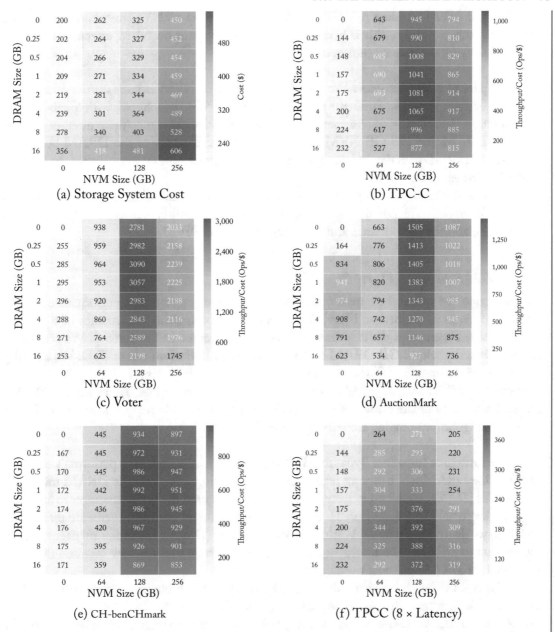

Figure 5.6: **Storage Hierarchy Recommendation**—(a) The total cost of the DRAM, NVM, and SSD devices used in a multi-tier storage system. (b-f) The performance/price numbers of candidate storage hierarchies on different benchmarks. Given a system cost budget and a target workload, the recommendation system performs a grid search to identify the storage hierarchy with the highest performance/price number.

and 128 GB NVM. Adding a 1 GB DRAM buffer on top of NVM increases throughput by 15% on this workload. This is because it reduces time spent on NVM operations by 21%, thereby justifying the data migration overhead.

Impact of NVM Latency: We look at the impact of NVM latency on the selection of storage hierarchy. Figure 5.6f presents the results for the TPC-C benchmark with the 8× latency configuration. The storage system that delivers the highest performance/price number consists of 4 GB DRAM and 128 GB NVM on top of SSD. The capacity of the DRAM buffer has increased from 2 GB with the 2× latency configuration. This shows that the utility of the DRAM buffer has increased due to slower NVM operations.

The results in Figure 5.6 illustrate how the selection of a multi-tier storage system for a given workload depending on the working set size, the frequency of persistent writes, the system cost budget, and the performance and cost characteristics of NVM.

5.6.5   DATA MIGRATION POLICIES

In this section, we look at the impact of data migration policies on runtime performance and the number of writes performed on NVM. We begin by comparing the performance of the buffer manager when it employs the lazy and eager policies presented in Section 5.2. We consider a storage hierarchy with 2 GB DRAM and 128 GB NVM buffers on top of SSD. We quantify the performance impact of four data flow optimizations: (1) bypassing DRAM ($\mathcal{D}_r$, $\mathcal{D}_w$) and (2) bypassing NVM ($\mathcal{N}_r$, $\mathcal{N}_w$) while serving read and write operations. To derive insights that are applicable for a broader range of NVM technologies, we do this analysis across three NVM latency configurations ranging from 2–8× DRAM latency.

Performance Impact of Bypassing DRAM: Figure 5.7 illustrates the performance impact of bypassing DRAM while serving reads and write operations. We vary the DRAM migration frequencies ($\mathcal{D}_r$, $\mathcal{D}_w$) in lockstep from 1–1,000. We configured the buffer manager to adopt an eager policy for NVM ($\mathcal{N}_r$, $\mathcal{N}_w = 1$). Since the DRAM migration frequencies are updated in lockstep, we denote them by $\mathcal{D}$. With the baseline policy ($\mathcal{D} = 1$), the buffer manager eagerly moves data to DRAM. The results in Figure 5.7 demonstrate that the lazy migration policies work well for DRAM on most workloads.

For the TPC-C benchmark shown in Figure 5.7a, the throughput observed when $\mathcal{D}$ is 100 is 65% higher than that with the eager migration policy on the 2× latency configuration. The reasons for this are twofold. First, the lazy policy reduces the data migration between NVM and DRAM. Second, it ensures that only frequently referenced data are moved to DRAM. The performance gap drops to 19% on the 8× latency configuration. This is because the lazy policy amplifies the performance impact of slower NVM operations.

The benefits of lazy data migration are more prominent on the write-intensive Voter workload. Bypassing DRAM while performing writes nearly doubles the throughput, as shown

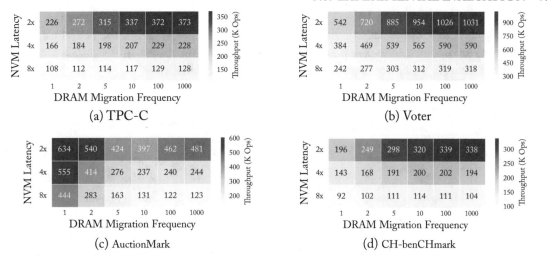

Figure 5.7: **Performance Impact of Bypassing DRAM**—Comparison of the buffer manager's throughput when it adopts lazy and eager data migration policies for DRAM. We measure the performance impact of these policies across different NVM latency configurations and DRAM migration frequencies ($\mathcal{D}$).

in Figure 5.7b. With the lazy policy, the buffer manager directly flushes dirty blocks to NVM instead of first writing them on DRAM. Since DRAM write latencies are comparable to those of NVM, particularly on the 2× latency configuration, bypassing DRAM during writes shrinks the overall write latency.

Unlike other workloads, eager policy works well for the AuctionMark workload, as depicted in Figure 5.7c. It outperforms the lazy policy ($\mathcal{D} = 10$) by 60% on the 2× latency configuration. This is because the workload's working set fits in the DRAM buffer and shifts over time. But the lazy policy delays the migration of hot data from NVM to DRAM, thereby reducing the utility of the DRAM buffer. The performance gap shrinks to 37% with a lazier policy ($\mathcal{D} = 100$). The reduction in data movement between DRAM and NVM dampens the impact of delayed migration of the working set.

Lastly, on the CH-benCHmark workload, the lazy policy delivers 72% higher throughput than its eager counterpart, as shown in Figure 5.7d. Unlike AuctionMark, the working set of this workload is more stable. Even though the lazy policy results in delayed migration, the buffer manager eventually loads the working set in the DRAM buffer. This illustrates that the optimal migration policy depends on the workload characteristics.

Performance Impact of Bypassing NVM: Figure 5.8 illustrates the performance impact of bypassing NVM while serving reads and write operations. In this experiment, we vary the

NVM migration frequencies ($\mathcal{N}_r$, $\mathcal{N}_w$) in lockstep from 1 through 1000. We configured the buffer manager to adopt an eager policy for DRAM ($\mathcal{D}_r$, $\mathcal{D}_w = 1$). Since the NVM migration frequencies are updated in lockstep, we denote them by $\mathcal{N}$. The results in Figure 5.8 show that eager migration ($\mathcal{N} = 1$) works well for NVM on most workloads.

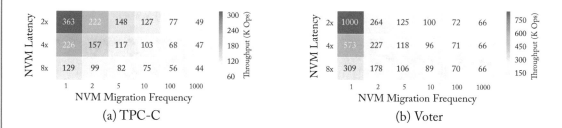

(a) TPC-C   (b) Voter

Figure 5.8: **Performance Impact of Bypassing NVM**—Comparison of the buffer manager's throughput when it adopts lazy and eager data migration policies for NVM. We measure the performance impact of these policies across different NVM latency configurations and NVM migration frequencies ($\mathcal{N}$).

For the TPC-C benchmark shown in Figure 5.8a, the throughput observed when $\mathcal{N}$ is set to 10 is 65% lower than that with the eager policy on the 2× latency configuration. This is because the time spent on SSD operations increases by 15× due to bypassing NVM during writes. The performance impact of lazy migration marginally drops to 39% on the 8× latency configuration. Slower NVM operations dampen the effect of writes landing on SSD.

The performance impact of NVM bypass is more prominent on the Voter workload shown in Figure 5.8b. The throughput drops by 90% when $\mathcal{N}$ is set to 10 on the 2× latency configuration. These results illustrate that while lazy migration policies work well for DRAM, eager policies are a better fit for NVM.

Impact of NVM Bypass on Writes to NVM: Although lazy data migration negatively impacts runtime performance, it reduces the number of writes performed on NVM. Figure 5.9 presents the impact of NVM bypass on the number of NVM writes. For the TPC-C benchmark, as shown in Figure 5.9a, the buffer manager performs 5.8× fewer writes to NVM with a lazy migration policy ($\mathcal{N} = 10$) in comparison to eager migration. The impact of NVM bypass on the number of writes performed on NVM is equally pronounced on the Voter workload as shown in Figure 5.9b. Adopting the lazy migration policy ($\mathcal{N} = 10$) reduces the number of NVM writes by 5.5×.

These results illustrate that the optimal data migration policy must be chosen depending on the runtime performance requirements and write endurance characteristics of NVM.

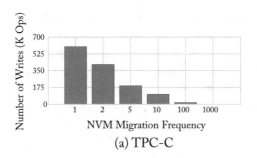

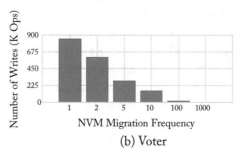

(a) TPC-C (b) Voter

Figure 5.9: **Impact of Bypassing NVM on Writes to NVM**—Comparison of the number of writes performed on NVM when the buffer manager adopts lazy and eager data migration policies for NVM. We measure the impact of these policies across different NVM migration frequencies ($\mathcal{N}$).

Impact of Storage Hierarchy: We next consider how the optimal data migration policy varies across storage hierarchies. In this experiment, we consider 2 three-tier storage hierarchies with 256 MB and 8 GB DRAM buffers. We configured both systems to use a 128 GB NVM buffer on top of SSD. The results for the TPC-C benchmark depicted in Figure 5.10 show that the utility of lazy data migration varies across storage systems.

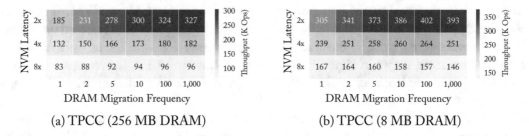

(a) TPCC (256 MB DRAM) (b) TPCC (8 MB DRAM)

Figure 5.10: **Impact of Storage Hierarchy**—Comparison of the optimal data migration policy decision for bypassing DRAM across different storage hierarchies, NVM latency configurations, and DRAM migration frequencies.

On the first system, as shown in Figure 5.10a, the throughput with lazy migration ($\mathcal{D} = 100$) is 75% higher than that with its eager counterpart. The performance gap between the policies on this system is larger than that observed with a larger DRAM buffer (1 GB) in Figure 5.7a. This is because the lazy policy increases the utility of the smaller DRAM buffer by not polluting it with colder data. For this system, the optimal migration frequency remains unchanged even on slower latency configurations.

The results for the second system shown in Figure 5.10b illustrate that the lazy policy delivers 31% higher throughput on the 2× latency configuration. The utility of lazy migration is not as prominent on this system since the capacity of the DRAM buffer is one-eighth of that of the NVM buffer. The eager policy ($\mathcal{D} = 1$) outperforms its lazy counterpart on the 8× latency configuration. This is because the latter policy amplifies the impact of slower NVM operations, particularly when the relative size of the DRAM buffer compared to the NVM buffer is large.

We conclude that the optimal migration policy depends not only on the workload and device characteristics, but also on the relative size of the DRAM buffer compared to the NVM buffer.

5.6.6   BUFFER MANAGEMENT POLICY COMPARISON

In this section, we compare our proposed data migration policy against that presented by van Renen et al. [190]. We refer to the former and latter policies by $\mathcal{A}$ and $\mathcal{B}$, respectively. We developed $\mathcal{A}$ based on the insights presented in Section 5.6.5. This policy consists of lazy migration for DRAM ($\mathcal{D}_r = 100$, $\mathcal{D}_w = 100$) and NVM during reads ($\mathcal{N}_r = 5$), and eager migration for NVM during writes ($\mathcal{N}_w = 1$). We configured $\mathcal{B}$ following the guidelines in [190]. $\mathcal{B}$ consists of eager migration for DRAM ($\mathcal{D}_r = 1$, $\mathcal{D}_w = 1$), and lazy migration for NVM during reads ($\mathcal{N}_r = \infty$) and writes ($\mathcal{N}_w = 2$). These policies differ in two ways. With the former policy, the buffer manager initially moves data into NVM and lazily migrates it to DRAM. It frequently bypasses DRAM during writes and directly persists data on NVM. With $\mathcal{B}$, the buffer manager initially moves data into DRAM and stores data evicted from DRAM on NVM. It bypasses NVM during writes in order to ensure that only frequently referenced data is stored on NVM.

The results in Figure 5.11 illustrate that $\mathcal{A}$ works well across different workloads. For the TPC-C workload shown in Figure 5.11a, it outperforms $\mathcal{B}$ by 3.1×. The reasons for this are twofold. First, with the latter policy, the buffer manager bypasses NVM during writes. Although this scheme reduces the number of writes to NVM by 2×, it increases the time spent by the buffer manager on SSD operations by 8.8×. The former policy circumvents this problem by absorbing more writes on NVM. The buffer manager often reclaims space in the NVM buffer by discarding unmodified blocks. Second, bypassing DRAM during reads ($\mathcal{D}_r = 100$) reduces the data migration overhead between NVM and DRAM and ensures that only frequently referenced blocks are stored on DRAM. The performance gap between these policies shrink on the 8× NVM latency configuration since slower NVM operations reduce the utility of lazy migration for DRAM.

The results in Figure 5.11b illustrate the utility of eager migration to NVM during writes. $\mathcal{A}$ outperforms $\mathcal{B}$ by 6.5× on this workload. With the former policy, the buffer manager directly persists data on NVM instead of first buffering it on DRAM. Since DRAM write latencies are comparable to those of NVM, particularly on the 2× latency configuration, bypassing DRAM during writes reduces the overall write latency, thereby improving runtime performance.

With policy $\mathcal{B}$, NVM latency does not impact runtime performance. The throughput only drops by 16% when we transition from a 2× latency configuration to a 8× configuration. This is

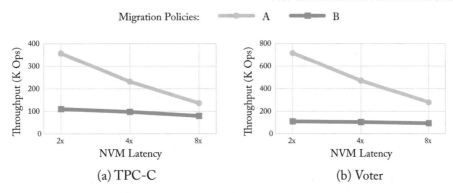

Migration Policies: ——— A ——— B

(a) TPC-C   (b) Voter

Figure 5.11: **Performance Impact of Buffer Management Policies**—The impact of different buffer management policies on runtime performance across different NVM latency configurations.

because lazy migration to NVM increases the time spent on SSD operations, thereby reducing the impact of slower NVM operations.

5.6.7   ADAPTIVE DATA MIGRATION

In the previous experiments, we examined the utility of a *fixed* data migration policy. But identifying the optimal data migration policy is challenging due to diversity of workloads and storage hierarchies. Thus, we now examine the ability of buffer manager to automatically adapt the management policy at runtime. In this experiment, the buffer manager begins executing the workload with an eager policy for both DRAM ($\mathcal{D} = 1$) and NVM ($\mathcal{N} = 1$). During execution, it adapts the policy using the simulated annealing (SA) algorithm presented in Section 5.3. This technique searches for the policy that maximizes the throughput given a target workload and storage hierarchy. We use an operation sequence with 100 M entries. We configure the duration of a tuning step to be 1 M operations to ensure that the impact of policy changes are prominently visible to the SA algorithm.

The results in Figure 5.12 show that the buffer manager converges to a near-optimal policy for different workloads without requiring any manual tuning. For the TPC-C and Voter workloads, tuning the data migration policy increases throughput by 81% and 77%, respectively. The buffer manager converges to a hybrid policy, with lazy migration for DRAM and eager migration for NVM on both workloads. The throughput converges to a global optima over time. We attribute this to the gradual cooling mechanism in SA that decreases the probability of accepting worse policies.

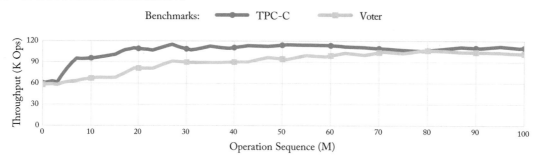

Figure 5.12: **Adaptive Data Migration**—The impact of buffer management policy adaptation on runtime performance across different workloads.

5.7   SUMMARY

This chapter explored the changes required in the buffer manager to leverage the unique properties of NVM in systems that still include DRAM and SSD. We introduced a taxonomy of data migration policies for DRAM and NVM. Our evaluation shows that a NVM-based storage hierarchy outperforms a similarly priced DRAM-SSD system by up to 10×. We demonstrate that our continuous adaptation mechanism allows the DBMS to achieve a near-optimal data migration policy for an arbitrary workload without requiring any manual tuning.

Thus far, this book has focused on implications of NVM for storage management, logging and recovery algorithms, and buffer management. Lastly, we examine the implications of NVM for index data structures in the next chapter.

CHAPTER 6

Indexing

Multi-threaded concurrency is one of the keys to unlocking high performance in main-memory databases. To achieve concurrency on modern CPUs, several systems—both research and commercial—implement latch-free index structures to avoid bottlenecks inherent in latching (locking) protocols. For instance, MemSQL uses latch-free skip-lists [169], while Microsoft's Hekaton main-memory OLTP engine uses the Bw-tree [70], a latch-free B+tree.

The algorithms for latch-free index designs are often complex. They rely on atomic CPU hardware primitives such as compare-and-swap (CAS) to atomically modify index state. These atomic instructions are limited to a single word, and non-trivial data structures—such as a latch-free B+tree—usually require multi-word updates, e.g., to handle operations like node splits and merges. These operations have to be broken up into multiple steps, thereby exposing intermediate states to other threads. As a result, the algorithms must handle subtle race conditions that may occur when intermediate states are exposed. In addition, some designs sacrifice performance to achieve latch-freedom. An example is the Bw-tree [126] that uses a mapping table to map logical page identifiers to physical pointers. Nodes in the Bw-tree store logical pointers and must dereference the mapping table on each node access during traversal of the index. Such indirection leads to degraded performance on modern CPUs.

Storing a latch-free index on NVM potentially enables both high performance and fast recovery. But, it further complicates implementation of latch-free indexes. The added complexity is mainly caused by the fact that CAS and other atomic hardware instructions do not persist their updates to NVM automatically and atomically. An update only modifies the target word in the processor cache and does not automatically update the target word in NVM. In case of a power failure, the volatile cache content is lost and the data in NVM may be left in an inconsistent state. Hence, we need a persistence protocol to ensure that an index recovers correctly after a system crash.

In this chapter, we propose the BzTree, a high-performance latch-free B+tree design for main-memory databases that has the following benefits.

Reduced Complexity: The BzTree implementation makes use of PMwCAS: a high-performance, multi-word, compare-and-swap operation that also provides persistence guarantees when used on NVM [200]. The PMwCAS operation is implemented in software and require no special hardware support other than a CAS (or equivalent) instruction. It is itself latch-free and either atomically installs all new values or fails the operation without exposing intermediate state. Using PMwCAS to build a latch-free index has two major advantages. First, the PMwCAS guarantees that all multi-word updates are atomic, thus avoiding the need to handle complex race conditions that result from exposing intermediate state during multi-word operations. Second, PMwCAS allows the BzTree to avoid logical-to-physical indirection used, for example, in the Bw-tree [126]. The BzTree stores direct memory pointers in both index and leaf nodes.

High Performance: Using the YCSB workload on volatile RAM, we show that the BzTree outperforms the Bw-tree. This demonstrates that the BzTree outperforms a state-of-the-art index designed for DRAM-based systems. Given its portability, we also experimentally demonstrate that the penalty for running the BzTree on NVM is low: on realistic workloads, the overhead of persistence is 8% on average. We also show that use of PMwCAS exhibits negligible contention even for larger multi-word operations. Even for highly skewed YCSB access patterns, the failure rate for updating multiple words across multiple BzTree nodes is only 0.2% on average.

Seamless Portability to NVM: The same BzTree implementation can run on both volatile DRAM and on NVM without *any* code changes. PMwCAS guarantees that upon success of an update (in this case to B+tree nodes), the operation will be durable on NVM and persist across failures. Remarkably, recovery is handled entirely by the PMwCAS library without any BzTree specific recovery code.

The rest of this chapter is organized as follows. In Section 6.1, we present the necessary background on the PMwCAS primitive. Section 6.3 presents the BzTree node layout and single-node updates, while Section 6.4 covers structure modifications. Durability and recoverability on NVM are covered in Section 6.5. We present our experimental evaluation in Section 6.6 and conclude the chapter in Section 6.7.

6.1   PERSISTENT MULTI-WORD CAS

The BzTree relies on an efficient and persistent multi-word compare-and-swap operation, named PMwCAS, to update state in a latch-free and persistent manner. The design is based on a volatile version by Harris et al. [94], which we enhance to guarantee persistence on NVM (details in [200]). The approach uses a descriptor to track metadata for the operation (details described later); these descriptors are pooled and eventually reused. The API for the PMwCAS is as follows.

- AllocateDescriptor(callback = default): Allocate a descriptor that will be used throughout the PMwCAS operation. The user can provide a custom callback function for recycling memory pointed to by the words in the PMwCAS operation.

- `Descriptor::AddWord(address, expected, desired)`: Specify a word to be modified. The caller provides the address of the word, expected value, and desired value.

- `Descriptor::ReserveEntry(addr, expected, policy)`: Similar to `AddWord` except the new value is left unspecified; returns a pointer to the `new_value` field so it can be filled in later. Memory referenced by `old_value`/`new_value` will be recycled according to the specified recycling policy.

- `Descriptor::RemoveWord(address)`: Remove the word previously specified as part of the `PMwCAS`.

- `PMwCAS(descriptor)`: Execute the `PMwCAS` and return true if succeeded.

- `Discard(descriptor)`: Cancel the `PMwCAS` (only valid before calling `PMwCAS`). No specified word will be modified.

The API is identical for both volatile and persistent `MWCAS`. Under the hood, `PMwCAS` provides all the needed persistence guarantees, without additional actions by the application.

To use `PMwCAS`, the application first allocates a descriptor and invokes the `AddWord` or `ReserveEntry` method once for each word to be modified. It can use `RemoveWord` to remove a previously specified word if needed. `AddWord` and `ReserveEntry` ensure that target addresses are unique and return an error if they are not. Calling `PMwCAS` executes the operation, while `Discard` aborts it. A failed `PMwCAS` will leave all target words unchanged. This behavior is guaranteed across a power failure when operating on NVM.

6.1.1 DURABILITY

When running on NVM, the `PMwCAS` provides durability guarantees through the use of instructions to selectively flush or write back a cache line, e.g., via the cache line write-back (`CLWB`) or cache line flush (`CLFLUSH` without write-back) instructions on Intel processors [23]. These instructions are carefully placed to ensure linearizable reads and writes and also guarantee correct recovery in case of a crash or power failure. This is achieved by using a single *dirty bit* on all modified words that are observable by other threads during the `PMwCAS`. For example, each modification that installs a descriptor address (or target value) sets a dirty bit to signify that the value is volatile, and that a reader must flush the value and unset the bit before proceeding. This protocol ensures that any dependent writes are guaranteed that the value read will survive power failure.

6.1.2 EXECUTION

Internally, `PMwCAS` makes use of a *descriptor* that stores all the information needed to complete the operation. Figure 6.1 depicts an example descriptor for three target words. A descriptor contains, for each target word: (1) the target word's address; (2) the expected value to compare against; (3) the new value; (4) the dirty bit; and (5) a memory recycling policy. The policy field indicates whether the new and old values are pointers to memory objects and, if so, which

PMWCAS Status	Undecided			
PMWCAS Size	3 Sub-operations			

Target Word's Address	Expected Old Value	New Value	Dirty Bit	Memory Recycling Policy
Address—1	Value O	Value N	0	None
Address—2	Pointer X	Pointer Y	1	Free One
Address—3	Pointer Q	Pointer R	1	Free One

Figure 6.1: PMwCAS **Descriptor Table**—Contents of the descriptor table used by threads to share information about the PMwCAS operation.

objects are to be freed on the successful completion (or failure) of the operation. The descriptor also contains a status word tracking the operation's progress. The PMwCAS operation itself is latch-free; the descriptor contains enough information for any thread to help complete (or roll back) the operation. The operation consists of two phases.

Phase 1: This phase attempts to install a pointer to the descriptor in each target address using a *double-compare single-swap* (RDCSS) operation [94]. RDCSS applies change to a target word only if the values of two words (including the one being changed) match their specified expected values. That is, RDCSS requires an additional "expected" value to compare against (but not modify) compared to a regular CAS. RDCSS is necessary to guard against subtle race conditions and maintain a linearizable sequence of operations on the same word. Specifically, we must guard against the installation of a descriptor for a completed PMwCAS (p_1) that might inadvertently overwrite the result of another PMwCAS (p_2), where p_2 should occur after p_1 (details in [200]).

A descriptor pointer in a word indicates that a PMwCAS is underway. Any thread that encounters a descriptor pointer helps complete the operation before proceeding with its own work, making PMwCAS cooperative (typical for latch-free operations). We use one high-order bit (in addition to the dirty bit) in the target word to signify whether it is a descriptor or regular value. Descriptor pointer installation proceeds in a target address order to avoid deadlocks between two competing PMwCAS operations that might concurrently overlap.

Upon completing Phase 1, a thread persists the target words whose dirty bit is set. To ensure correct recovery, this must be done before updating the descriptor's status field and advancing to Phase 2. We update status using CAS to either Succeeded or Failed (with the dirty bit set) depending on whether Phase 1 succeeded. We then persist the status field and clear its dirty bit. Persisting the status field "commits" the operation, ensuring its effects survive even across power failures.

Phase 2: If Phase 1 succeeds, the PMwCAS is guaranteed to succeed, even if a failure occurs—recovery will roll forward with the new values recorded in the descriptor. Phase 2 installs the final values (with the dirty bit set) in the target words, replacing the pointers to the descriptor. Since the final values are installed one by one, it is possible that a crash in the middle of Phase 2 leaves some target fields with new values, while others point to the descriptor. Another thread might have observed some of the newly installed values and make dependent actions (e.g., performing a PMwCAS of its own) based on the read. Rolling back in this case might cause data inconsistencies. Therefore, it is crucial to persist status before entering Phase 2. The recovery routine (covered next) can then rely on the status field of the descriptor to decide if it should roll forward or backward. If the PMwCAS fails in Phase 1, Phase 2 becomes a rollback procedure by installing the old values (with the dirty bit set) in all target words containing a descriptor pointer.

Recovery: Due to the two-phase execution of PMwCAS, a target address may contain a descriptor pointer or normal value after a crash. Correct recovery requires that the descriptor be persisted before entering Phase 1. The dirty bit in the status field is cleared because the caller has not started to install descriptor pointers in the target fields; any failure that might occur before this point does not affect data consistency upon recovery.

The PMwCAS descriptors are pooled in a memory location known to recovery. Crash recovery then proceeds by scanning the descriptor pool. If a descriptor's status field signifies success, the operation is rolled forward by applying the target values in the descriptor; if the status signifies failure it is rolled back by applying the old values. Uninitialized descriptors are simply ignored. Therefore, recovery time is determined by the number of in-progress PMwCAS operations during the crash; this is usually on the order of number of threads, meaning very fast recovery. In fact, in an end-to-end recovery experiment for the BzTree, we measured an average recovery time of 145 μs when running a write-intensive workload with 48 threads.

Memory Management: Latch-free data structure implementations require a mechanism to manage memory lifetime and garbage collection; since there are no locks protecting memory deallocation, the system must ensure no thread can dereference a block of memory before it is freed. The BzTree uses a high-performance epoch-based recycling scheme [127]. A thread joins the current epoch before each operation it performs on the index to protect the memory it accesses from reclamation. It exits the epoch when it finishes its operation. When all the threads that joined an epoch $\mathcal{E}$ have completed and exited, the garbage collector reclaims the memory occupied by the descriptors deallocated in $\mathcal{E}$. This ensures that no thread can possibly dereference a pointer after its memory is reclaimed.

Since the PMwCAS is latch-free, descriptor memory lifetime is managed by the epoch-based recycling scheme. This ensures that no thread can possibly dereference a descriptor pointer after its memory is reclaimed and reused by another PMwCAS. If any of the 8-byte expected or target values are pointers to larger memory objects, these objects can also be managed by the same memory reclamation scheme. Each word in the descriptor is marked with a memory recycling policy that denotes whether and what memory to free on completion of the operation. For instance, if a PMwCAS succeeds, the user may want memory behind the expected (old) value to be freed once the descriptor is deemed safe to recycle. Section 6.5 discusses the details of the interplay between PMwCAS and memory reclamation.

6.2   BzTREE ARCHITECTURE AND DESIGN

6.2.1   ARCHITECTURE

The BzTree is a high-performance main-memory B+tree. Internal nodes store search keys and pointers to child nodes. Leaf nodes store keys and either record pointers or actual payload values. Keys can be variable or fixed length. Our experiments assume leaf nodes store 8-byte record pointers as payloads (common in main-memory databases [70]), though we also discuss how to handle full variable-length payloads. The BzTree is a range access method that supports standard atomic key-value operations (insert, read, update, delete, range scan). Typical of most access methods, it can be deployed as a stand-alone key-value store, or embedded in a database engine to support ACID transactions, where concurrency control takes place outside of the access method as is common in most systems (e.g., within a lock manager) [97, 127].

Persistence Modes: We assume a system model with a single-level store where NVM is attached directly to the memory bus. The system may also contain DRAM which is used as working storage. A salient feature of the BzTree is that its design works for both volatile and persistent environments. In volatile mode, BzTree nodes are stored in volatile DRAM. Content is lost after a system failure. This mode is appropriate for use in existing main-memory system designs (e.g., Microsoft Hekaton [70]) that already contain recovery infrastructure to recover indexes. In durable mode, both internal and leaf nodes are stored in NVM. The BzTree guarantees that all updates are persistent and the index can recover quickly to a correct state after a failure. For disaster recovery (media failure), the BzTree must rely on common solutions like database replication.

Metadata: Besides nodes, there are only two other 64-bit values used by the BzTree:

- *Root pointer*. This is a 64-bit pointer to the root node of the index. When running in persistence mode, this value is persisted in a known location to find the index upon restart.

- *Global index epoch*. When running in persistence mode, the BzTree is associated with an *index epoch* number. This value is drawn from a global counter (one per index) that is initially zero for a new index and incremented *only* when the BzTree restarts after a crash. This value is persisted in a known location, and is used for recovery purposes and to detect in-flight operations (e.g., space allocations within nodes) during a crash. We elaborate on the use of this value in Sections 6.3 and 6.5.

6.2.2   COMPLEXITY AND PERFORMANCE

The BzTree design addresses implementation complexities and performance drawbacks of state-of-the-art latch-free range indexes.

Implementation Complexities: State-of-the-art range index designs usually rely on atomic primitives to update state. This is relatively straightforward for single-word updates. For example, the Bw-tree [126] updates a node using a single-word CAS to install a pointer to a delta record within a mapping table. Likewise, designs like the MassTree [138] use a CAS on a status word to arbitrate node updates. The implementation becomes more complex when handling multi-location updates, such as node splits and merges that grow (or shrink) an index. The Bw-tree breaks multi-node operations into steps that can be installed with a single atomic CAS; similar approaches are taken by other high-performance indexes to limit latching across nodes. These multi-step operations expose intermediate state to threads that concurrently access the index. This means the implementation must have special logic in place to allow a thread to (a) recognize when it is accessing an incomplete index (e.g., seeing an in-progress split or node delete) and (b) take cooperative action to help complete an in-progress operation. This logic leads to code "bloat" and subtle race conditions that are difficult to debug [135].

As we will see, the BzTree uses the PMwCAS primitive to update index state. We show that this approach performs well even when updating multiple nodes atomically. The BzTree thus avoids the subtle race conditions for more complex multi-node operations. In fact, using cyclomatic complexity analysis,[1] we show that the BzTree design is at least half as complex as the Bw-tree and MassTree [138], two state-of-the-art index designs.

Performance Considerations: Some latch-free designs such as the Bw-tree rely on indirection through a mapping table to isolate updates (and node reorganizations) to a single location. Bw-tree nodes store logical node pointers, which are indexes into the mapping table storing the physical node pointers. This approach comes with a tradeoff. While it avoids propagation of pointer changes up the index, e.g., to parent nodes, it requires an extra pointer dereference when accessing each node. This effectively doubles the amount of pointer dereferences during index traversal, leading to reduced performance, as we show in our experimental evaluation (Section 6.6).

The BzTree does not rely on indirection to achieve latch-freedom. Interior index nodes store direct pointers to child nodes to avoid costly extra pointer dereferences during traversal. As we show later in Section 6.6, this translates into higher performance when compared to the state-of-the-art in latch-free index design.

---

[1]Cyclomatic complexity is a quantitative measure of the number of linearly independent paths through source code.

6.3   BzTREE NODES

In this section, we begin by describing the BzTree node organization and then discuss how the BzTree supports latch-free reads and updates on these nodes. We then describe node consolidation: an operation that reorganizes a node to reclaim dead space and speed up search. We defer discussion of multi-node operations such as splits and merges until Section 6.4.

6.3.1   NODE LAYOUT

The BzTree node representation follows a typical slotted-page layout, where fixed-size metadata grows "downward" into the node, and variable-length storage (key and data) grow "upward." Specifically, a node consists of: (1) a fixed-size header, (2) an array of fixed-size record metadata entries, (3) free space that buffers updates to the node, and (4) a record storage block that stores variable-length keys and payloads. All fixed-sized metadata is packed into 64-bit aligned words so that it can easily be updated in a latch-free manner using PMwCAS.

Header: The header is located at the beginning of a node and consists of three fields as depicted in Figure 6.2a: (1) a `node size` field (32 bits) that stores the size of the entire node, (2) a `status word` field (64 bits) that stores metadata used for coordinating updates to a node (content discussed later in this section), and (3) a `sorted count` field (32 bits), representing the last index in the record metadata array in sorted order; any entries beyond this point might be unsorted and represent new records added to the node.

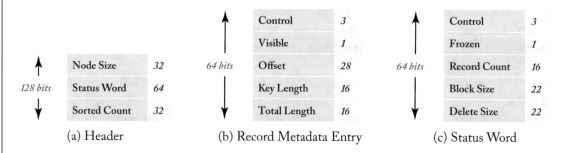

Figure 6.2: **Node Layout**—Node layout and details for the BzTree.

Record Metadata Array: Figure 6.2b depicts an entry in the record metadata array that consists of: (1) flag bits (4 bits) that are broken into PMwCAS `control bits`[2] (3 bits) used as internal metadata for the PMwCAS (e.g., to mark dirty words that require a flush) along with a `visible` flag (1 bit) used to mark a record as visible; (2) an `offset` value (28 bits) points to the full record entry in the key-value storage block; (3) a `key length` field (16 bits) stores the

---

[2]PMwCAS relies on these bits to function property. A detailed description is available in [200].

variable-length key size; and (4) a `total length` field (16 bits) stores the total length of the record block; subtracting `key length` from this value provides the record payload size.

Free Space: Free space is used to absorb modifications to a node such as record inserts. This free space sits between the fixed-size record metadata array and the record storage block. The record metadata array grows "downward" into this space, while the data storage block grows "upward." However, internal index nodes do not contain free space; as we will discuss later, these nodes are search-optimized and thus do not buffer updates, as doing so results in degraded binary search performance.

Record Storage Block: Entries in this block consist of contiguous key-payload pairs. Keys are variable-length byte strings. Payloads in internal BzTree nodes are fixed-length (8-byte) child node pointers. In this chapter, we assume payloads stored in leaf nodes are 8-byte record pointers (as is common in main-memory databases [70]). However, the BzTree also supports storing full variable-length payloads within leaf nodes. We discuss how to update both types of payloads later in this section.

Status Word: The status word, depicted in Figure 6.2c, is a 64-bit value that stores node metadata that changes during an update. For leaf nodes, this word contains the following fields: (1) `PMwCAS control bits` (3 bits) used to atomically update the word; (2) a `frozen` flag (1 bit) that signals that the node is immutable; (3) a `record count` field (16 bits) that stores the total number of entries in the record metadata array; (4) a `block size` field (22 bits) storing the number of bytes occupied by the record storage block at the end of the node; and (5) a `delete size` field (22 bits) that stores the amount of logically deleted space on the node, which is useful for deciding when to merge or reorganize the node. Status words for *internal nodes* only contain the first two fields; this is because we do not perform singleton updates on internal nodes and thus do not need the other fields. We opt to replace internal nodes wholesale (e.g., when adding or deleting a record) for search performance reasons.

Internal and Leaf Node Differences: Besides status word format, internal and leaf nodes differ in that internal nodes are immutable once created, while leaf nodes are not. Internal nodes only store records in sorted order by key (for fast binary search) and do not contain free space. Leaf nodes, on the other hand, contain free space to buffer inserts (and updates if the leaf nodes store full record payloads). This means that leaf nodes consist of both sorted records (records present during node creation) and unsorted records (records added to the page incrementally). We chose this approach because the vast majority of updates in a B+tree occur at the leaf level, thus it is important to have leaf nodes quickly absorb record updates "in place." On the other hand, internal index nodes are read-mostly and change less frequently, thus can tolerate whole-sale replacement, e.g., when adding a new key as a result of a node split. In our experience, keeping internal index nodes search-optimized leads to better performance than an alternative approach that organizes internal nodes with both sorted and unsorted key space [126].

6.3.2   LEAF NODE OPERATIONS

This section describes the latch-free read and update operations on BzTree leaf nodes. For writes, the basic idea is to employ the PMwCAS to manipulate the page and record metadata atomically in a latch-free manner, for both reserving space (in the case of copying variable length data into the page) and making the update "visible" to concurrent threads accessing the page. Readers access pages uncontested; they are not blocked by writers. Table 6.1 summarizes the PMwCAS operations associated with all the tree operations.

Table 6.1: PMwCAS **Summary Table**—The size of the PMwCAS operations associated with different node and structure modification operations.

Tree Operation	PMwCAS Size
Node operations	
Insert (allocation, completion)	2,2
Delete	2
Update (record pointer, inlined payload)	3,2
Node consolidation	2
SMOs	
Node split (preparation, installation)	1,3
Node merge (preparation, installation)	2,3

Inserts

New records are added to the free space available in the node. To insert a new record r, a thread first reads the frozen bit. If it is set, this means the page is immutable and may no longer be part of the index (e.g., due to a concurrent node delete). In this case, the thread must re-traverse the index to find the new incarnation of the "live" leaf node. Otherwise, the thread reserves space for r in both the record metadata array and record storage block. This is done by performing a 2-word PMwCAS on the following fields: (1) the node's status word to atomically increment the record count field by one and add the size of r to the block size value; and (2) the record metadata array entry to flip the offset field's high-order bit and set the rest of its bits equal to the global index epoch.[3] If this PMwCAS succeeds, the reservation is a success. The offset field is overridden during this phase to remember the allocation's index epoch. We refer to this

---

[3]Note that setting this field atomically along with the reservation is safe, since it will only succeed if the space allocation succeeds.

value as the allocation epoch and use it for recovery purposes (explained later). We steal the high-order bit to signal whether the value is an allocation epoch (set) or actual record offset (unset).

The insert proceeds by copying the contents of r to the storage block and updating the fields in the corresponding record metadata entry, initializing the visible flag to 0 (invisible). Once the copy completes, the thread flushes r (using CLWB or CLFLUSH) if the index must ensure persistence. It then reads the status word value s to again check the frozen bit, aborting and retrying if the page became frozen (e.g., due to a concurrent structure modification). Otherwise, the record is made visible by performing a 2-word PMwCAS on (1) the 64-bit record metadata entry to set the visible bit and also set the offset field to the actual record block offset (with its high-order bit unset) and (2) the status word, setting it to s (the same value initially read) to detect conflict with a concurrent thread trying to set the frozen bit. If the PMwCAS succeeds, the insert is a success. Otherwise, the thread re-reads the status word (ensuring the frozen bit is unset) and retries the PMwCAS.

The BzTree must be able to detect concurrent inserts of the same key to enforce, for instance, unique key constraints. We implement an optimistic protocol to detect concurrent key operations as follows. When an insert operation first accesses a node, it searches the sorted key space for its key and aborts if the key is present. Otherwise, it continues its search by scanning the unsorted key space. If it sees any record with an unset visible flag and an allocation epoch value equal to the current *global index epoch*, this means it has encountered an in-progress insert that *may* be for the same key. An entry with an unset visible flag and an allocation epoch *not* equal to the *global index epoch* means it is either deleted or its allocation was in-progress during a crash from a previous incarnation of the index and can be ignored (details in Section 6.5.3). Instead of waiting for the in-progress insert to become visible, the thread sets an internal *recheck* flag to remember to re-scan the unsorted key space and continues with its insert. The *recheck* flag is also set if the thread loses a PMwCAS to reserve space for its insert since the concurrent reservation may be for the same key. Prior to setting its own visibility bit, the thread re-scans the unsorted key space if the *recheck* flag is set and examines all prior entries before its own position. Upon encountering a duplicate key, the thread zeroes out its entry in the record storage block and sets its offset value to zero; these two actions signify a failed operation that will be ignored by subsequent searches. If the thread encounters an in-progress operation during its scan, it must wait for the record to become visible, since this represents an operation that serialized behind the insert that *may* contain a duplicate key.

Delete

To delete a record, a thread performs a 2-word PMwCAS on (1) a record's metadata entry to unset its visible bit and set its offset value to zero, signifying a deleted record and (2) the node status word to increment the delete size field by the size of the target record. If the PMwCAS fails due to a concurrent delete or conflict on the status word, the thread retries the delete. If the failure is due to a concurrent operation that set the `frozen` bit on the node, the delete must re-traverse the index to retry on a mutable leaf node. Incrementing `delete size` allows the BzTree to determine when to delete or consolidate a node (Section 6.4).

Update

There are two methods to update an existing record, depending on whether a leaf node stores record pointers or full payloads.

- **Record Pointers:** If leaf nodes contain record pointers and the user wishes to update a record in-place, the BzTree is passive and the update thread can traverse the pointer to access the record memory directly. If the update requires swapping in a *new* record pointer, this can be done in place within the record storage block. To do this, a thread reads both (a) the record metadata entry m to ensure it is not deleted and (b) the status word s to ensure the node is not frozen. It then performs a 3-word `PMwCAS` consisting of: (1) the 64-bit pointer in the storage block to install the new pointer; (2) the record's metadata entry, setting it to m (the same value as it read) to detect conflict with a competing delete trying to modify the word; and (3) the status word, setting it to s (the same value it read) to detect conflict with a competing flip of the frozen bit.

- **Inline Payloads:** If leaf nodes store full payloads, the update follows the same protocol as an insert by (1) allocating space in the metadata array and record storage block and (2) writing a (key, `update_payload`) record into the record block that describes the update. The `update_payload` can be either a full payload replacement or a "byte diff" describing only the part(s) of the payload that have changed. Unlike inserts, we treat concurrent updates to the same key as a natural race, supporting the "last writer wins" protocol. This means there is no need to detect concurrent updates to the same key.

Upsert

The BzTree supports the upsert operation common in most key-value stores. If the record exists in the leaf node, the thread performs an update to that record. If the record does not exist, the thread performs an insert. In this case if the insert fails due to another concurrent insert, the operation can retry to perform an update.

Reads

BzTree update operations do not block readers. A reader traverses the index to the target leaf node. If the leaf node stores record pointers, a thread first performs a binary search on the sorted key space. If it does not find its search key (either the key does not exist or was deleted in the sorted space), it performs a sequential scan on the unsorted key space. If the key is found, it returns the record to the user. If leaf nodes store full record payloads, the search first scans the unsorted key space starting from the most recent entry, as recent update records will represent the latest payload for a record. If the key is not found, the search continues to the sorted key space.

A read returns the most recent record it finds on the node that matches its search key. It ignores all concurrent update activity on the node by disregarding both the `frozen` bit and any in-progress record operations (unset `visible` bits). These concurrent operations are treated as natural races, since (a) any record-level concurrency must be handled outside the BzTree and (b) the frozen bit does not matter to reads, as it is used by operations attempting to reorganize the node to serialize with updates.

Range Scans

The BzTree supports range scans as follows. A user opens a scan iterator by specifying a `begin_key` and an optional `end_key` (null if open-ended) defining the range they wish to scan. The scan then proceeds one leaf node at a time until termination. It begins by entering an epoch to ensure memory stability and uses the `begin_key` to find the initial leaf node. When entering a page, the iterator constructs a response array that lists the valid records (i.e., visible and not deleted) on the node in sorted order. In essence, the response array is a snapshot copy of the node's valid records in its record storage block. After copying the snapshot, the iterator exits its epoch so as to not hold back memory garbage collection. It then services record-at-a-time `get_next` requests out of its snapshot. Once it exhausts the response array, the iterator proceeds to the next leaf node by entering a new epoch and traversing the tree using a "greater than" search on the largest key in the response array; this value represents the high boundary key of the previous leaf node and will allow the traversal to find the next leaf node position in the scan. This process repeats until the iterator can no longer satisfy the user-provided range boundaries, or the user terminates the iterator.

6.3.3   LEAF NODE CONSOLIDATION

Eventually a leaf node's search performance and effective space utilization degrade due to side effects of inserts or deletes. Search degrades due to (a) the need to sequentially scan the unsorted key space (in the case of many inserts) and/or (b) a number of deletes adding to the "dead space" within the sorted key space, thereby inflating the cost of binary search. The BzTree will occasionally consolidate (reorganize) a leaf node to increase search performance and eliminate dead space. Consolidation is triggered when free space reaches a minimum threshold, or the amount of logically deleted space on the node is greater than a configurable threshold.

To perform consolidation of a node $\mathcal{N}$, a thread first performs a single-word `PMwCAS` on the $\mathcal{N}$'s status word to set its frozen flag. This prevents any ongoing updates from completing and ensures the consolidation process sees a consistent snapshot of $\mathcal{N}$'s records. The process then scans $\mathcal{N}$ to locate pointers to all live records on the page—ignoring deleted and invisible records—and calculates the space needed to allocate a fresh node (the size of all valid records plus free space). If this space is beyond a configurable max page size, the process invokes a node split (covered in Section 6.4). Otherwise, it allocates memory for a new node $\mathcal{N}'$ along with some free space to buffer new node updates. It then initializes the header and copies over all live records from $\mathcal{N}$ to $\mathcal{N}'$ in key-sequential order. Now, $\mathcal{N}'$ contains all sorted records and is ready to replace $\mathcal{N}$.

Making $\mathcal{N}'$ visible in the index requires "swapping out" a pointer to $\mathcal{N}$ at its parent node $\mathcal{P}$ to replace it with a pointer to $\mathcal{N}'$. To do this, the thread uses its path stack (a stack recording node pointers during traversal) to find a pointer to $\mathcal{P}$. If this pointer represents a frozen page, the thread must re-traverse the index to find the valid parent. It then finds the record r in $\mathcal{P}$ that stores the child pointer to $\mathcal{N}$ and performs an in-place update using a 2-word PMwCAS on (1) the 64-bit child pointer in r to install the pointer to $\mathcal{N}'$ and (2) $\mathcal{P}$'s status word to detect a concurrent page freeze. If this PMwCAS succeeds, $\mathcal{N}'$ is now live in the index and $\mathcal{N}$ can be garbage collected. However, $\mathcal{N}$ cannot be immediately freed, since this process is latch-free and other threads may still have pointers to $\mathcal{N}$. The BzTree handles this case by using an epoch-based garbage collection approach to safely free memory.

Concurrency During Consolidation: Freezing a node prior to consolidation will cause any in-progress updates on that node to fail, as they will detect the set frozen bit when attempting a PMwCAS on the status word. The failed operations will then retry by re-traversing the tree to find a new "live" leaf node. If they again land on a frozen node, this is a signal to help along to complete the consolidation instead of "spinning" by continuously re-traversing the index hoping for a live node. In this case, each thread will start its own consolidate process and attempt to install it at the parent. This effectively makes threads race to install a consolidated node, although one will ultimately win. Afterward, each thread resumes its original operation.

6.3.4 INTERNAL NODE OPERATIONS

Updates to existing records on internal nodes are performed in place following the protocol discussed in the previous section for installing a new child pointer. To maintain search optimality of internal nodes, record inserts and deletes (e.g., part of splitting or deleting a child node) create a completely new version of an internal node. In other words, an insert or delete in an internal node immediately triggers a consolidation. This process is identical to the leaf node consolidation steps just discussed: a new node will be created (except with one record added or removed), and its pointer will be installed at the parent.

6.4 STRUCTURE MODIFICATIONS

We now describe the latch-free algorithms used in the BzTree for structure modification operations (SMOs). Like single-node updates, the basic idea for SMOs is to employ the PMwCAS to update page state atomically and in a latch-free manner. This involves manipulating metadata like frozen bits, as well as manipulating search pointers within index nodes to point to new page versions (e.g., split pages).

We begin with a presentation of the node split and node merge algorithms. We then discuss the interplay between the algorithms when commingling structural changes and data changes. We also explain why threads concurrently accessing the tree are guaranteed to not observe inconsistencies, which simplifies both implementation and reasoning about correctness.

6.4.1 PRIORITIZING STRUCTURE MODIFICATIONS

Triggering SMOs in the BzTree relies on a simple deterministic policy. A split is triggered once a node size passes a configurable `max_size` threshold (e.g., 4 KB). Likewise, a node delete/merge is triggered once a node's size falls below a configurable `min_size`.

If an update thread encounters a node in need of an SMO, it temporarily suspends its operation to perform the SMO before continuing its operation (we do not force readers to perform SMOs). Given that SMOs are relatively heavyweight, prioritizing them over (lightweight) single-record operations is important. Otherwise, in a latch-free race, single-record operations would always win and effectively starve SMOs.

6.4.2 NODE SPLIT

Node splits are broken into two phases: (1) a preparation phase that allocates and initializes new nodes with the SMO changes and (2) an installation phase that atomically installs the new nodes in the index. We now describe the split details with the aid of Figure 6.3.

Preparation: To split a node $\mathcal{N}$, we first perform a `PMwCAS` on its status word to set the `frozen` bit, as depicted in Figure 6.3a. We then scan $\mathcal{N}$ to find all valid records and calculate a separator key k that provides a balanced split. We then allocate and initialize three new nodes: (1) a new version of $\mathcal{N}$ (call it $\mathcal{N}'$) that contains all valid records with keys less than or equal to k; (2) a new sibling node $\mathcal{O}$ that contains all valid records with keys greater than k; and (3) a new version of $\mathcal{N}$'s parent node $\mathcal{P}$ (call it $\mathcal{P}'$) that replaces the child pointer of $\mathcal{N}$ with a pointer to $\mathcal{N}'$ and adds a new search record consisting of key k and a pointer to the new child $\mathcal{O}$. All nodes are consolidated (search-optimized) and store sorted records.

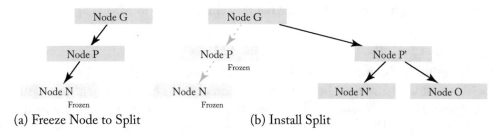

Figure 6.3: **Node Split**—Node split in the BzTree.

Installation: Installation of a split involves "swapping out" $\mathcal{P}$ to replace it with $\mathcal{P}'$, thereby making the new split nodes $\mathcal{N}'$ and $\mathcal{O}$ visible in the index. Figure 6.3b depicts this process. The installation is atomic and involves using a 3-word PMwCAS to modify the following words: (1) the status word of $\mathcal{P}$ to set its frozen bit, failure to set the bit means it conflicts with another update to $\mathcal{P}$; (2) the 64-bit child pointer to $\mathcal{P}$ at its parent $\mathcal{G}$ ($\mathcal{N}$'s grandparent) to swap in the new pointer to $\mathcal{P}'$; and (3) $\mathcal{G}$'s status word to detect a concurrent page freeze. If the PMwCAS succeeds, the split is complete, and the old nodes $\mathcal{P}$ and $\mathcal{N}$ are sent to the epoch-protected garbage collector. On failure, a thread retries the split, and the memory for nodes $\mathcal{N}'$, $\mathcal{P}'$, and $\mathcal{O}$ can be deallocated immediately since they were never seen by another thread.

6.4.3 NODE MERGE

The BzTree performs node merges in a latch-free manner similar to node splits. Before triggering a delete of a node $\mathcal{N}$, we first find a sibling that will absorb $\mathcal{N}$'s existing records. We chose $\mathcal{N}$'s left sibling $\mathcal{L}$ if (1) it shares a common parent[4] $\mathcal{P}$ and (2) is small enough to absorb $\mathcal{N}$'s records without subsequently triggering a split (defeating the purpose of a merge). Otherwise, we look at $\mathcal{N}$'s right sibling $\mathcal{R}$, verifying it has enough space to absorb $\mathcal{N}$'s records without a split. If neither $\mathcal{R}$ nor $\mathcal{L}$ satisfy the merge constraints, we allow $\mathcal{N}$ to be underfull until these constraints are met. In the remainder of this section, we assume $\mathcal{N}$ merges with its sibling $\mathcal{L}$.

Preparation: To initiate the delete, we first perform a PMwCAS on the status word of both $\mathcal{L}$ and $\mathcal{N}$ to set their frozen bit. We then allocate and initialize two new nodes: (1) a new version of the left sibling $\mathcal{L}'$ containing its own valid records and all of $\mathcal{N}'s$ valid records; and (2) a new version of $\mathcal{N}$ and $\mathcal{L}$'s parent $\mathcal{P}'$ that replaces the child pointer of $\mathcal{L}$ with a pointer to $\mathcal{L}'$ and removes the search record containing the separator key between $\mathcal{L}$ and $\mathcal{N}$ along with the child pointer to $\mathcal{N}$.

Installation: Installation of the node delete and merge involves installing the new version of $\mathcal{P}'$ in the index that makes the merged child node $\mathcal{L}'$ visible and removes $\mathcal{N}$ and $\mathcal{L}$. This operation is identical to that of node split that replaces the parent $\mathcal{P}$ with $\mathcal{P}'$ by both freezing $\mathcal{P}$ as well as updating its parent $\mathcal{G}$ to install the new child pointer to $\mathcal{P}'$.

6.4.4 INTERPLAY BETWEEN ALGORITHMS

The BzTree offloads the handling of ACID transactions to a higher software layer of the system. This could, for instance, be a logical concurrency control component in a decoupled database system [126]. The index itself is responsible for correctly serializing conflicting data and structural changes. We now describe how BzTree ensures that threads do not observe the

---

[4]We chose to avoid merges that cross parent nodes to minimize the number of modified nodes.

effects of in-progress changes.

Co-operative `PMwCAS`: B+tree implementations typically rely on latches for preventing threads from observing changes performed by concurrent threads. The BzTree instead employs `PMwCAS` to accomplish this. As described in Section 6.1, we employ a latch-free `PMwCAS` library. The `PMwCAS` operation is cooperative, in that any thread (reader or writer) that encounters an in-progress `PMwCAS` will first help along to complete the operation before continuing with its own. This policy effectively serializes `PMwCAS` operations that might conflict. It also ensures the atomicity of operations within the BzTree. Since all updates to the index are performed using `PMwCAS`, updates will either succeed uncontested, or the `PMwCAS` help-along protocol will arbitrate conflict and abort some conflicting operations.

Record Operations and Structure Modifications: BzTree employs the status word to correctly serialize conflicting data and structural changes that might conflict with each other. For instance, an in-progress consolidate or SMO will first set the frozen bit within a node. This causes all in-flight record-level operations to fail their `PMwCAS` due to conflict on the status word. These record operations will then retry and either see (a) the frozen version of a node that requires maintenance, for which it will attempt to complete or (b) a new (unfrozen) version of the node that is ready for record updates.

Serializing Structure Modifications: The BzTree uses a cooperative approach for serializing conflicting SMOs. Consider a node deletion operation. To delete node $\mathcal{N}$, the BzTree first checks if its left sibling $\mathcal{L}$ is alive. If it observes that $\mathcal{L}$ is frozen, then it detects that another structural change is in progress. In this case, the BzTree serializes the deletion of $\mathcal{N}$ (if still needed) after that of $\mathcal{L}$.

6.5   BZTREE DURABILITY AND RECOVERY

In this section, we illustrate how BzTree ensures recoverability of the tree across system failures using `PMwCAS`. BzTree stores the tree either on DRAM when used in volatile mode, or on NVM when used in durable mode. In volatile mode, the BzTree does not flush the state of the tree to durable storage. However, when used in durable mode, it persists the tree on NVM to preserve it across system failures. The BzTree does *not* need to employ a specific recovery algorithm. It instead relies on the recovery algorithms of a persistent memory allocator and the `PMwCAS` library to avoid persistent memory leaks and ensure recoverability, respectively. We now describe these algorithms in detail.

6.5.1   PERSISTENT MEMORY ALLOCATION

A classic volatile memory allocator with an `allocate` and `free` interface does not ensure correct recovery when used on NVM. If the allocator marks a memory chunk as being in use (due to allocate), and the application (e.g., BzTree) fails to install the allocated chunk on NVM before a crash, then this causes a persistent memory leak. In this state, the memory chunk is "homeless" in that it can neither be seen by the application nor by the memory allocator after a crash.

While creating a safe and correct persistent memory allocator is outside the scope of this chapter, there have been many proposals. We assume availability of a three-stage allocator [178] that provides the following states: (1) allocate, (2) activated, and (3) free. The application first requests the allocation of a memory chunk. The allocator updates the chunk's meta-data to indicate that it has been allocated and returns it to the application. During recovery after a system failure, the allocator reclaims all allocated memory chunks. To retain the ownership of the memory chunk even after a failure, the application must separately request that the allocator activate the memory chunk. At this point in time, the application owns the memory chunk and is responsible for its lifetime, including any cleanup after a failure.

The application must carefully interact with the allocator in the activation process, through an interface (provided by the allocator) that is similar to posix_memalign which accepts a reference of the target location for storing the address of the allocated memory. This design is employed by many existing NVM systems [10, 159, 178, 197]. The application owns the memory only after the allocator has successfully persisted the address of the newly allocated memory in the provided reference.

6.5.2   DURABILITY

There are two cases by which the BzTree handles durability of index data.

- **Variable-length Data:** Newly inserted records as well as new node memory (allocated as part of a consolidate, split, or delete/merge) represents variable-length data in the BzTree. To ensure durability, the BzTree flushes all variable-length data before it can be read by other threads. That is, newly inserted record memory on a node is flushed before the atomic flip of its visible bit. Likewise, new node memory is flushed before it is "linked into" the index using a PMwCAS. This flush-before-visible protocol ensures that variable-length data in the BzTree is durable when it becomes readable to concurrent threads.

- **Word-size Data:** The durability of word-size modifications is handled by the PMwCAS operation. As mentioned in Section 6.1, the PMwCAS ensures durability of all words it modifies upon acknowledging success. Thus, modifications like changing the node status word and reserving and updating a record's metadata entry are guaranteed to be durable when modified using the PMwCAS. In addition, all modifications performed by the PMwCAS are guaranteed to be durable to concurrent readers.

The BzTree avoids inconsistencies arising from write-after-read dependencies. That is, it guarantees that a thread *cannot* read a volatile modification made by another thread. Otherwise, any action taken after the read (such as a dependent write) might not survive across a crash and lead to an inconsistent index. As mentioned above, the flush-before-visible protocol ensures this property for variable-length modifications to the BzTree. Likewise, the PMwCAS ensures this property for word-sized modifications.

6.5.3   RECOVERY

Memory Lifetime: The PMwCAS library maintains a pool of descriptors at a well-defined location on NVM. Each word descriptor contains a field specifying a memory recycling policy. This policy defines how the memory pointed to by the old value and new value fields should be handled when the PMwCAS operation concludes. The PMwCAS library supports two memory recycling policies: NONE and FREE-ONE. With the former policy, there is no need for recycling memory. The BzTree uses this policy for modifying non-pointer values, such as the status word in nodes. With the latter policy, the PMwCAS library frees the memory pointed to by the old (or new) value depending on whether the PMwCAS operation succeeds (or fails). The BzTree uses this policy when allocating and installing a new node in the tree. To *activate* the node memory, BzTree provides a memory reference to the descriptor word responsible for holding a pointer to the node memory. This ensures an atomic transfer of the activated memory pointer to the descriptor. The memory lifetime is then handled by the PMwCAS library. In case of a failure, the node's memory is reclaimed by the recovery algorithm. This obviates the need for BzTree to implement its own memory recycling mechanism.

Recovery Steps: During recovery from a system failure, the allocator first runs its recovery algorithm to reclaim memory chunks that have been reserved but not yet activated. Then, the PMwCAS library executes its recovery algorithm to ensure that the effects of all successfully completed PMwCAS operations are persisted. As covered in Section 6.1, upon restart after a crash, any in-flight PMwCAS operations marked as succeeded will roll forward, otherwise they will roll back. For operations involving memory pointer swaps, the PMwCAS will ensure that allocated and active memory dereferenced by its descriptors will be correctly handled according to the provided memory recycling policy.

Aborted Space Allocations: While PMwCAS recovery can handle recovery of 64-bit word modifications, including pointer swaps and node memory allocations, it cannot handle recovery of dangling record space allocations within a node. As detailed in Section 6.3.2, an insert[5] is broken into two atomic parts: ❶ record space allocation and ❷ record initialization (copying key bytes and populating metadata) and making the record visible. The BzTree must be able to detect and recover failed inserts that allocated space within a node in ❶, but crashed during ❷ before a record was fully populated and made visible. The BzTree uses the allocation epoch for this purpose (as described in Section 6.3.2, this value is temporarily stored in the offset field until ❷ completes). Since this field is populated atomically during ❶, any subsequent failure before completion of ❷ will be detected after recovery increments the *global index epoch*. Doing

---

[5]And update if leafs contain full record payloads.

so will invalidate any searches—such as those done by inserts checking for duplicate keys—that encounter an allocation from a previous epoch. This dangling node space will be reclaimed when the node is rebuilt during consolidation or a structure modification.

6.6 EXPERIMENTAL EVALUATION

We implemented the BzTree in approximately 3,000 lines of C++ code, using the PMwCAS library to ensure atomicity and durability of tree updates [200]. This library employs the Win32 native InterlockedCompareExchange64 to perform CAS. NVM devices based on new material technologies (e.g., Intel 3D XPoint) are not yet commercially available. We instead target flash-backed NVDIMMs. These NVDIMMs are DRAM whose data content is saved to flash storage on power failure. We conduct experiments on a workstation running Windows Server 2012 on an Intel Xeon E7-8890 CPU (at 2.2 GHz) with 24 physical cores.

Evaluation Workloads
We use the YCSB benchmark in our evaluation. A detailed description of this benchmark is presented in Appendix B. Both BzTree and Bw-tree are treated as standalone key-value record stores that accept read (Get), write (Insert/Delete/Update/Upsert), and range scan operations. By default, the write operations in the workload mixtures are Upserts. We configure the distribution of the keys accessed by the index operations to be based on the following distributions.

- **Random:** 64-bit integers from a Uniform distribution.
- **Zipfian:** 64-bit integers from a Zipfian distribution.
- **Monotonic:** 64-bit monotonically increasing integer.

We generate a skewed workload using the Zipfian distribution. Unless mentioned otherwise, our primary performance metric is throughput measured in *operations per second*. We use 48 worker threads equal to the number of logical cores on our experiment machine. We use 8-byte keys and values, and configure the default page size for both BzTree and Bw-tree to be 1 KB. In all our experiments, we prefill the index with 1 M records. We observed similar trends when the index is prefilled with ten million records. The BzTree, by default, assumes that keys are variable length and uses the offset field in the record metadata entry to dereference keys (there is no fixed-length optimization). We execute all the workloads three times under each setting and report the average throughput.

6.6.1 DESIGN COMPLEXITY

As minimized complexity is one of our primary goals, we begin by quantifying the BzTree design complexity compared to the Bw-tree. The Bw-tree's latch-free tree algorithms make use of a single-word CAS [126]. Its complexity stems from the fact that multi-word updates temporarily leave the index in an inconsistent state that other threads must detect and handle. The

BzTree instead uses PMwCAS to atomically install changes at multiple tree locations, and this reduces its complexity considerably. Consider the node split algorithm: if the node split operation propagates only up to the great-grandparent node, it involves atomic updates to five tree locations. With a single-word CAS approach, the developer must explicitly handle many of the 2^5 (32) possible intermediate states that could be exposed to concurrent threads.[6] In contrast, with PMwCAS, the developer only needs to reason about two tree states: the initial state with none of the locations mutated, and the final state with all the five locations successfully mutated. More broadly, PMwCAS shrinks the state space associated with mutating k tree locations from 2^k states to k states.

To quantify the reduction in design complexity, we measure the lines of code (LOC) of the node split algorithm in BzTree and Bw-tree. While the Bw-tree implementation contains 750 LOC, the one in BzTree only contains 200 LOC. This is because the BzTree implementation handles fewer tree states. A relative reduction in LOC does not necessarily imply a more maintainable data structure. We therefore measured the *cyclomatic complexity* (CC) of these algorithms. CC is a quantitative measure of the number of linearly independent paths through the function's source code and represents the function's complexity. Higher values of CC, therefore, correspond to more complex functions that are harder to debug and maintain. CC of the node split algorithms in BzTree and Bw-tree are 7 and 12, respectively. This demonstrates that PMwCAS reduces the design complexity of BzTree's algorithms.

6.6.2 RUNTIME PERFORMANCE

We now provide an analysis of the runtime performance of BzTree compared to the Bw-tree on different workload mixtures and key access distributions. For each configuration, we scale up the number of worker threads. The worker threads process tree operations in a closed loop. These experiments are run with both indexes in volatile DRAM mode to (a) showcase the peak performance of the BzTree (we study durability in the next section) and (b) provide a fair comparison to the Bw-tree since its design targets volatile DRAM with no straightforward extension to NVM.

Random Key Access Distribution: We first consider the results on the read-only workload with random key distribution shown in Figure 6.4a. These results provide an upper bound on the tree's performance because none of the operations modify the tree. The most notable observation from this experiment is that BzTree delivers 28% higher throughput than Bw-tree. This is primarily because BzTree employs raw pointers to inter-link tree nodes meaning readers do not have to use indirection to locate child nodes.

The benefits of BzTree algorithms are more prominent on the write-intensive workloads in Figures 6.4c and 6.4d, where BzTree's throughput is 1.7× higher and 2.4× higher than that

---

[6]This is because each tree location can either be updated or not at a given point in time. Although some of these intermediate states might never be observed in practice, we note that the state space grows exponentially.

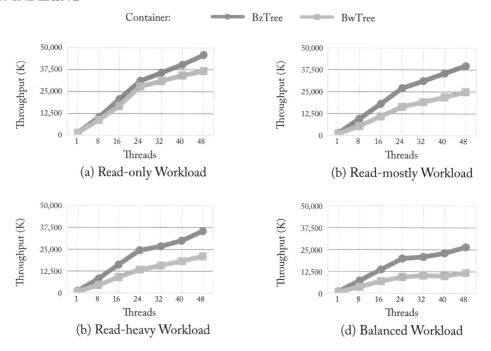

Figure 6.4: **Random Key Access Distribution**—The throughput of BzTree and Bw-tree for the YCSB benchmark with different workload mixtures.

of Bw-tree, respectively. We attribute this gap to the reduction in algorithm complexity and BzTree's ability to perform in-place updates.

Zipfian Key Access Distribution: Figures 6.5a and 6.5b present the throughput of BzTree and Bw-tree on different workloads with the Zipfian key distribution. The benefits of BzTree's reader-friendly algorithms are prominent on the read-only workload, where BzTree outperforms Bw-tree by 33%. By skipping the layer of indirection through the mapping table, readers can traverse BzTree faster than Bw-tree. Unlike Bw-tree, BzTree supports inlined updates in leaf nodes and always keeps the interior nodes consolidated. This reduces pointer chasing, thereby enabling a faster read path.

On the balanced workload in Figure 6.5b, BzTree's throughput is 4.3× higher than that of Bw-tree. Since most of key accesses are directed to a few leaf nodes with the Zipfian key distribution, the in-place update design of BzTree reduces the need for frequent node splits in comparison to Bw-tree. This shrinks the amount of work performed by writers in BzTree, since the split operations take more time to complete compared to single record writes.

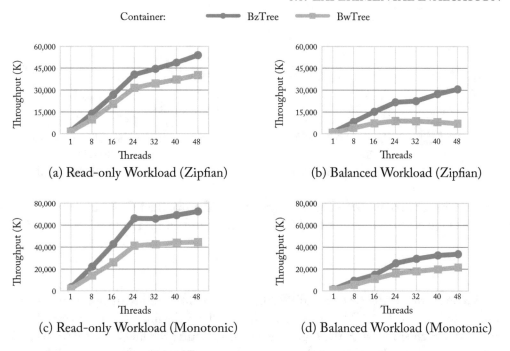

Figure 6.5: **Zipfian and Monotonic Key Access Distributions**—The throughput of BzTree and Bw-tree for the YCSB benchmark.

Monotonic Key Access Distribution: The performance of Bw-tree and BzTree on workloads with the monotonic key distribution is shown in Figures 6.5c and 6.5d. We observe that on the balanced workload, BzTree and Bw-tree deliver 34 M and 21 M operations per second, respectively. The benefits of processor caching are prominent on this workload since keys are monotonically increasing. This is a pathological configuration for concurrent writers since they always contend on the same node. It is an approximate upper bound on the worst-case behavior of BzTree's latch-free algorithms on write-intensive workloads.

6.6.3   DURABILITY

We now examine the cost of persistence by measuring the runtime performance of BzTree in volatile and durable modes on different workload mixtures based on the random key access distribution. As shown in Figures 6.6a and 6.6b, the persistence overhead is 5% and 12% on the read-mostly and balanced workloads, respectively. We attribute the small drop in throughput to the overhead of using PMwCAS in durable mode as opposed to volatile version [200].

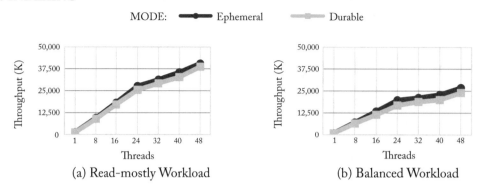

MODE: — Ephemeral   — Durable

(a) Read-mostly Workload

(b) Balanced Workload

Figure 6.6: **Cost of Persistence**—The throughput of BzTree for the YCSB benchmark in volatile and durable modes across different workload mixtures based on the random key access distribution.

In durable mode, the BzTree additionally uses the CLFLUSH instruction to write back the modified tree contents to NVM. Since CLFLUSH invalidates the line from the cache, this results in compulsory cache miss when the same data is accessed after the line has been flushed. Future processors will support the CLWB instruction, which unlike CLFLUSH, does not invalidate the line and instead only transitions it to a non-modified state [23]. We expect that such a lightweight cache-line flushing instruction will further increase BzTree's throughput in durable mode by improving its caching behavior. This experiment illustrates that the same BzTree implementation can be used for indexes in both DRAM and NVM with a moderate cost to seamlessly support persistence.

6.6.4   SCAN PERFORMANCE

We next examine the performance of BzTree and Bw-tree on different workload mixtures of the YCSB benchmark containing range scan operations. In this experiment, we configure the scan predicate's key range so that the scan operation starts from a uniformly random starting offset, and returns at most 10 matching records. The most notable observation from the results shown in Figure 6.7 is that BzTree scales better than Bw-tree. On the read-mostly workload with range scan operations, as shown in Figure 6.7a, the BzTree's throughput with 48 worker threads is 28.5× that of its single-threaded performance. In contrast, Bw-tree's throughput with 48 worker threads is 16.4× that of its single-threaded performance. This is mainly due to less pointer chasing and memory accesses in the BzTree. The Bw-tree must always perform delta updates to pages (new memory prepended to a node representing an update), even for 8-byte payload changes. This causes the scan to perform pointer chases over delta chains, e.g., when constructing a page snapshot to service get-next requests.

The BzTree's throughput on the read-mostly workload is 1.8× higher than that of Bw-tree. We attribute this to the reduction in indirection overhead of range scan operation that forms 90% of the read-mostly workload. On the balanced workload, as shown in Figure 6.7b, the BzTree outperforms Bw-tree by 2.7×. This performance gap is realized by virtue of the reduction in algorithm complexity and BzTree's ability to perform in-place updates, compared to the Bw-tree's usage of delta updates. We observe that the absolute throughput of BzTree on the balanced workload is 2.1× higher than that on the read-mostly workload. This is because range scan is more expensive than the write operation, and the latter operation is more often executed in the balanced workload.

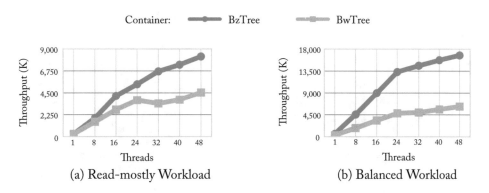

(a) Read-mostly Workload   (b) Balanced Workload

Figure 6.7: **Scan Performance**—The throughput of BzTree and Bw-tree on different workload mixtures containing range scan operations.

6.6.5   PMWCAS STATISTICS

To perform record updates and install structure modifications, the BzTree uses the PMwCAS operation with the word count varying from 1–3. We analyzed the failure frequency of PMwCAS operations in the BzTree across varying degrees of contention on the balanced workload. We observe an increase of 0.02–0.12% in the fraction of failed PMwCAS operations going from 8–48 threads. This is primarily because multiple worker threads concurrently attempt to split the same leaf node and only one thread succeeds. A key takeaway is that on all configurations, the overall fraction of failed PMwCAS operations remains less than 0.2%.

6.6.6   SENSITIVITY ANALYSIS

We now analyze how the key size and unsorted free space size affects the runtime performance of BzTree on the YCSB benchmark. We ran the read-only and read-heavy workloads based on the random key distribution.

Key Size: In this experiment, we fix the page size to be 1 KB, and vary the key size from 8–128 B. The key observation from the results in Figure 6.8a is that the throughput drops by 39% when we increase the key size on the read-only workload. We attribute this to more expensive key comparisons in case of longer keys, both in the interior and leaf nodes. The performance impact of key size is more prominent on the read-heavy workload where we observe a throughput drop of 46%. This is because with longer keys, the leaf nodes are filled faster with fewer keys, and this leads to more frequent node splits that negatively affects throughput.

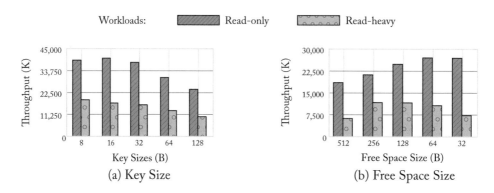

Figure 6.8: **Impact of Key Size and Free Space Size**—The throughput of BzTree while running the YCSB benchmark under different key size and free space size settings.

Free Space Size: Lastly, we examine the impact of the size of the free space on the BzTree's performance. We fix the page size to be 1 KB, and vary the free space size from 32–5122 B. The BzTree uses the remaining space in the leaf node to store the sorted keys, as described in Section 6.3.1. Figure 6.8b shows that the throughput increases by 45% when we decrease the free space size. This is because readers need to perform fewer key comparisons in leaf nodes as the free space can only contain fewer keys. Reducing the free space in this manner, however, increases the frequency of node split operations and reduces space utilization. This is illustrated on the read-heavy workload, where BzTree delivers its peak throughput when the free space size is 128 B. We attribute this to more node splits and key comparisons under smaller and larger free space size settings, respectively.

6.6.7   MEMORY FOOTPRINT

We next compare the peak memory footprint of BzTree and Bw-tree data structures while running the balanced workload in the YCSB benchmark. We observe that BzTree's footprint is 1.6× smaller than that of Bw-tree for trees whose sizes range from 100 K–10 M keys. For instance, when we prefill the index with 10 M keys, the peak memory footprint of BzTree and Bw-tree are 228 MB and 365 MB, respectively. We attribute this to the compact node layout of BzTree and its ability to buffer updates in place.

6.6.8   EXECUTION TIME BREAKDOWN

In this experiment, we analyze the time that BzTree spends in its internal components during execution. We examine the balanced workload in the YCSB benchmark with uniform key access distribution. We use profiling tools available in Windows Server to track the cycles executed within the different components of BzTree [141]. We start this profiling after prefilling the index. The cycles are classified into four categories: (1) leaf node search, (2) internal node search, (3) PMwCAS, and (4) other miscellaneous components. This last category includes the time spent in copying data and performing tasks such as garbage collection.

The most notable result for this experiment, as shown in Figure 6.9, is that even on the balanced workload, BzTree only spends 12% of its time on performing PMwCAS operations. This is because it spends the bulk of the time on traversing the tree and searching the leaf and internal nodes. We observe that the proportion of the time that BzTree spends on searching nodes increases from 61–78% when the workload is not write-intensive. This explains why the BzTree optimizations are more beneficial for the balanced workload.

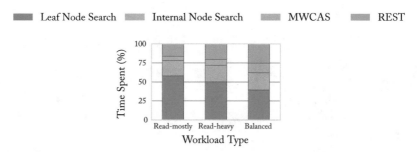

Figure 6.9: **Execution Time Breakdown**—The time that BzTree spends in its internal components when running the balanced workload.

6.7   SUMMARY

It is challenging to design, debug, and extend latch-free indexing structures. This is because "traditional" latch-free designs rely on a single-word CAS instruction that requires the developer to carefully stage every atomic action so that each action leaves the tree in an intermediate state that is recognizable to concurrent accessors. Upcoming NVM environments will only make this task more difficult due to durability guarantees and the interplay with volatile CPU caches.

With the BzTree design we demonstrate that using PMwCAS, a multi-word compare-and-swap with durability guarantees, helps reduce index design complexity tremendously. Our experimental evaluation shows that even though PMwCAS is computationally more expensive than a hardware-based single-word CAS, the simplicity that we gain by using PMwCAS improves not only the maintainability but also the performance of the BzTree. A cyclomatic complexity analysis shows that the BzTree is at least half as complex as state-of-the-art main-memory index designs (the Bw-tree and MassTree). Another benefit of the BzTree design is its flexibility: the same design can be used on both volatile DRAM and NVM, with a roughly 8% overhead to ensure persistence. In addition, existing B+tree implementations that achieve durability on NVM often employ complex algorithms for ensuring recoverability. The BzTree, on the other hand, does not rely on custom recovery techniques: it relies on the general-purpose PMwCAS to roll forward (or back) its in-flight word modifications before becoming online and active. This allows for near-instantaneous recovery of the BzTree index and is a defining feature of its design.

CHAPTER 7

Related Work

In this chapter, we provide a discussion of related work. We begin with a discussion of work related to the general themes in this book, then examine specific areas in depth.

The design of a DBMS's architecture is predicated on the target storage hierarchy. There are essentially two types of DBMS architectures: disk-oriented [36, 186] and memory-oriented systems [16, 70, 82, 107, 108]. The former is exemplified by the first DBMSs, such as IBM's System R [36], where the system is predicated on the management of blocks of tuples on disk using an in-memory cache; the latter by IBM's IMS/VS Fast Path [82], where the system performs updates on in-memory data and relies on the disk to ensure durability.

The need to ensure that all changes are durable has dominated the design of systems with both disk-oriented and memory-oriented architectures [38, 63, 145]. This has involved optimizing the layout of data for each storage layer depending on how fast it can perform random accesses [80]. Further, updates performed on tuples stored in memory need to be propagated to an on-disk representation for durability. Previous studies have shown that the overhead of managing this data movement for OLTP workloads is considerable [91]. The advent of NVM offers an intriguing blend of the two storage mediums. This book explores the changes required in DBMS architectures to leverage NVM. It has benefited from prior work and in some cases built upon it.

7.1   LOGGING AND RECOVERY

Safe RAM is one of the first projects that explored the use of NVM in software applications [62]. Copeland et al. define Safe RAM as a memory with enough backup power so that its contents can be safely copied to disk in case of a power failure. Using simulations, they demonstrate the improvement in transactional throughput and latency when they replace the disk with the Safe RAM. Agrawal et al. present recovery algorithms for a hypothetical database machine in which the memory is non-volatile [26]. They extend the write-ahead logging protocol to leverage NVM. This scheme does not require the DBMS to persist updated pages on NVM at the time of committing a transaction (i.e., NO-FORCE policy). This allows a hot page to be updated in memory by several transactions without it ever being written to disk. This freedom, however, comes at the expense of high data duplication and slow recovery.

More recently, Fang et al. propose a NVM-centric DBMS architecture where in-memory log buffers and disk-based log files are replaced by a single log in NVM [76]. They extend the ARIES WAL protocol to NVM and address the problems of detecting partial writes and holes, and ensuring recoverability. Wang et al. present a passive group commit method for a distributed logging protocol extension to Shore-MT [199]. Instead of issuing a barrier for every processor at commit time, the DBMS tracks when all of the records required to ensure the durability of a transaction are flushed to NVM. This scheme reduces log contention. It considers a log record as committed when it is written to a NVM buffer. When the log buffer is full, it is flushed to disk. To establish the ordering of log records, the protocol assigns a global sequence number based on a logical clock to each record. This work is based on the Shore-MT engine [105], which means that the DBMS records page-level before-images in the undo logs before performing in-place updates. This results in high data duplication.

PCMLogging is a logging protocol designed for a three-tier storage system with DRAM, NVM, and SSD [79]. This scheme involves writing implicit log records in modified pages. When a transaction is committed, PCMLogging flushes all the modified pages to NVM to ensure that the database contains the latest changes. To remove the effects of uncommitted transactions, the DBMS keeps track of a list of running transactions and the pages that they modified on NVM. The DBMS does not apply in-place updates on pages stored on NVM so that the changes can be rolled back if needed. This protocol does not leverage the byte-addressability property of NVM and employs a physical undo mechanism.

Pelley et al. introduced a group commit mechanism to persist transactions' updates in batches to reduce the number of write barriers required for ensuring correct ordering on NVM [164]. The authors explore three NVM-centric DBMS architectures based on Shore-MT [105]. These architectures do not leverage the byte-addressability property of NVM.

MARS [58] is an in-place updates engine optimized for NVM that relies on a hardware-assisted primitive that allows multiple writes to arbitrary locations to happen atomically. MARS does away with undo log records by keeping the changes isolated using this primitive. Similarly, it relies on this primitive to apply the redo log records at the time of commit. In comparison, our WBL approach is based on non-volatile pointers, a software-based primitive, and uses existing (or upcoming) synchronization instructions. It removes the need to record redo information in the WAL, but still needs to store undo log records until the transaction commits.

SOFORT [155, 156] is a hybrid storage engine designed for both OLTP and OLAP workloads. The engine is designed to not perform any logging and uses MVCC. It targets a two-tier storage system with DRAM and NVM. The engine stores the primary copy of the data on NVM, and supports the maintenance of auxiliary data structures on DRAM and NVM. To support hybrid workloads, SOFORT manages data in read-optimized main storage for OLAP and write-optimized delta storage for OLTP [29, 179]. The engine periodically merges the contents of the delta storage into main storage to limit the size of the delta. SOFORT manages the main storage on NVM and supports near-instantaneous recovery after a system failure. Similar to SOFORT, we also make use of non-volatile pointers [10], but we use these pointers differently. SOFORT's non-volatile pointers are a combination of page ID and offset. We eschew the page abstraction in our engines since NVM is byte-addressable, and thus we use raw pointers that map to data's location in NVM.

REWIND is a userspace library for efficiently managing persistent data structures on NVM using WAL to ensure recoverability [53]. SiloR is an efficient parallelized logging, checkpointing, and recovery subsystem for in-memory DBMSs [210]. Oh et al. present a per-page logging approach for replacing a set of successive page writes to the same logical page with fewer log writes [150].

FOEDUS is a scalable OLTP engine designed for a two-tier storage system with DRAM and NVM [110]. It is based on the *dual page* primitive that points to a pair of logically equivalent pages, a mutable volatile page in DRAM containing the latest changes, and an immutable snapshot page on NVM. With logical equivalence, the existence of a volatile page implies that it contains the latest modifications. The absence of such a page implies that the snapshot page contains all the changes. FOEDUS accomplishes physical independence between volatile and snapshot pages by deriving the latter from the write-ahead log. This obviates the need for synchronization between these two physical entities. The engine employs a log gleaner that constructs snapshot pages in DRAM and sequentially writes them to NVM. FOEDUS reduces read amplification by routing the read operation to the appropriate version. The engine adopts an optimistic concurrency control scheme based on the Masstree and the Foster B-Tree data structures [84, 138]. During recovery, the log gleaner creates snapshot pages using the contents of the WAL log. Although FOEDUS delivers high performance, it relies on canonical WAL and does not leverage the byte-addressability property of NVM.

The instant-recovery protocol comprises of on-demand single-tuple redo and single-transaction undo mechanisms to support almost instantaneous recovery from system failures [83, 90]. While processing transactions, the DBMS reconstructs the desired version of the tuple on demand using the information in the write-ahead log. The DBMS can, therefore, start handling new transactions almost immediately after a system failure. The downside is that the DBMS performance is lower than that observed after the traditional ARIES-style recovery while the recovery is not yet complete. This protocol works well when the DBMS runs on a slower durable storage device. But with NVM, WBL enables the DBMS to deliver high performance than instant recovery immediately after recovery as it does not require an on-demand redo process.

NV-logging focuses on the cost-effective use of NVM [100]. This protocol only uses NVM for storing the database log since NVM is more expensive than SSD. The authors propose a per-transaction decentralized logging scheme that works around the contention associated with a centralized log buffer. The DBMS maintains a private log for each transaction. The log records are created in DRAM and later flushed to a circular log buffer on NVM. The recovery scheme is a variant of the ARIES protocol. Although NV-logging is cost-effective, this approach only leverages the low-latency sequential writes of NVM and does not exploit its ability to efficiently support random writes and fine-grained data access. Unlike WBL, all these systems require that the changes made to persistent data must be preceded by logging.

7.2   FILE-SYSTEMS

Beyond DBMSs, researchers have explored using NVM in file-systems. Baker et al. evaluate the utility of battery-backed DRAM as a client-side file cache in a distributed filesystem to reduce write traffic to file servers, and as a write buffer for write-optimized file systems to reduce server disk accesses [39].

Rio is a persistent file cache that relies on an uninterruptible power supply to provide a safe, in-memory buffer for filesystem data [131]. It reduces transaction latency by absorbing synchronous writes to disk without losing data during system crashes. The authors propose a safe synchronization technique that writes dirty file cache data reliably to disk during the last stage of a system crash.

BPFS uses a variant of shadow paging on NVM to support fine-grained atomic updates by relying on a special hardware instruction that ensures ordering between writes in different epochs [60]. It uses a copy-on-write technique and 8-byte in-place atomic updates to provide metadata and data consistency. SCMFS is a NVM-centric filesystem that utilizes the OS's virtual memory management module to map files to large contiguous virtual address ranges [202]. It supports efficient NVM accesses but does not offer any consistency guarantees for both metadata and data.

PMFS is another filesystem from Intel Labs that is explicitly tailored for byte-addressable NVM [11, 73]. Unlike BPFS, it leverages in-place atomic updates with fine-grained logging for ensuring metadata consistency, and a copy-on-write technique for guaranteeing data consistency. It optimizes memory-mapped I/O by directly mapping NVM to the application's address space and using large page mappings. PMFS assumes a simpler hardware barrier primitive for flushing NVM stores to a power fail-safe destination.

Direct access storage (DAX) is a mechanism for enabling direct access to files stored on NVM without copying the data to the page cache [3, 5, 93, 112]. This requires only one copy between the file and the user buffers, thus improving the file I/O performance. EXT4 DAX extends the EXT4 file system to support direct mapping of NVM by bypassing the buffer cache [64]. It relies on journaling for atomic metadata updates. Unlike the EXT4 file system, EXT4 DAX does not support atomic updates to data. Aerie provides direct access for file data I/O using user-level leases for NVM updates [196]. It journals metadata but does not support atomic data updates and memory mapping.

NOVA is a log-structured file system that provides synchronous file system semantics on NVM [203]. Each inode in NOVA has a separate log, thereby allowing concurrent updates across files without synchronization. NOVA uses a copy-on-write technique for writes by allocating new pages. It relies on logging and lightweight journaling for complex atomic updates. During recovery, NOVA scans all the logs to reconstruct the memory allocator's state. NOVA-

Fortis extends NOVA by supporting lightweight file-system snapshots and providing protection against media errors and corruption due to software errors [204]. It demonstrates that a NVM-aware file-system can provide reliability guarantees with a tolerable performance impact.

Kwon et al. present the architecture of a three-tier file-system that transparently migrates data among different levels in the storage system [116]. It supports performance-isolated access to NVM using a per-application log. This file-system is optimized for a specific NVM technology that is 2× slower than DRAM. So it does not cache NVM-resident data on DRAM. For the same reason, it bypasses DRAM while performing synchronous write operations.

Renen et al. present a buffer manager that eagerly migrates data from SSD to DRAM [190]. When a page is evicted from DRAM, the buffer manager considers admitting it into the NVM buffer. The fundamental idea is to only admit recently referenced pages. The buffer manager maintains an admission queue to keep track of pages considered for admission and only admits pages that were recently denied admission.

In Chapter 5, we introduced a taxonomy of data migration policies that subsumes the specific schemes adopted by prior systems. We derive insights that are applicable for a broader range of three-tier storage systems and NVM technologies. In particular, we explore how the optimal data migration policy depends on workload and storage system characteristics.

7.3   REPLICATION

With the WBL logging protocol described in Chapter 4, the DBMS can recover from system and transaction failures. However, it cannot cope up with media failures or corrupted data. This is because it relies on the integrity of durable data structures (e.g., the log) during recovery. These failures are instead overcome through replication, wherein the DBMS propagates changes made by transactions to multiple servers [86, 174]. When the primary server incurs a media failure, replication ensures that there is no data loss since the secondary servers can be configured to maintain a transactionally consistent copy of the database.

Mojim provides reliable and highly available NVM by using a two-tier architecture that supports an additional level of redundancy and efficiently replicates the data stored on NVM [208]. It allows programmers to use fault-tolerant memory storage in their applications but does not provide the transactional semantics required by a DBMS.

RAMCloud is a DRAM-based storage system that can be used as a low-latency key-value store [154]. While both Mojim and RAMCloud provide reliable memory-based storage, the former exports a memory-like interface to the applications and the latter supports a key-value interface. Unlike RAMCloud, Mojim does not shard memory. It instead relies on fail-over to recover from failures.

7.4   MEMORY MANAGEMENT

A NVM-aware memory allocator differs from a volatile memory allocator in three ways [37, 178, 198]. The first difference is that it provides a *durability* mechanism to ensure that modifications to data stored on NVM are persisted [144]. This is necessary because the changes made by a transaction to a location on NVM may still reside in volatile processor caches when the transaction commits. If a power failure happens before the changes reach NVM, then these changes are lost [47].

The allocator exposes a special API call to provide this durability. Internally, the allocator first writes out the cache lines containing the data from any level of the cache hierarchy to NVM using CLWB, the optimized cache flushing instruction that is part of the newly proposed NVM-related instruction set extensions [19]. Then, it issues a SFENCE instruction to ensure that the stores are ordered ahead of subsequent instructions. At this point, the stores may reside in the memory controller's write-pending queue (WPQ). In case of a power failure or shutdown, the *asynchronous DRAM refresh* (ADR) instructions of newer NVM platforms automatically flushes the WPQ [177], thus ensuring that the data is durable.

The second variation is that the allocator provides a *naming* mechanism for allocations so that pointers to memory locations are valid even after the system restarts [37, 156]. The allocator ensures that the virtual memory addresses assigned to a memory-mapped region never change. With this mechanism, a pointer to a NVM location is mapped to the same virtual location after the OS or DBMS restarts. We refer to these pointers as non-volatile pointers.

Lastly, the allocator ensures the *atomicity* of all the memory allocations so that after a system failure all memory regions are either allocated or available for use [178]. Allocator guarantees that there are no torn data writes, dangling references, and persistent memory leaks by decoupling memory allocations into two steps: (1) reserve and (2) activate. After the reserve step, the DBMS can use the reserved memory region for storing ephemeral data. In case of a failure, however, the allocator reclaims this memory region. To ensure that it owns a memory region even after a failure, the DBMS must request the allocator to separately activate the memory region by updating the meta-data associated with that region. Under this two-step process, the DBMS first initializes the contents of a memory region after the reserve step but before it activates it.

Mnemosyne and NV-heaps use software transactional memory to support transactional updates to data stored on NVM [59, 197]. While the former supports word-based transactions, the latter supports node-based transactions. The primitives provided by these systems allow programmers to use NVM in their applications but do not provide the transactional semantics required by a DBMS.

Moraru et al. propose NVMalloc, a NVM-aware that helps with wear-leveling and protects memory against erroneous writes [144]. They augment the CPU caches with a set of counters to keep track of the number of dirty cache lines that are yet to be written back to NVM.

WAlloc is another efficient wear-aware NVM allocator [207]. These allocators perform wear-leveling in software.

NVM-Malloc belongs to a family of allocators that assume that wear-leveling will be done in hardware [178]. It prevents memory leaks by decoupling memory allocations into two steps. It manages a single memory pool and uses relative pointers to keep track of objects. It uses a segregated-fit algorithm for blocks smaller than 2 KB, and employs a best-fit technique for larger blocks.

Persistent Memory Development Kit (PMDK) is a collection of NVM-centric libraries and tools [10]. The libpmemobj library provides a transactional object store on NVM and internally uses a NVM allocator. This allocator employs a a segregated-fit algorithm with multiple size classes for smaller blocks less than 256 KB and a best-fit technique for larger blocks. To reduce fragmentation, it splits a 256 KB chunk into smaller blocks. But, it does not contain a defragmentation mechanism.

Makalu is a fail-safe NVM allocator that employs a recovery-time garbage collector to maintains internal consistency [46]. It reduces the allocation persistence overhead by lazily persisting unnecessary metadata and by using the garbage collector to avoids NVM leaks. Makalu's allocation strategy is similar to that of NVM-Malloc. Unlike NVM-Malloc, it only ensures the durability of a subset of allocator metadata and reconstructs missing metadata during recovery. Makalu uses regular volatile pointers and maps the memory pool at a fixed location to ensure that the pointers are valid across restarts. However, this can result in the un-mapping of other objects that have been already mapped in the address range.

PAllocator is a special-purpose NVM allocator that uses multiple files to dynamically expand and shrink the managed NVM pools [158, 160]. Instead of using thread-local pools, PAllocator uses one allocator object per physical core. This works well for DBMSs that spawn and terminate several threads during query processing. It defragments memory by leveraging the hole punching feature of sparse files. It supports fast recovery by persisting the bulk of the metadata and internally use hybrid DRAM-NVM data structures.

X-Mem is a memory management framework that automatically places data-structures in a two-tier storage system with DRAM and NVM [74]. It allocates objects of different data structures in disjoint regions of memory to preserve semantic information at the granularity of a single allocation. X-Mem contains a profiling tool that identifies the access pattern to a data structure and improves performance by automatically mapping memory regions of the data structure to DRAM or NVM.

7.5   HARDWARE SUPPORT

Persistent caches simplify NVM software development by obviating the need for a persistency model. Such caches can be constructed by ensuring that a battery backup is available to flush the cache contents to NVM upon failure [146, 147], or by not caching NVM accesses [199]. However, high NVM latency precludes its use as a processor cache [209], and it is unclear how to provide battery backup for systems with large caches. Our DBMS architectures only assume volatile caches.

Kolli et al. present a synchronous ordering (SO) scheme to formalize the memory persistency model implied by Intel's NVM-centric ISA extensions [19, 113, 114]. These extensions ensure correct ordering of NVM writes [52, 53, 74, 197, 202]. SO presents fewer opportunities for overlapping program execution and persist operations. To increase this overlap, the authors propose delegated ordering. This technique decouples persist order enforcement from thread execution by buffering persists in hardware.

BPFS uses barriers to divide program execution into epochs within which stores may be concurrently persisted [60]. It supports epoch barriers by tagging cache blocks with the current epoch ID on every store. Since epoch barriers obviate stalls, this technique increases overlap between program execution and persist operations compared to SO. However, it is tightly coupled with cache management and requires write permissions to be discarded when epochs are drained. Delegated ordering decouples cache management from the path taken by NVM writes.

Pelley et al. introduce a taxonomy of persistency models ranging from conservative (strict persistency) to very relaxed (strand persistency) models [163]. They demonstrate that exposing additional persist concurrency to the NVM controller improves performance. They present a variant of epoch barriers that improves performance by managing inter-thread persist dependencies. However, they do not propose hardware implementations for the persistency models. Joshi et al. propose efficient persist barriers that support buffered epoch persistency [106]. Adoption of such persistency models will improve the performance of NVM-centric DBMSs.

Kiln export a transactional storage system interface to NVM by guaranteeing the atomicity, durability, and consistency properties [209]. It assumes that processor caches are persistent and leverages the implicit data versioning in caches. LOC adopts a custom hardware logging mechanism and multi-versioned caches to minimize intra- and inter-transaction dependencies [132]. Unlike these systems, DBMSs need to additionally provide the isolation guarantee between concurrently executing transactions.

7.6   SOFTWARE TESTING

Lantz et al. propose Yat [119], a hypervisor-based testing framework for NVM-centric software systems. It adopts a record-and-replay technique. During execution, it records all NVM writes by logging hypervisor exits. It replaces instructions related to ensuring persistence on NVM with illegal instructions so that they can be traced via hypervisor exits. Yat splits the memory trace into segments that are delimited by persistence barriers. It lets writes within a segment to different NVM locations to be reordered. During replay, it considers all possible segment reorderings and invokes the recovery procedure after each execution. The authors restrict the number of examined reorderings to bound testing time.

Oukid et al. present an automated testing framework that does not require software instrumentation [157]. This framework performs on-line testing and improves code coverage by not examining similar scenarios. It automatically crashes the evaluated software system and invokes the system's recovery procedure. The authors focus on improving software quality by efficiently covering a wide range of NVM-related errors within a reasonable time-frame.

7.7   LATCH-FREE INDEXES

Modern devices with multi-core processors and high-capacity memory mandate highly concurrent indexes. This gave rise to the design of Bw-tree, a latch-free index built on top of the single-word CAS primitive [126]. Although such an index delivers high performance, it is challenging to design, debug, and extend. The developers must carefully design every SWCAS-based latch-free algorithm so that each atomic action leaves the tree in a valid intermediate state for other threads [78, 188]. We employ the stronger MWCAS primitive to simplify BzTree's design.

Other state-of-the-art data structures include ART and MassTree. ART is a trie-based data structure that employs an adaptive node structure and adopts an optimistic lock coupling synchronization algorithm [122, 124, 125]. MassTree is a hybrid cache-conscious B-tree/trie data structure that eschews traditional latch coupling [138]. Unlike BzTree, its synchronization algorithm relies on clever use of atomic operations and hand-over-hand latching. With this approach, developers need to keep track of the latches being held along different control flow paths to release the correct set of locks. This increases the design complexity of the data structure. In addition, MassTree and ART, by design, do not ensure durability on NVM.

7.8   MULTI-WORD CAS

A multi-word CAS instruction (MWCAS) simplifies latch-free programming of high-performance data structures as exemplified in BzTree. A general-purpose MWCAS implementation is not available in hardware. Prior work has focused on realizing MWCAS in software using the hardware-provided SWCAS [28, 88, 98, 102]. The PMwCAS library we use is based on the volatile MWCAS primitive proposed by Harris et al. [94]. MWCAS and transactional memory systems are similar in that they require either all or none of the sub-operations to succeed [98]. Software transactional memory systems have limited adoption due to high-performance overhead [180]. In contrast, hardware transactional memory (HTM) [104, 206] exhibits lower-performance overhead and can help simplify the latch-free design. However, HTM suffers from spurious transaction aborts either due to transaction size or because of CPU cache associativity [135]. The PMwCAS library does not use HTM.

7.9   PERSISTENT INDEXES

The advent of NVM triggered the development of different persistent indexes [55, 56, 159, 191, 205]. Since NVM devices are expected to have limited write endurance, these indexes focus on reducing the number of stores to NVM. Write atomic B+tree accomplishes this by using an indirection slot array to minimize the movement of index entries and adopts a redo-only logging algorithm for ensuring durability [56].

CDDS B+tree is a multi-versioned B+tree [191]. Instead of performing in-place updates and logging, it relies on versioning to guarantee recoverability and consistency. CDDS, by design, performs a lot of cache line flushes, which degrades its performance. In contrast, NV-Tree [205] employs an append-only update strategy and re-constructs internal index nodes during recovery. However, it requires the internal nodes to be stored in consecutive memory blocks. FPTree [159] is a hybrid DRAM-NVM index that keeps the internal nodes in volatile memory and stores the leaf nodes on NVM, requiring the overhead of a partial index rebuild during recovery. It exploits hardware transactional memory and fine-grained locks to handle concurrent internal and leaf node accesses.

BzTree (Chapter 6) design differs from these approaches in three ways. First, the BzTree does not require custom recovery code. Prior persistent NVM index designs employ sophisticated logging and recovery algorithms. These logging algorithms record all the tree updates to persistent storage to achieve persistence, and periodically write out checkpoints to speed up recovery. For example, the FPTree's node split algorithm requires the writer to log information about the node being split and the newly allocated leaf node. Depending on when the crash occurs within the algorithm, the writer either rolls the split operation forward or backward. Developing correct logging and recovery algorithms are challenging and contributes to the increased design complexity of these data structures. In addition, existing designs often require the reconstruction of internal index nodes after a system failure. In contrast, BzTree does not require a tree-level recovery algorithm. Second, the BzTree design works seamlessly across both volatile and persistent environments. To our knowledge, the BzTree is the only index design flexible enough to function and perform well in both environments. Lastly, The BzTree is the only design that is latch-free and highly concurrent, while also ensuring persistence guarantees on NVM.

CHAPTER 8

Future Work

We see several directions for future work on NVM-centric DBMSs. A subset of the directions here focus on DBMS components that have not been explored in this book, while others represent new questions arising from this work.

8.1 QUERY OPTIMIZATION

Cost-based query optimizers in modern DBMSs are designed to take into consideration the gap between sequential and random I/O costs of durable storage devices. They, however, do not account for read/write asymmetry exhibited by NVM while performing sequential and random I/O [40, 165]. The optimizer must, therefore, differentiate between reads and writes, and take into consideration the convergence of sequential and random accesses in NVM.

The table and index scan algorithms retrieve the tuples satisfying a given predicate by scanning through the associated table and index respectively. The original cost functions of these algorithms in the optimizer only distinguish between sequential and random accesses. We can adapt these functions to indicate that these accesses are reads. Similarly, when the result of a sub-tree in an execution plan is needed multiple times by the associated parent node, the DBMS materializes it. The cost function for this materialization operation should indicate that the associated accesses to storage are writes.

We can adapt the cost function of a join algorithm by considering the two phases of the algorithm. The function should account for writing and reading all the data one time each. All the reads during the join phase tend to be sequential, while the writes in the partitioning phase are random. We note that these adapted cost functions still do not account for the byte-addressability of NVM [194].

8.2 QUERY PROCESSING ALGORITHMS

The algorithms backing the relational operators in main-memory DBMSs are designed to have low computational complexity and to exploit the processor caches in modern multi-core chips [27, 51, 80, 92]. We now need to redesign these algorithms to also reduce the number of writes to durable storage, given the read-write asymmetry and limited write-endurance of NVM [42, 49, 55, 81, 193].

The cache-friendly implementation of the hash-join algorithm partitions the input tables so that every pair of partitions can fit within the CPU caches. Unfortunately, the partitioning phase necessitates writing out the entire tables back on NVM in their partitioned form [55]. One can avoid this by keeping track of *virtual partitions* of the tables that only contain the identifiers of the tuples that belong to a given partition, and accesses the records in place during the join phase. In this manner, virtual partitioning avoids data copying to reduce the number of writes at the expense of additional reads.

For sorting NVM-resident data, the DBMS can use a hybrid write-limited sorting algorithm called *segment sort* [49, 193]. This algorithm sorts a fraction of the input using the write-intensive faster external merge-sort algorithm, and the remaining fraction using the write-limited slower selection sort algorithm. The selection sort algorithm involves multiple read passes over the input, and writes each element of the input only once at its final location. The DBMS uses the fraction as a knob for constraining the write-intensiveness of the algorithm with respect to its symmetric-I/O counterpart at the cost of lower performance.

Like with sorting, there are also join algorithms that are designed for asymmetric NVM storage. The *segmented Grace hash-join*, which unlike the regular Grace join, materializes only a fraction of the input partitions, and continuously iterates over the rest of the input to process the remaining partitions [193]. The associated read-amplification does not hurt performance given the read-write asymmetry. We note that it is important that write-limited algorithms converge to the I/O-minimal behavior of their counterparts that are designed for symmetric I/O at lower write-intensity levels.

8.3 ACCESS METHODS

Given the read-write asymmetry in NVM, it is important to redesign the persistent data structures that are used as access methods in a DBMS so that they perform fewer writes to NVM [53, 56, 130, 159, 205]. In a persistent NVM-aware B+tree index, the foremost change is to keep the entries in the leaf node unsorted so that the tree performs fewer writes and cache line flushes when it is mutated [126, 191]. Unsorted key-value entries in the leaf node require an expensive linear scan. This operation is sped up by hashing the keys, and using the hashes as a filter to avoid comparing the keys [159].

Another design optimization is to selectively enforce persistency where the tree only persists its leaf nodes and reconstructs its inner nodes during recovery [205]. In a storage hierarchy containing DRAM and NVM, the tree can persist the leaf nodes on NVM and maintain the inner nodes on DRAM. During recovery from a system failure, the tree rebuilds all the inner nodes that it placed in DRAM. Although this approach increases the recovery latency of the tree, the associated improvements in search and update operations during regular processing justify it [159].

A DBMS can also leverage the asymmetric I/O property by temporarily relaxing the balance of the B+tree [192]. Such imbalance (potentially) causes extra reads to access the tree but reduces the number of writes. This is a good trade-off for NVM because reads are less expensive than the writes and reduces wear-down of the storage device. By periodically re-balancing the tree and reducing the number of writes, a NVM-aware B+tree outperforms the regular B+tree across different workloads. We note that other data structures used as access methods in a DBMS, such as hash tables, must also be redesigned for NVM.

8.4 LARGER-THAN-MEMORY DATABASES

The fundamental limitation of memory-oriented DBMSs is that their improved performance is only achievable when the database is smaller than the amount of physical memory available in the system. If the database does not fit in memory, then the OS will start to page virtual memory, and main memory accesses will cause page faults. In a three-tier storage hierarchy with DRAM, NVM, and SSDs, the DBMS ensures that the "hot" data resides on DRAM. It then migrates the "cold" data to the NVM and SSD layers over time as the data ages and is likely to be updated. The latency of a transaction that accesses a cold tuple will be higher in a three-tier storage hierarchy. This is because NVM supports faster reads than SSD. During update operations, however, the DBMS quickly writes to the log and database on NVM. Eventually, the DBMS migrates the cold data to SSD.

We note that WBL protocol described in Chapter 4 can be used even in such a three-tier storage hierarchy. In this case, the DBMS uses a SSD to store the less frequently accessed tuples in the database. It stores the log and the more frequently accessed tuples on NVM. As bulk of the data is stored on SSD, the DBMS only requires a less expensive NVM device with smaller storage capacity. In Chapter 5, we examine impact of dynamic data placement on a three-tier storage hierarchy containing NVM. However, the traces used in our experiments are obtained from a DBMS that employs WAL. We plan to explore the utility of WBL in a three-tier storage hierarchy in future work.

8.5 SQL EXTENSIONS

The DBMS should contain certain SQL extensions to allow the user to control data placement on NVM [13, 21]. For instance, the user can indicate that certain performance-critical tables and materialized views should reside on NVM using the ON_NVM attribute. When this attribute is specified for a tablespace, the DBMS creates all the tables and materialized views within this tablespace on NVM.

```
ALTER TABLESPACE nvm_table_space DEFAULT ON_NVM;
```

By default, the DBMS stores all the columns in a table tagged with the ON_NVM attribute on NVM. However, the user can choose to store only a subset of the columns on NVM if desired. For instance, the following SQL statement excludes the ORDER_TAX column in the ORDERS table from being stored on NVM.

```
ALTER TABLE orders ON_NVM EXCLUDE(order_tax);
```

8.6   TESTING

Testing the correctness of a NVM DBMS is challenging. This is because the ordering of writes to NVM is outside the control of the system. For instance, cache-line evictions can happen at any time, and the DBMS cannot completely control the behavior of processor caches. Yat is a hypervisor-based framework for testing the correctness of NVM-oriented systems [119]. It adopts a record and replay method to simulate architectural failure conditions that are specific to NVM. After capturing a sequence of write and fence operations by the DBMS, Yat tests all permissible ordering of the operations to provide extensive coverage of possible error conditions. When it detects a system failure, it reports the exact sequence of operations that led to the failure. This information is useful for identifying the root cause of the failure. We plan to test the Peloton DBMS using NVM software validation frameworks in future work.

8.7   HIGH AVAILABILITY

With the WBL logging protocol, the DBMS can recover from system and transaction failures. However, it cannot cope up with media failures or corrupted data. This is because it relies on the integrity of durable data structures (e.g., the log) during recovery. These failures are instead overcome through replication, wherein the DBMS propagates changes made by transactions to multiple servers [86, 174]. When the *primary* server incurs a media failure, replication ensures that there is no data loss since the *secondary* servers can be configured to maintain a transactionally consistent copy of the database.

The round-trip latency between the primary and secondary server is on average a couple of orders of magnitude higher than the durable write latency of NVM. The networking cost is, thus, the major performance bottleneck in replication. A faster replication standard, such as the NVMe over Fabrics [18, 20], is required for efficient transaction processing in a replicated environment containing NVM [208]. With this technology, the additional latency between a local and remote NVM device is expected to be less than a few microseconds. As every write must be replicated in most usage models, we expect a logging scheme designed for NVM to outperform WAL in this replicated environment because it incurs fewer writes.

CHAPTER 9

Conclusion

In this book, we presented the design and implementation of DBMS architectures that are explicitly tailored for NVM. It focused on three aspects of a DBMS: (1) logging and recovery, (2) storage and buffer management, and (3) indexing.

In Chapter 3, we presented the fundamentals of storage methods in a NVM DBMS. We implemented three storage engines with different architectures and then developed optimized variants of each of these engines that better make use of NVM's characteristics. Our analysis showed that the NVM-optimized engines outperform their traditional counterparts while reducing the number of writes to the storage device by more than half on write-intensive workloads. We attribute this to the reduction in redundant data that the NVM-optimized engines store when a transaction modifies the database. We found that the NVM access latency has the most impact on the runtime performance of these engines, more so than the workload skew or the number of modifications to the database in the workload.

We next described WBL, a NVM-optimized logging and recovery protocol, in Chapter 4. WBL not only improved the runtime performance of the DBMS, but it also enabled it to recovery nearly instantaneously from system failures. The way that WBL achieved this is by tracking what parts of the database have changed rather than how it was changed. With WBL, a NVM DBMS directly flushes the changes made by transactions to the database instead of recording them in the log. By ordering writes to NVM correctly, it guarantees that all transactions are durable and atomic. Our evaluation showed that WBL reduces the system's recovery time by 100×.

We explored the fundamentals of buffer management in a three-tier storage system including DRAM, NVM, and SSD in Chapter 5. We described a set of data migration optimizations enabled by NVM. The key idea is that since the DBMS can directly operate on NVM-resident data, the buffer manager can adopt a lazy data migration policy for copying data over to DRAM. We illustrated that these optimizations have to be tailored depending on the characteristics of the storage hierarchy and the workload. We then made the case for adaptive data migration, a continuous adaptation mechanism in the buffer manager that achieves a near-optimal data migration policy for an arbitrary workload and storage hierarchy without requiring any manual tuning.

Lastly, in Chapter 6, we examined the implications of NVM for index data structures. With the BzTree design we demonstrated that using PMwCAS, a multi-word compare-and-swap with durability guarantees, helps reduce index design complexity tremendously. Our analysis showed that even though PMwCAS is computationally more expensive than a hardware-based single-word CAS, the simplicity that we gain by using PMwCAS improves not only the maintainability but also the performance of the BzTree. A cyclomatic complexity analysis showed that the BzTree is at least half as complex as state-of-the-art main-memory index designs.

All together, the work described in this book illustrates that rethinking the key algorithms and data structures employed in a DBMS for NVM not only improves performance and operational cost, but also simplifies development and enables the DBMS to support near-instantaneous recovery.

APPENDIX A

Non-Volatile Memory Emulation

NVM storage devices are currently prohibitively expensive and only support small capacities. For this reason, we use a NVM hardware emulator developed by Intel Labs [73] in this book. In this chapter, we present the architecture of the hardware emulator and the interfaces that it exports to applications. We then describe the internals of the NVM-aware memory allocator that we developed specifically for DBMSs.

A.1 NVM HARDWARE EMULATOR

Intel has developed a NVM hardware emulator, called persistent memory evaluation platform (PMEP), that models the latency and bandwidth characteristics of upcoming NVM technologies [73, 208]. This emulator supports tunable read latencies and read/write bandwidths. It enables us to evaluate multiple hardware profiles that are not specific to a particular NVM technology. Unlike NVM simulators, like PCM-SIM [134], this emulator enables us to better understand the impact of cache evictions, prefetching, and speculative execution on long-running DBMS workloads.

NVM technologies have higher read and write latency than DRAM. PMEP emulates the latency for the NVM partition using custom CPU microcode. The microcode estimates the additional cycles that the CPU would have to wait if DRAM is replaced by slower NVM and then stalls the CPU for those cycles. The accuracy of the latency emulation model has been validated by comparing the performance of several applications on emulated NVM and slower NUMA memory [73]. PMEP emulates the write bandwidth of NVM by limiting the number of DDR operations performed per microsecond.

The emulator is implemented on a dual-socket Intel Xeon processor-based platform. Each processor has 8 cores that run at 2.6 GHz and supports 4 DDR3 channels with 2 DIMMs per channel. The cores on each processor share a 20 MB L3 cache. The emulator's custom BIOS partitions the available DRAM memory into emulated NVM and regular (volatile) memory. Half of the memory channels on each processor are reserved for emulated NVM while the rest are used for regular memory. The emulated NVM is visible to the OS as a single NUMA node that interleaves memory (i.e., cache lines) across the two sockets. We configure the latency and bandwidth for the NVM partition by writing to CPU registers through the OS kernel. We refer interested readers to [73] for more technical details on the emulator.

We divide the NVM partition into two sub-partitions. The first sub-partition is available to software as a NUMA node. The second sub-partition is managed by persistent memory file system (PMFS), a file system optimized for persistent memory [73]. Applications allocate and access memory in the first sub-partition using `libnuma` library or tools such as `numactl` [2, 7]. We refer to this interface provided by the emulator as the *NUMA interface*.

Applications can also use regular POSIX file system interface to allocate and access memory in the second sub-partition through the *PMFS interface*. The sustained bandwidth of NVM is likely to be lower than that of DRAM. We therefore use the PMEP's throttling mechanism to reduce the NVM bandwidth to be 8× lower (9.5 GB/s) than DRAM. We now discuss the two emulator interfaces and how we utilize them.

A.1.1   NUMA INTERFACE

This interface allows us to evaluate the performance of DBMSs on NVM without making major modifications to the source code. All memory allocations for an application are assigned to the special NUMA node using `numactl`. Any read or write to memory are slowed down according to the emulator's latency setting. One potential drawback of this interface is that the DBMS's program code and OS data structures related to the DBMS's processes also reside in NVM. Furthermore, memory for other unrelated processes in the system could be allocated to the NUMA node. We did not observe this issue in our trials because of the default Linux memory policy that favors allocations from regular (volatile) memory nodes. In addition, the DBMS's program code is likely to be cached in the on-chip CPU caches, minimizing the overhead of fetching from the NVM.

A.1.2   PMFS INTERFACE

The emulator also supports a file system interface that allows us to deploy DBMSs using NVM with DRAM. Traditional file systems that operate at block granularity and in a layer above the block device abstraction are not best suited for fast, byte-addressable NVM. This is because the overhead of translating between two different address spaces (i.e., virtual addresses in memory and blocks in the block device) and maintaining a page cache in a traditional file system is significant. PMFS is a lightweight file system developed at Intel Labs that addresses this issue by completely avoiding page cache and block layer abstractions [73]. PMFS includes several optimizations for byte-addressable NVM that provide a significant performance improvement over traditional file systems (e.g., EXT4). Typically, in a block-oriented filesystem, file I/O requires two copies; one involving the block device and another involving the user buffer. PMFS, however, requires only one copy between the file and the user buffers. This improves the file I/O performance by 7–10× compared to block-oriented filesystems. PMFS also allows applications to access NVM using memory-mapped I/O.

Both of the above interfaces use memory from the emulated NVM. The key difference, however, is that the filesystem interface supports a naming mechanism that ensures that file offsets are valid after the system restarts. The downside of the filesystem interface is that it requires the application's writes to go through the kernel's virtual filesystem (VFS) layer. In contrast, when the application uses the allocator interface, it can write to and read from NVM directly within userspace. However, the allocator interface does not automatically provide a naming mechanism that is valid after a system restart. We use a memory allocator that is designed for NVM to overcome this limitation.

A.2   NVM-AWARE MEMORY ALLOCATOR

An NVM-aware memory allocator for a DBMS needs to satisfy two essential requirements. The first is that it should provide a *durability* mechanism to ensure that modifications to data stored on NVM are persisted. This is necessary because the changes made by a transaction to a location on NVM may still reside in volatile CPU caches when the transaction commits. If a power failure happens before the changes reach NVM, then these changes are lost. The allocator exposes a special API call to provide this durability mechanism.

Internally, the allocator first writes back the modifications to NVM using the cache-line write back (CLWB) instruction [23], as shown in Figure 2.1. This instruction writes back the modified data in the cache-lines to NVM. Unlike the cache-line flush (CLFLUSH) instruction that is generally used for flushing operations, CLWB does not invalidate the line from the cache and instead only transitions it to a non-modified state. This reduces the possibility of a compulsory cache miss when the same data is accessed momentarily after the line has been flushed. After flushing the cache lines, it issues a SFENCE instruction to ensure that the stores are ordered ahead of any subsequent operations. Otherwise, these changes might not be globally visible to other operations. From here on, we refer to this durability mechanism as the *sync* primitive.

The second requirement is that it should provide a *naming* mechanism for allocations so that pointers to locations in memory are valid even after the system restarts. The allocator ensures that the virtual memory addresses assigned to a memory-mapped region never change. With this mechanism, a pointer to a NVM location is mapped to the same virtual location after the OS or DBMS restarts. We refer to these pointers as *non-volatile pointers* [156].

The NVM allocator that we use in our evaluation is based on the open-source NVM-related *libpmem* library [10]. We extended this allocator to follow a rotating best-fit allocation policy and to support multi-threaded usage. The allocator directly maps the NVM to its address space. Unlike the filesystem interface, accessing a region of memory obtained from this allocator does not require copying data to user buffers. After an OS restart, the allocator reclaims memory that has not been persisted and restores its internal metadata to a consistent state. This recovery mechanism is required only after the OS restarts and not after the DBMS restarts, because the allocator handles memory management for all applications.

To show that accessing NVM through the allocator interface is faster than using the filesystem interface, we compare them using a micro-benchmark. In this experiment, the application performs durable writes to NVM using the two interfaces with sequential and random access patterns. The application performs durable writes using the filesystem's *fsync* system call and the allocator's sync primitive. We vary the size of the data chunk that the application writes from 1–256 bytes. The results in Figure A.1 show that NVM-aware allocator delivers 10–12× higher write bandwidth than the filesystem. The performance gap is more evident when the application writes out small data chunks sequentially. We also note that the gap between sequential and random write bandwidth is lower than that observed in other durable storage technologies.

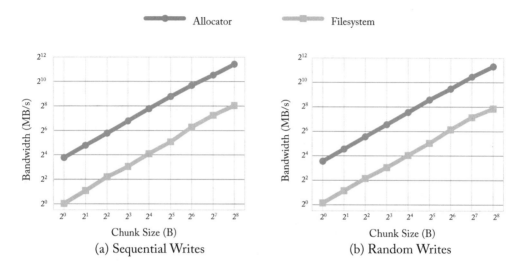

Figure A.1: **Write Bandwidth of Emulator Interfaces**—Comparison of the durable write bandwidth of Intel Lab's NVM emulator using the allocator and filesystem interfaces.

A.3   INTEL OPTANE NVM DIMMS

Intel has announced the availability of Optane NVM DIMMs[1] [65]. These modules are compatible with standard DDR4 DIMMs and will be supported by Xeon server platforms. The device characteristics of this technology have not been publicly disclosed as of late 2018 (e.g., power consumption, read and write latencies, and endurance ratings). Optane DIMMs support the SNIA NVM Programming Model, an industry standard for the interface between applications and operating systems that provide access to NVM [14]. The Persistent Memory Development Kit (PMDK) includes libraries that support several usage models of these DIMMs (e.g., transactional object store, log storage) [10]. Since the device characteristics of this technology are not available, we discuss the implications of the design assumptions listed in Chapter 1.

---

[1]These modules have been known under the Apache Pass codename.

- **Byte-Addressability:** Optane DIMMs bring 3D XPoint memory onto the DDR4 memory bus. The size of an atomic write operation will, therefore, likely remain close to that of a cache-line (i.e., 64 B) as opposed to a disk block (i.e., 4096 B).

- **High Write Throughput:** These modules are compatible with standard DDR4 DIMMs. So they will likely deliver higher write throughput compared to SSD. However, the performance gap between sequential and random write throughput of these modules might still be significant. If so, we will need to adapt the protocols and data structures presented in this book depending on the device characteristics. Since traditional DBMSs and the DBMS architectures advocated here are designed for two ends of a design spectrum (i.e., large and small performance gaps, respectively), we anticipate that a hybrid approach will work well on these DIMMs. For example, we can extend the write-behind logging protocol (Section 4.3) to manage the database as a log. However, the timestamp gap tracking technique will still be sufficient to ensure the atomicity property.

- **Read-Write Asymmetry:** Optane DIMMs will likely exhibit read-write asymmetry. So reducing the number of writes using NVM-aware data structures and algorithms will improve the runtime performance of the DBMS.

APPENDIX B

Benchmarks

We now describe the benchmarks used in our evaluations in this book. We ported these benchmarks in a good faith to follow the original spirit of each benchmark's specification.

B.1 YCSB

The Yahoo! Cloud Services Benchmark (YCSB) is a workload that is representative of large-scale services provided by web-scale companies [61]. It is a key-value store workload. We configure each tuple to consist of a unique key and ten columns of random string data, each 100 bytes in size. Thus, the total size of a tuple is approximately 1 KB.

The workload used for this analysis consists of two transaction types, a `read` and an `update` transaction. The read randomly selects a key and reads a single tuple. The update randomly selects a key and updates all 10 non-key values for the tuple selected. We use five types of workload mixtures that allow us to vary the I/O operations that the DBMS executes. These mixtures represent different ratios of *read* and *update* transactions:

- **Read-Only:** 100% *reads*
- **Read-Heavy:** 90% *reads*, 10% *updates*
- **Balanced:** 50% *reads*, 50% *updates*
- **Write-Heavy:** 10% *reads*, 90% *updates*

In addition to the read-write mix, we also control the amount of skew that determines how often a tuple is accessed by transactions. We use YCSB's Zipfian distribution to model temporal skew in the workloads, meaning that newer items are accessed much more frequently than older items. The amount of skew is controlled by the Zipfian constant $s > 0$, where higher values of s generate higher skewed workloads. We pick values of s in the range of 0.5–1.5, which is representative of a range of skewed workloads. We refer to workloads with $s = 0.5$ and $s = 1.5$ as *low-skew* and *high-skew* workloads, respectively.

B.2 TPC-C

This benchmark is an industry standard for evaluating the performance of OLTP systems [189]. The benchmark simulates an order-processing application, and consists of nine tables and five different transaction types. Only two of the transaction types modify tuples, but they make up 88% of a TPC-C workload. For simplicity, we have configured transactions to only access data from a single warehouse. Thus, all transactions are single-sited (i.e., there are no distributed transactions) because warehouses are mapped to partitions.

B.3   VOTER

This is an OLTP benchmark that simulates a phone-based election application. It is derived from the software system used to record votes for a television talent show. The workload consists of many short-lived transactions that each update a small number of tuples. Users call in to vote for a contestant which invokes a new transaction that updates the total number of votes for each contestant. A separate transaction is periodically invoked to display the vote totals for all contestants.

B.4   CH-BENCHMARK

This is a complex HTAP workload that is derived from a transactional workload based on the order entry processing of TPC-C and a corresponding TPC-H-equivalent OLAP query suite. It is useful to evaluate DBMSs designed to serve both OLTP and OLAP workloads. CH-benCHmark extends the TPC-C benchmark with 22 additional analytical queries.

B.5   AUCTIONMARK

This is an OLTP benchmark that models the workload characteristics of an on-line auction site [30]. The database and workload properties are derived from information extracted from a well-known auction site. The workload consists of ten transactions, two of which are periodically executed to process recently ended auctions. The user-to-item ratio follows a highly skewed Zipfian distribution. The total number of transactions that target each item is temporally skewed, as items receive more activity as the auction approaches its closing.

APPENDIX C

H-Store DBMS

H-Store is a distributed, memory-oriented DBMS that targets modern hardware (e.g., DRAM, multi-core processors) and OLTP workloads [161]. Its architecture is designed to eliminate the overhead of the legacy architectural components in a disk-oriented system [107]. We provide a brief overview of the H-Store DBMS.

C.1 ARCHITECTURAL OVERVIEW

An H-Store instance is a cluster of shared-nothing nodes [185]. Each *node* is a single physical computer system that hosts an H-Store process that contains one transaction coordinator that manages one or more partitions. The *transaction coordinator* at different nodes communicate with each other during the execution of distributed transactions. A *partition* is a disjoint subset of the entire database.

Each partition is assigned a single-threaded *execution engine* that is responsible for running transactions. The execution engine communicates with other engines through the transaction coordinator. It has exclusive access to the data at its partition. If a transaction needs to access data at a partition, then this request has to be sent to that partition's engine for execution.

H-Store's *storage manager* manages tuples in main memory using a row-oriented format. The DBMS replicates partitions to ensure the durability and availability of data in the event of a node failure. It replicates data in two ways: (1) replicating partitions on multiple nodes and (2) replicating a table at all partitions (i.e., each partition has a copy of the entire table). H-Store executes the majority of the application's transactions as pre-defined *stored procedures*. Each stored procedure consists of a set of parameterized queries, and control code that contains invocations of those queries intermixed with application logic.

H-Store's architecture is divided into two parts: (1) the front-end transaction coordinator and (2) the back-end execution engine and storage manager. The front-end consists of the networking libraries for communicating with the application's clients and the transaction coordinators. The back-end execution engine and storage manager for each partition contains the query plan execution and data management logic.

C.1.1 TRANSACTION COORDINATOR

Unlike disk-oriented systems, H-Store uses a lightweight concurrency control scheme when executing multiple transactions at a partition. It runs transactions one-at-a-time at each partition. When a transaction executes in H-Store, it has exclusive access to the data and indexes at the required partitions. H-Store uses timestamp-based concurrency control scheme for scheduling transactions [44]. Serializing transactions at each partition in this manner improves performance on OLTP workloads where most transactions only access a single entity in the database at a time.

C.1.2   EXECUTION ENGINE

A single-threaded execution engine manages every partition in H-Store. It has exclusive access to the data at that partition. The engine's thread blocks on a queue waiting for tasks to perform. These tasks can either instruct the engine to start a new transaction or to execute a fragment of a distributed query plan on behalf of a transaction running at another partition. In the latter case, the coordinators ensure that no transaction is allowed to place a task at an engine's queue unless the transaction holds the lock for that engine's partition.

C.1.3   STORAGE LAYER

The storage manager of each partition maintains separate indexes for the database tables that only contain entries for the tuples associated with that particular partition. So, an execution engine cannot directly access data stored in another partition at the same node. The in-memory storage area for tables is split into separate pools for fixed-sized and variable-length blocks. The storage manager organizes the tables' tuples unsorted within the pools. It supports hash table and B-tree data structures for unique and non-unique indexes. The values of the entries in these indexes are tuple offsets in the pools.

C.1.4   RECOVERY MECHANISM

Since H-Store is a DRAM-centric DBMS, it must ensure that all of a transaction's changes are durable and recoverable if a node crashes. It is critical that it provides this guarantee with minimal performance impact. H-Store employs a lightweight, logical logging scheme that has less overhead than existing techniques used in disk-oriented systems. With this scheme, the DBMS only records the high-level operation that the transaction executed (e.g., a query invocation) instead of recording the physical changes made by the transaction. Logical logging reduces the amount of data that needs to be written to durable storage compared to physical logging, since the DBMS only needs to record *what* the operation was rather than the changes it applied to the database. However, recovering the database using logical logging takes longer since the DBMS needs to re-execute the recorded operations.

C.1.5   REPLICATION

Since logical logging increases the time taken to rebuild the database after a node failure, H-Store uses a replication scheme that allows it to keep running even if one node crashes. A collection of nodes that all contain the same partitions is termed as a replica set. Each node manages its own logical log and database snapshots. To elect a node as the master of the replica set, the system uses the Paxos consensus protocol [117]. The other nodes in the replica set are referred to as slave nodes. When the master node crashes, the DBMS runs a new election round using the consensus protocol to promote one of the slaves as the new master.

Bibliography

[1] Apache Cassandra. http://datastax.com/documentation/cassandra/2.0/ 24

[2] Control NUMA policy for processes or shared memory. http://linux.die.net/man/8/numactl 146

[3] Direct access for files (DAX). https://www.kernel.org/doc/Documentation/filesystems/dax.txt 132

[4] H-Store. http://hstore.cs.brown.edu 8

[5] LIBNVDIMM: Non-volatile devices. https://www.kernel.org/doc/Documentation/nvdimm/nvdimm.txt 132

[6] Linux perf framework. https://perf.wiki.kernel.org/index.php/Main_Page 30, 34, 38

[7] NUMA policy library. http://linux.die.net/man/3/numa 146

[8] OLTPBenchmark.com. http://oltpbenchmark.com 87

[9] Peloton database management system. http://pelotondb.org 49, 62

[10] Persistent memory development kit (PMDK). http://pmem.io/ 118, 130, 135, 147, 148

[11] Persistent memory file system (PMFS). https://github.com/linux-pmfs/pmfs 132

[12] PostgreSQL. https://www.postgresql.org/ 87

[13] SAP HANA administration guide: Load/unload a column table into/from memory. http://help.sap.com/saphelp_hanaplatform/helpdata/en/c1/33165bbb57101493c5fb19b5b8607f/content.htm 141

[14] SNIA NVM programming model. https://www.snia.org/forums/sssi/nvmp 148

[15] VoltDB. http://voltdb.com 20

[16] Oracle TimesTen products and technologies. *Technical Report*, February 2007. 76, 129

[17] Intel's 3D memory is 1,000 times faster than modern storage. https://www.engadget.com/2015/07/28/intel-3d-memory-1000-times-faster/, July 2015. 2, 47

[18] JEDEC announces support for NVDIMM hybrid memory modules. `https://www.jedec.org/news/pressreleases/jedec-announces-support-nvdimm-hybrid-memory-modules`, 2015. 142

[19] Intel architecture instruction set extensions programming reference. `https://software.intel.com/sites/default/files/managed/b4/3a/319433--024.pdf`, 2016. 134, 136

[20] NVM express over fabrics specification. `http://www.nvmexpress.org/specifications`, 2016. 142

[21] Oracle in-memory database white paper. `http://www.oracle.com/technetwork/database/in-memory/overview/twp-oracle-database-in-memory-2245633.html`, 2016. 141

[22] HPE unveils computer built for the era of big data. `https://news.hpe.com/a-new-computer-built-for-the-big-data-era/`, May 2017. 2, 47

[23] A new breakthrough in persistent memory gets its first public demo. `https://itpeernetwork.intel.com/new-breakthrough-persistent-memory-first-public-demo/`, May 2017. 2, 7, 43, 47, 70, 103, 124, 147

[24] Intel optane SSD 905P series. `https://www.intel.com/content/www/us/en/products/memory-storage/solid-state-drives/gaming-enthusiast-ssds/optane-905p-booktitle.html`, 2018. 89

[25] AGIGARAM. DDR3 NVDIMM. `http://www.agigatech.com/ddr3.php` 47

[26] R. Agrawal and H. V. Jagadish. Recovery algorithms for database machines with non-volatile main memory. In *IWDM*, 1989. DOI: 10.1007/3-540-51324-8_41 50, 56, 80, 129

[27] A. Ailamaki, D. J. DeWitt, M. D. Hill, and M. Skounakis. Weaving relations for cache performance. In *VLDB*, 2001. 139

[28] J. H. Anderson, S. Ramamurthy, and R. Jain. Implementing wait-free objects on priority-based systems. In *PODC*, 1997. DOI: 10.1145/259380.259443 137

[29] M. Andrei, C. Lemke, G. Radestock, R. Schulze, C. Thiel, R. Blanco, A. Meghlan, M. Sharique, S. Seifert, S. Vishnoi, et al. SAP HANA adoption of non-volatile memory. *VLDB*, 10(12):1754–1765, 2017. DOI: 10.14778/3137765.3137780 130

[30] V. Angkanawaraphan and A. Pavlo. AuctionMark: A Benchmark for High-Performance OLTP Systems. `http://hstore.cs.brown.edu/projects/auctionmark` 152

[31] J. Arulraj, J. Levandoski, U. F. Minhas, and P.-A. Larson. BzTree: A high-performance latch-free range index for non-volatile memory. In *VLDB*, 2018. 4

[32] J. Arulraj and A. Pavlo. How to build a non-volatile memory database management system. In *SIGMOD*, 2017. DOI: 10.1145/3035918.3054780 3, 5

[33] J. Arulraj, A. Pavlo, and S. Dulloor. Let's talk about storage and recovery methods for non-volatile memory database systems. In *SIGMOD*, 2015. DOI: 10.1145/2723372.2749441 4, 56, 62

[34] J. Arulraj, A. Pavlo, and P. Menon. Bridging the archipelago between row-stores and column-stores for hybrid workloads. In *SIGMOD*, 2016. DOI: 10.1145/2882903.2915231 4, 51, 53

[35] J. Arulraj, M. Perron, and A. Pavlo. Write-behind logging. In *VLDB*, 2017. DOI: 10.14778/3025111.3025116 3, 4, 81

[36] M. M. Astrahan et al. System R: Relational approach to database management. In *ACM TODS*, vol. 1, June 1976. DOI: 10.1016/b978-0-934613-53-8.50042-x 1, 129

[37] A. Badam and V. S. Pai. SSDAlloc: Hybrid SSD/RAM memory management made easy. In *NSDI*, 2011. 134

[38] P. Bailis, C. Fournier, J. Arulraj, and A. Pavlo. Research for practice: Distributed consensus and implications of NVM on database management systems. In *Queue*, vol. 14, July 2016. DOI: 10.1145/2949033 129

[39] M. Baker, S. Asami, E. Deprit, J. Ousterhout, and M. Seltzer. Non-volatile memory for fast, reliable file systems. In *ASPLOS*, 1992. DOI: 10.1145/143365.143380 132

[40] D. Bausch, I. Petrov, and A. Buchmann. Making cost-based query optimization asymmetry-aware. In *DaMoN*, ACM, 2012. DOI: 10.1145/2236584.2236588 139

[41] D. Beaver, S. Kumar, H. C. Li, J. Sobel, P. Vajgel, and F. Inc. Finding a needle in haystack: Facebook's photo storage. In *OSDI*, 2010. 80

[42] N. Ben-David et al. Parallel algorithms for asymmetric read-write costs. In *SPAA*, 2016. DOI: 10.1145/2935764.2935767 139

[43] J. Bergstra and Y. Bengio. Random search for hyper-parameter optimization. In *Journal of Machine Learning Research*, vol. 13, 2012. 85

[44] P. A. Bernstein and N. Goodman. Timestamp-based algorithms for concurrency control in distributed database systems. In *Proc. of the 6th International Conference on Very Large Data Bases*, vol. 6, pages 285–300, VLDB Endowment, 1980. DOI: 10.21236/ada087996 154

[45] P. A. Bernstein, V. Hadzilacos, and N. Goodman. *Concurrency Control and Recovery in Database Systems*. Addison-Wesley Longman Publishing Co., Inc., Boston, MA, 1986. 1, 23, 75

[46] K. Bhandari, D. R. Chakrabarti, and H.-J. Boehm. Makalu: Fast recoverable allocation of non-volatile memory. In *SIGPLAN Notices*, 2016. DOI: 10.1145/3022671.2984019 135

[47] K. Bhandari et al. Implications of CPU caching on byte-addressable non-volatile memory programming. In *HPL Tech Report*, 2012. 134

[48] T. Bingmann. STX B+ tree C++ template classes. http://panthema.net/2007/stx-btree/ 20, 42

[49] G. E. Blelloch, J. T. Fineman, P. B. Gibbons, Y. Gu, and J. Shun. Sorting with asymmetric read and write costs. In *SPAA*, 2015. DOI: 10.1145/2755573.2755604 139, 140

[50] B. H. Bloom. Space/time trade-offs in hash coding with allowable errors. In *Communications of the ACM*, 1970. DOI: 10.1145/362686.362692 23, 30

[51] P. Boncz, S. Manegold, and M. L. Kersten. Database architecture optimized for the new bottleneck: Memory access. In *VLDB*, 1999. 139

[52] D. R. Chakrabarti, H.-J. Boehm, and K. Bhandari. Atlas: Leveraging locks for non-volatile memory consistency. In *ACM SIGPLAN Notices*, vol. 49, 2014. DOI: 10.1145/2714064.2660224 136

[53] A. Chatzistergiou, M. Cintra, and S. D. Viglas. REWIND: Recovery write-ahead system for in-memory non-volatile data-structures. In *PVLDB*, 2015. DOI: 10.14778/2735479.2735483 63, 131, 136, 140

[54] F. Chen, M. Mesnier, and S. Hahn. A protected block device for persistent memory. In *MSST*, 2014. DOI: 10.1109/msst.2014.6855541 2

[55] S. Chen, P. B. Gibbons, and S. Nath. Rethinking database algorithms for phase change memory. In *CIDR*, 2011. 5, 137, 139, 140

[56] S. Chen and Q. Jin. Persistent B+-trees in non-volatile main memory. In *PVLDB*, vol. 8, 2015. DOI: 10.14778/2752939.2752947 63, 137, 138, 140

[57] H. Chu. MDB: A memory-mapped database and backend for OpenLDAP. *Technical Report*, OpenLDAP, 2011. 22, 28, 42

[58] J. Coburn, T. Bunker, M. Schwarz, R. Gupta, and S. Swanson. From ARIES to MARS: Transaction support for next-generation, solid-state drives. In *SOSP*, 2013. DOI: 10.1145/2517349.2522724 5, 130

[59] J. Coburn, A. M. Caulfield, A. Akel, L. M. Grupp, R. K. Gupta, R. Jhala, and S. Swanson. NV-heaps: Making persistent objects fast and safe with next-generation, nonvolatile memories. In *ASPLOS*, ACM, 2011. DOI: 10.1145/2248487.1950380 134

[60] J. Condit, E. B. Nightingale, C. Frost, E. Ipek, B. Lee, D. Burger, and D. Coetzee. Better I/O through byte-addressable, persistent memory. In *SOSP*, 2009. DOI: 10.1145/1629575.1629589 132, 136

[61] B. F. Cooper, A. Silberstein, E. Tam, R. Ramakrishnan, and R. Sears. Benchmarking cloud serving systems with YCSB. In *SoCC*, 2010. DOI: 10.1145/1807128.1807152 151

[62] G. Copeland, T. Keller, R. Krishnamurthy, and M. Smith. The case for safe RAM. In *VLDB*, 1989. 129

[63] J. Corbet. LFCS: Preparing Linux for nonvolatile memory devices. In *LWN*, April 2013. 129

[64] J. Corbet. Supporting filesystems in persistent memory. https://lwn.net/Articles /610174/, 2014. 132

[65] I. Cutress and B. Tallis. Intel launches optane DIMMS up to 512 GB: Apache pass is here. https://www.anandtech.com/show/12828/intel-launches-optane-dimms-up-to-512gb-apache-pass-is-here, May 2018. 148

[66] J. Dean and S. Ghemawat. LevelDB. http://leveldb.googlecode.com 23

[67] J. DeBrabant, J. Arulraj, A. Pavlo, M. Stonebraker, S. Zdonik, and S. Dulloor. A prolegomenon on OLTP database systems for non-volatile memory. In *ADMS@VLDB*, 2014. 2, 3, 24

[68] J. DeBrabant, A. Pavlo, S. Tu, M. Stonebraker, and S. Zdonik. Anti-caching: A new approach to database management system architecture. In *VLDB*, 2013. DOI: 10.14778/2556549.2556575 3, 10, 16

[69] D. J. DeWitt, R. H. Katz, F. Olken, L. D. Shapiro, M. R. Stonebraker, and D. Wood. Implementation techniques for main memory database systems. In *SIGMOD Record*, vol. 14, 1984. DOI: 10.1145/602260.602261 54, 76, 81

[70] C. Diaconu, C. Freedman, E. Ismert, P.-A. Larson, P. Mittal, R. Stonecipher, N. Verma, and M. Zwilling. Hekaton: SQL server's memory-optimized OLTP engine. In *SIGMOD*, 2013. DOI: 10.1145/2463676.2463710 2, 51, 77, 101, 106, 109, 129

[71] D. E. Difallah, A. Pavlo, C. Curino, and P. Cudré-Mauroux. Oltp-bench: An extensible testbed for benchmarking relational databases. In *PVLDB*, vol. 7, 2013. DOI: 10.14778/2732240.2732246 12, 87

[72] A. Driskill-Smith. Latest advances and future prospects of STT-RAM. In *Non-Volatile Memories Workshop*, 2010. 2, 47

[73] S. R. Dulloor, S. K. Kumar, A. Keshavamurthy, P. Lantz, D. Subbareddy, R. Sankaran, and J. Jackson. System software for persistent memory. In *EuroSys*, 2014. DOI: 10.1145/2592798.2592814 2, 7, 12, 24, 44, 86, 132, 145, 146

[74] S. R. Dulloor, A. Roy, Z. Zhao, N. Sundaram, N. Satish, R. Sankaran, J. Jackson, and K. Schwan. Data tiering in heterogeneous memory systems. In *EuroSys*, 2016. DOI: 10.1145/2901318.2901344 135, 136

[75] A. Eldawy, J. Levandoski, and P.-Å. Larson. Trekking through Siberia: Managing cold data in a memory-optimized database. In *PVLDB*, vol. 7, VLDB Endowment, 2014. DOI: 10.14778/2732967.2732968 77

[76] R. Fang, H.-I. Hsiao, B. He, C. Mohan, and Y. Wang. High performance database logging using storage class memory. In *ICDE*, 2011. DOI: 10.1109/icde.2011.5767918 129

[77] M. Franklin. Concurrency control and recovery. In *The Computer Science and Engineering Handbook*, 1997. DOI: 10.1201/b16768-15 8, 9, 21, 49, 50, 51, 56, 80

[78] K. Fraser. Practical lock-freedom. Ph.D. thesis, University of Cambridge, 2004. 137

[79] S. Gao, J. Xu, B. He, B. Choi, and H. Hu. PCMLogging: Reducing transaction logging overhead with PCM. In *CIKM*, 2011. DOI: 10.1145/2063576.2063977 130

[80] H. Garcia-Molina and K. Salem. Main memory database systems: An overview. In *IEEE TKDE*, 1992. DOI: 10.1109/69.180602 129, 139

[81] V. Garg, A. Singh, and J. R. Haritsa. On improving write performance in PCM databases. *Technical Report, TR-2015–01*, IISc, 2015. 139

[82] D. Gawlick and D. Kinkade. Varieties of concurrency control in IMS/VS Fast Path. *Technical Report*, Tandem, 1985. 129

[83] G. Graefe, W. Guy, and C. Sauer. Instant recovery with write-ahead logging: Page repair, system restart, and media restore. In *Synthesis Lectures on Data Management*, Morgan & Claypool Publishers, 2015. DOI: 10.2200/s00710ed2v01y201603dtm044 62, 70, 131

[84] G. Graefe, H. Kimura, and H. Kuno. Foster B-trees. In *TODS*, vol. 37, 2012. DOI: 10.1145/2338626.2338630 131

[85] G. Graefe, H. Volos, H. Kimura, H. Kuno, J. Tucek, M. Lillibridge, and A. Veitch. In-memory performance for big data. In *VLDB*, vol. 8, 2014. DOI: 10.14778/2735461.2735465 77

[86] J. Gray, P. Helland, P. O'Neil, and D. Shasha. The dangers of replication and a solution. In *SIGMOD Record*, vol. 25, 1996. DOI: 10.1145/235968.233330 133, 142

[87] J. Gray, P. McJones, M. Blasgen, B. Lindsay, R. Lorie, T. Price, F. Putzolu, and I. Traiger. The recovery manager of the system R database manager. In *ACM Computing Surveys*, vol. 13, June 1981. DOI: 10.1145/356842.356847 22

[88] M. Greenwald. Two-handed emulation: How to build non-blocking implementations of complex data-structures using DCAS. In *PODC*, 2002. DOI: 10.1145/571873.571874 137

[89] R. A. Hankins and J. M. Patel. Data morphing: An adaptive, cache-conscious storage technique. In *VLDB*, 2003. 43

[90] T. Härder, C. Sauer, G. Graefe, and W. Guy. Instant recovery with write-ahead logging. In *Datenbank-Spektrum*, 2015. DOI: 10.1007/s13222-015-0204-3 62, 70, 131

[91] S. Harizopoulos, D. J. Abadi, S. Madden, and M. Stonebraker. OLTP through the looking glass, and what we found there. In *SIGMOD*, 2008. DOI: 10.1145/3226595.3226635 1, 8, 76, 129

[92] S. Harizopoulos, V. Liang, D. J. Abadi, and S. Madden. Performance tradeoffs in read-optimized databases. In *VLDB*, 2006. 139

[93] R. Harris. Windows leaps into the NVM revolution. http://www.zdnet.com/articl e/windows-leaps-into-the-nvm-revolution/, April 2016. 132

[94] T. L. Harris, K. Fraser, and I. A. Pratt. A practical multi-word compare-and-swap operation. In *DISC*, 2002. DOI: 10.1007/3-540-36108-1_18 102, 104, 137

[95] A. Hassan et al. Energy-efficient in-memory data stores on hybrid memory hierarchies. In *DaMoN*, ACM, 2015. DOI: 10.1145/2771937.2771940 77

[96] M. Hedenfalk. Copy-on-write B+ Tree. http://www.bzero.se/ldapd/ 22, 42

[97] J. M. Hellerstein, M. Stonebraker, and J. R. Hamilton. Architecture of a database system. In *Foundations and Trends in Databases*, vol. 1, 2007. DOI: 10.1561/1900000002 1, 75, 106

[98] M. Herlihy. A methodology for implementing highly concurrent data objects. In *ACM TOPLAS*, vol. 15, November 1993. DOI: 10.1145/142111.964613 137

[99] W. W. Hsu, A. J. Smith, and H. C. Young. Characteristics of production database workloads and the TPC benchmarks. In *IBM Systems Journal*, vol. 40, 2001. DOI: 10.1147/sj.403.0781 5, 87

[100] J. Huang, K. Schwan, and M. K. Qureshi. NVRAM-aware logging in transaction systems. In *VLDB*, December 2014. DOI: 10.14778/2735496.2735502 49, 131

[101] Y. E. Ioannidis and E. Wong. *Query Optimization by Simulated Annealing*, vol. 16, ACM, 1987. DOI: 10.1145/38713.38722 83

[102] A. Israeli and L. Rappoport. Disjoint-access-parallel implementations of strong shared memory primitives. In *PODC*, 1994. DOI: 10.1145/197917.198079 137

[103] B. L. Jacob, P. M. Chen, S. R. Silverman, and T. N. Mudge. An analytical model for designing memory hierarchies. In *IEEE Transactions on Computers*, vol. 45, 1996. DOI: 10.1109/12.543711 84, 85

[104] C. Jacobi, T. Slegel, and D. Greiner. Transactional memory architecture and implementation for IBM System Z. In *MICRO*, 2012. DOI: 10.1109/micro.2012.12 137

[105] R. Johnson, I. Pandis, N. Hardavellas, A. Ailamaki, and B. Falsafi. Shore-MT: A scalable storage manager for the multicore era. In *EDBT*, 2009. DOI: 10.1145/1516360.1516365 130

[106] A. Joshi, V. Nagarajan, M. Cintra, and S. Viglas. Efficient persist barriers for multicores. In *MICRO*, ACM, 2015. DOI: 10.1145/2830772.2830805 136

[107] R. Kallman et al. H-Store: A high-performance, distributed main memory transaction processing system. In *VLDB*, 2008. DOI: 10.14778/1454159.1454211 2, 76, 129, 153

[108] A. Kemper and T. Neumann. HyPer: A hybrid OLTP&OLAP main memory database system based on virtual memory snapshots. In *ICDE*, 2011. 2, 129

[109] H. Kim et al. Evaluating phase change memory for enterprise storage systems: A study of caching and tiering approaches. In *FAST*, 2014. DOI: 10.1145/2668128 40, 67, 77

[110] H. Kimura. FOEDUS: OLTP engine for a thousand cores and NVRAM. In *SIGMOD*, 2015. DOI: 10.1145/2723372.2746480 5, 131

[111] S. Kirkpatrick, C. D. Gelatt, and M. P. Vecchi. Optimization by simulated annealing. In *Science*, vol. 220, American Association for the Advancement of Science, 1983. DOI: 10.1016/b978-0-08-051581-6.50059-3 83

[112] T. Klima. Using non-volatile memory (NVDIMM-N) as byte-addressable storage in windows server 2016. https://channel9.msdn.com/events/build/2016/p470 132

[113] A. Kolli. Architecting persistent memory systems. Ph.D. thesis, University of Michigan, 2017. 136

[114] A. Kolli, J. Rosen, S. Diestelhorst, A. Saidi, S. Pelley, S. Liu, P. M. Chen, and T. F. Wenisch. Delegated persist ordering. In *MICRO*, IEEE Press, 2016. DOI: 10.1109/micro.2016.7783761 136

[115] B. Kuszmaul. A comparison of fractal trees to log-structured merge (LSM) trees. *Technical Report*, Tokutek, 2014. 23

[116] Y. Kwon, H. Fingler, T. Hunt, S. Peter, E. Witchel, and T. Anderson. Strata: A cross media file system. In *SOSP*, 2017. DOI: 10.1145/3132747.3132770 75, 81, 133

[117] L. Lamport et al. Paxos made simple. *ACM SIGACT News*, 32(4):18–25, 2001. 155

[118] D. Laney. 3D data management: Controlling data volume, velocity and variety, February 2001. 1

[119] P. Lantz, S. Dulloor, S. Kumar, R. Sankaran, and J. Jackson. Yat: A validation framework for persistent memory software. In *ATC*, 2014. 136, 142

[120] P.-A. Larson, S. Blanas, C. Diaconu, C. Freedman, J. M. Patel, and M. Zwilling. High-performance concurrency control mechanisms for main-memory databases. In *VLDB*, 2011. DOI: 10.14778/2095686.2095689 51

[121] C. Lefurgy, K. Rajamani, F. Rawson, W. Felter, M. Kistler, and T. W. Keller. Energy management for commercial servers. In *Computer*, vol. 36, IEEE Computer Society Press, Los Alamitos, CA, 2003. DOI: 10.1109/mc.2003.1250880 77

[122] V. Leis. Query processing and optimization in modern database systems. Ph.D. thesis, Technische Universität München, 2016. 137

[123] V. Leis, M. Haubenschild, A. Kemper, and T. Neumann. Leanstore: In-memory data management beyond main memory. In *ICDE*, 2018. DOI: 10.1109/icde.2018.00026 77

[124] V. Leis, A. Kemper, and T. Neumann. The adaptive radix tree: ARTful indexing for main-memory databases. In *ICDE*, 2013. DOI: 10.1109/icde.2013.6544812 137

[125] V. Leis, F. Scheibner, A. Kemper, and T. Neumann. The ART of practical synchronization. In *DaMoN*, 2016. DOI: 10.1145/2933349.2933352 137

[126] J. Levandoski, D. Lomet, and S. Sengupta. The Bw-Tree: A B-tree for new hardware platforms. In *ICDE*, 2013. DOI: 10.1109/icde.2013.6544834 101, 102, 107, 110, 116, 120, 137, 140

[127] J. Levandoski, D. B. Lomet, S. Sengupta, R. Stutsman, and R. Wang. High performance transactions in deuteronomy. In *CIDR*, 2015. 105, 106

[128] J. J. Levandoski, P.-Å. Larson, and R. Stoica. Identifying hot and cold data in main-memory databases. In *ICDE*, 2013. DOI: 10.1109/icde.2013.6544811 77

[129] LevelDB. Implementation details of LevelDB. https://leveldb.googlecode.com/svn/trunk/doc/impl.html 29

[130] R.-S. Liu, D.-Y. Shen, C.-L. Yang, S.-C. Yu, and C.-Y. M. Wang. NVM Duet: Unified working memory and persistent store architecture. In *SIGARCH Computer Architecture News*, vol. 42, ACM, 2014. DOI: 10.1145/2541940.2541957 140

[131] D. E. Lowell and P. M. Chen. Free transactions with rio vista. In *SOSP*, 1997. DOI: 10.1145/269005.266665 132

[132] Y. Lu, J. Shu, L. Sun, and O. Mutlu. Loose-ordering consistency for persistent memory. In *ICCD*, IEEE, 2014. DOI: 10.1109/iccd.2014.6974684 136

[133] L. Ma et al. Larger-than-memory data management on modern storage hardware for in-memory OLTP database systems. In *DaMoN*, 2016. DOI: 10.1145/2933349.2933358 77

[134] P. Macko. A simple PCM block device simulator for Linux. https://code.google.com/p/pcmsim/people/list 145

[135] D. Makreshanski, J. Levandoski, and R. Stutsman. To lock, swap, or elide: On the interplay of hardware transactional memory and lock-free indexing. In *PVLDB*, vol. 8, 2015. DOI: 10.14778/2809974.2809990 107, 137

[136] N. Malviya, A. Weisberg, S. Madden, and M. Stonebraker. Rethinking main memory OLTP recovery. In *ICDE*, 2014. DOI: 10.1109/icde.2014.6816685 8, 9, 16, 22

[137] J. A. Mandelman, R. H. Dennard, G. B. Bronner, J. K. DeBrosse, R. Divakaruni, Y. Li, and C. J. Radens. Challenges and future directions for the scaling of dynamic random-access memory (DRAM). In *IBM Journal of Research and Development*, vol. 46, Riverton, NJ, IBM Corporation. DOI: 10.1147/rd.462.0187 77

[138] Y. Mao, E. Kohler, and R. T. Morris. Cache craftiness for fast multicore key-value storage. In *EuroSys*, 2012. DOI: 10.1145/2168836.2168855 107, 131, 137

[139] MemSQL. How MemSQL works. http://docs.memsql.com/4.1/intro/ 76

[140] J. Meza, Y. Luo, S. Khan, J. Zhao, Y. Xie, and O. Mutlu. A case for efficient hardware/software cooperative management of storage and memory, 2013. 77

[141] Microsoft. Profiling tools. https://docs.microsoft.com/en-us/visualstudio/profiling/profiling-feature-tour 127

[142] C. Mohan, D. Haderle, B. Lindsay, H. Pirahesh, and P. Schwarz. ARIES: A transaction recovery method supporting fine-granularity locking and partial rollbacks using write-ahead logging. In *ACM TODS*, vol. 17, 1992. DOI: 10.1145/128765.128770 9, 21, 51, 52

[143] D. Molka, D. Hackenberg, R. Schone, and M. S. Muller. Memory performance and cache coherency effects on an intel nehalem multiprocessor system. In *PACT*, 2009. DOI: 10.1109/pact.2009.22 28

[144] I. Moraru, D. Andersen, M. Kaminsky, N. Tolia, P. Ranganathan, and N. Binkert. Consistent, durable, and safe memory management for byte-addressable non volatile main memory. In *TRIOS*, 2013. DOI: 10.1145/2524211.2524216 2, 24, 25, 27, 30, 134

[145] M. Nanavati, M. Schwarzkopf, J. Wires, and A. Warfield. Non-volatile Storage: Implications of the datacenter's shifting center. In *Queue*, vol. 13, January 2016. 129

[146] D. Narayanan and O. Hodson. Whole-system persistence. In *SIGARCH Computer Architecture News*, vol. 40, 2012. DOI: 10.1145/2189750.2151018 135

[147] F. Nawab, D. R. Chakrabarti, T. Kelly, and C. B. Morrey III. Procrastination beats prevention: Timely sufficient persistence for efficient crash resilience. In *EDBT*, 2015. 135

[148] T. Neumann, T. Mühlbauer, and A. Kemper. Fast serializable multi-version concurrency control for main-memory database systems. In *SIGMOD*, 2015. DOI: 10.1145/2723372.2749436 51

[149] NVM Express Inc. NVM express over fabrics specification. http://www.nvmexpress.org/specifications, 2016. 69

[150] G. Oh, S. Kim, S.-W. Lee, and B. Moon. SQLite optimization with phase change memory for mobile applications. In *VLDB*, vol. 8, August 2015. DOI: 10.14778/2824032.2824044 131

[151] M. Olson, K. Bostic, and M. Seltzer. Berkeley DB. In *Proc. of the FREENIX Track: USENIX Annual Technical Conference*, 1999. 11

[152] E. J. O'Neil, P. E. O'Neil, and G. Weikum. The LRU-K page replacement algorithm for database disk buffering. In *SIGMOD*, 1993. DOI: 10.1145/170036.170081 76

[153] P. O'Neil, E. Cheng, D. Gawlick, and E. O'Neil. The log-structured merge-tree (LSM-tree). In *Acta Informatica*, vol. 33, June 1996. DOI: 10.1007/s002360050048 23, 29

[154] D. Ongaro, S. M. Rumble, R. Stutsman, J. Ousterhout, and M. Rosenblum. Fast crash recovery in RAMCloud. In *SOSP*, 2011. DOI: 10.1145/2043556.2043560 133

[155] I. Oukid. Architectural principles for database systems on storage-class memory. Ph.D. thesis, Technische Universität Dresden, 2017. 5, 130

[156] I. Oukid, D. Booss, W. Lehner, P. Bumbulis, and T. Willhalm. SOFORT: A hybrid SCM-DRAM storage engine for fast data recovery. In *DaMoN*, 2014. DOI: 10.1145/2619228.2619236 5, 130, 134, 147

[157] I. Oukid, D. Booss, A. Lespinasse, and W. Lehner. On testing persistent-memory-based software. In *DaMoN*, 2016. DOI: 10.1145/2933349.2933354 136

[158] I. Oukid, D. Booss, A. Lespinasse, W. Lehner, T. Willhalm, and G. Gomes. Memory management techniques for large-scale persistent-main-memory systems. *VLDB*, 2017. DOI: 10.14778/3137628.3137629 135

[159] I. Oukid, J. Lasperas, A. Nica, T. Willhalm, and W. Lehner. FPTree: A hybrid SCM-DRAM persistent and concurrent B-tree for storage class memory. In *SIGMOD*, 2016. DOI: 10.1145/2882903.2915251 5, 118, 137, 138, 140

[160] I. Oukid and W. Lehner. Data structure engineering for byte-addressable non-volatile memory. In *SIGMOD*, 2017. DOI: 10.1145/3035918.3054777 5, 135

[161] A. Pavlo. On scalable transaction execution in partitioned main memory database management systems. Ph.D. thesis, Brown University, 2013. 1, 153

[162] A. Pavlo, C. Curino, and S. Zdonik. Skew-aware automatic database partitioning in shared-nothing, parallel OLTP systems. In *SIGMOD*, 2012. DOI: 10.1145/2213836.2213844 31

[163] S. Pelley, P. M. Chen, and T. F. Wenisch. Memory persistency. In *ACM SIGARCH Computer Architecture News*, vol. 42, IEEE Press, 2014. DOI: 10.1145/2678373.2665712 136

[164] S. Pelley, T. F. Wenisch, B. T. Gold, and B. Bridge. Storage management in the NVRAM era. In *PVLDB*, vol. 7, 2013. DOI: 10.14778/2732228.2732231 5, 130

[165] S. Pelley, T. F. Wenisch, and K. LeFevre. Do query optimizers need to be SSD-aware? In *ADMS*, 2011. 139

[166] T. Perez and C. Rose. Non-volatile memory: Emerging technologies and their impact on memory systems. In *PURCS Technical Report*, 2010. 2

[167] M. Pezzini, D. Feinberg, N. Rayner, and R. Edjlali. Hybrid transaction/analytical processing will foster opportunities for dramatic business innovation. https://www.gartner.com/doc/2657815/, 2014. 1

[168] S. Pilarski and T. Kameda. Checkpointing for distributed databases: Starting from the basics. In *IEEE Transactions on Parallel and Distributed Systems*, 1992. DOI: 10.1109/71.159043 53

[169] A. Prout. The story behind MemSQL's skiplist indexes. http://blog.memsql.com/the-story-behind-memsqls-skiplist-indexes/, 2014. 101

[170] M. K. Qureshi, V. Srinivasan, and J. A. Rivers. Scalable high performance main memory system using phase-change memory technology. In *ISCA*, 2009. DOI: 10.1145/1555815.1555760 79

[171] R. Ramakrishnan and J. Gehrke. *Database Management Systems*, 3rd ed. McGraw-Hill, Inc., New York, 2003. 76

[172] L. E. Ramos, E. Gorbatov, and R. Bianchini. Page placement in hybrid memory systems. In *SC*, ACM, 2011. DOI: 10.1145/1995896.1995911 77

[173] S. Raoux, G. Burr, M. Breitwisch, C. Rettner, Y. Chen, R. Shelby, M. Salinga, D. Krebs, S.-H. Chen, H.-L. Lung, and C. Lam. Phase-change random access memory: A scalable technology. In *IBM Journal of Research and Development*, vol. 52, 2008. DOI: 10.1147/rd.524.0465 2, 47, 78

[174] D. Roberts. Efficient data center architectures using non-volatile memory and reliability techniques. Ph.D. thesis, University of Michigan, 2011. 133, 142

[175] O. Rodeh. B-trees, shadowing, and clones. In *Transactions on Storage*, 2008. DOI: 10.1145/1326542.1326544 22, 42

[176] M. Rosenblum and J. K. Ousterhout. The design and implementation of a log-structured file system. In *ACM Transactions on Computer Systems*, vol. 10, February 1992. DOI: 10.1007/978-1-4615-2221-8 23

[177] A. Rudoff. Deprecating the PCOMMIT instruction. https://software.intel.com/en-us/blogs/2016/09/12/deprecate-pcommit-instruction, 2016. 7, 134

[178] D. Schwalb, T. Berning, M. Faust, M. Dreseler, and H. Plattner. NVM Malloc: Memory allocation for NVRAM. In *ADMS*, 2015. 118, 134, 135

[179] D. Schwalb, G. K. BK, M. Dreseler, S. Anusha, M. Faust, A. Hohl, T. Berning, G. Makkar, H. Plattner, and P. Deshmukh. Hyrise-NV: Instant recovery for in-memory databases using non-volatile memory. In *DASFAA*, pages 267–282, 2016. DOI: 10.1007/978-3-319-32049-6_17 5, 130

[180] N. Shavit and D. Touitou. Software transactional memory. In *PODC*, 1995. DOI: 10.1145/224964.224987 137

[181] D.-J. Shin, S. K. Park, S. M. Kim, and K. H. Park. Adaptive page grouping for energy efficiency in hybrid pram-dram main memory. In *RACS*, ACM, 2012. DOI: 10.1145/2401603.2401689 77

[182] V. Sikka, F. Färber, W. Lehner, S. K. Cha, T. Peh, and C. Bornhövd. Efficient transaction processing in SAP HANA database: The end of a column store myth. In *SIGMOD*, 2012. DOI: 10.1145/2213836.2213946 80

[183] R. Stoica and A. Ailamaki. Enabling efficient OS paging for main-memory OLTP databases. In *DaMon*, 2013. DOI: 10.1145/2485278.2485285 77

[184] M. Stonebraker. Operating system support for database management. In *Communications of the ACM*, vol. 24, 1981. DOI: 10.1145/358699.358703 76

[185] M. Stonebraker. The case for shared nothing. In *IEEE Database Engineering Bulletin*, 9(1), 1986. 153

[186] M. Stonebraker, S. Madden, D. J. Abadi, S. Harizopoulos, N. Hachem, and P. Helland. The end of an architectural era: (It's time for a complete rewrite). In *VLDB*, 2007. DOI: 10.1145/3226595.3226637 2, 20, 39, 129

[187] D. B. Strukov, G. S. Snider, D. R. Stewart, and R. S. Williams. The missing memristor found. In *Nature*, no. 7191, 2008. DOI: 10.1038/nature06932 2, 47

[188] H. Sundell and P. Tsigas. Lock-free deques and doubly linked lists. In *JPDC*, vol. 68, July 2008. DOI: 10.1016/j.jpdc.2008.03.001 137

[189] The transaction processing council. TPC-C Benchmark (Revision 5.9.0). http://www.tpc.org/tpcc/, June 2007. 151

[190] A. van Renen et. al. Managing non-volatile memory in database systems. In *SIGMOD*, 2018. DOI: 10.1145/3183713.3196897 5, 75, 79, 82, 98, 133

[191] S. Venkataraman, N. Tolia, P. Ranganathan, and R. H. Campbell. Consistent and durable data structures for non-volatile byte-addressable memory. In *FAST*, 2011. 5, 25, 27, 30, 137, 138, 140

[192] S. D. Viglas. Adapting the B+-tree for asymmetric I/O. In *ADBIS*, 2012. DOI: 10.1007/978-3-642-33074-2_30 140

[193] S. D. Viglas. Write-limited sorts and joins for persistent memory. In *PVLDB*, vol. 7, 2014. DOI: 10.14778/2732269.2732277 139, 140

[194] S. D. Viglas. Data management in non-volatile memory. In *SIGMOD*, 2015. DOI: 10.1145/2723372.2731082 139

[195] V. Viswanathan, K. Kumar, and T. Willhalm. Intel memory latency checker. `https://software.intel.com/en-us/articles/intelr-memory-latency-checker` 30

[196] H. Volos, S. Nalli, S. Panneerselvam, V. Varadarajan, P. Saxena, and M. M. Swift. Aerie: Flexible file-system interfaces to storage-class memory. In *EuroSys*, 2014. DOI: 10.1145/2592798.2592810 132

[197] H. Volos, A. J. Tack, and M. M. Swift. Mnemosyne: Lightweight persistent memory. In R. Gupta and T. C. Mowry, Eds., *ASPLOS*, ACM, 2011. DOI: 10.1145/1961295.1950379 118, 134, 136

[198] C. Wang et al. NVMalloc: Exposing an aggregate SSD store as a memory partition in extreme-scale machines. In *IPDPS*, IEEE, 2012. DOI: 10.1109/ipdps.2012.90 134

[199] T. Wang and R. Johnson. Scalable logging through emerging non-volatile memory. In *PVLDB*, vol. 7, 2014. DOI: 10.14778/2732951.2732960 5, 130, 135

[200] T. Wang, J. Levandoski, and P. A. Larson. Easy lock-free indexing in non-volatile memory. In *SIGMOD*, 2017. DOI: 10.1109/icde.2018.00049 101, 102, 104, 108, 120, 123

[201] P. Wu et al. Algorithm-directed data placement in explicitly managed non-volatile memory. In *HPDC*, 2016. DOI: 10.1145/2907294.2907321 77

[202] X. Wu and A. Reddy. SCMFS: A file system for storage class memory. In *SC*, 2011. DOI: 10.1145/2063384.2063436 132, 136

[203] J. Xu and S. Swanson. Nova: A log-structured file system for hybrid volatile/non-volatile main memories. In *FAST*, 2016. 132

[204] J. Xu, L. Zhang, A. Memaripour, A. Gangadharaiah, A. Borase, T. B. Da Silva, S. Swanson, and A. Rudoff. Nova-fortis: A fault-tolerant non-volatile main memory file system. In *SOSP*, 2017. DOI: 10.1145/3132747.3132761 133

[205] J. Yang, Q. Wei, C. Chen, C. Wang, K. L. Yong, and B. He. NV-Tree: Reducing consistency cost for NVM-based single level systems. In *FAST*, 2015. 5, 137, 138, 140

[206] R. M. Yoo, C. J. Hughes, K. Lai, and R. Rajwar. Performance evaluation of Intel transactional synchronization extensions for high-performance computing. In *SC*, 2013. DOI: 10.1145/2503210.2503232 137

[207] S. Yu, N. Xiao, M. Deng, Y. Xing, F. Liu, Z. Cai, and W. Chen. Walloc: An efficient wear-aware allocator for non-volatile main memory. In *IPCCC*, 2015. DOI: 10.1109/pccc.2015.7410326 135

[208] Y. Zhang, J. Yang, A. Memaripour, and S. Swanson.   Mojim: A reliable and highly-available non-volatile memory system.   In *ASPLOS,* 2015. DOI: 10.1145/2786763.2694370 69, 86, 133, 142, 145

[209] J. Zhao, S. Li, D. H. Yoon, Y. Xie, and N. P. Jouppi. Kiln: Closing the performance gap between systems with and without persistence support. In *MICRO*, IEEE, 2013. DOI: 10.1145/2540708.2540744 135, 136

[210] W. Zheng, S. Tu, E. Kohler, and B. Liskov.   Fast databases with fast durability and recovery through multicore parallelism. In *OSDI*, 2014. 131

Authors' Biographies

JOY ARULRAJ

Joy Arulraj is an Assistant Professor of Database Systems in the School of Computer Science at Georgia Institute of Technology. His doctoral research focused on the design and implementation of non-volatile memory database management systems. He is a member of the Database Group and the Center for Experimental Research in Computer Systems at Georgia Tech. His work is also in collaboration with the Intel Science and Technology Center for Big Data, Microsoft Research, and Samsung Research.

ANDREW PAVLO

Andrew Pavlo is an Assistant Professor of Databaseology in the Computer Science Department at Carnegie Mellon University. At CMU, he is a member of the Database Group and the Parallel Data Laboratory. His work is also in collaboration with the Intel Science and Technology Center for Big Data.